"This is a book anyone can benefit from—whether you want to want sex, haven't been in the mood, or want to have sex with a partner who doesn't seem interested. I wish this book had been out when my kids were young. Now, for anyone with a family, it is a must-read. Don't miss it."

—Tammy Nelson, PhD, author of *Open Monogamy*, director of the Integrative Sex Therapy Institute, host of the podcast *The Trouble with Sex*, and TEDx speaker

Praise for **Parents in Love**

"Rebecca Howard Eudy has written a breakthrough book on sustaining a healthy sexual relationship while parenting. In a culture that too often de-eroticizes parents—especially mothers—this book offers a powerful alternative: one that embraces secure, satisfying, and sexual parenthood. Dr. Howard Eudy encourages couples to become intimate and erotic allies, showing how sexuality can energize their bond and help them grow as both partners and parents."

—Barry McCarthy, PhD, presenter, professor emeritus, and author of numerous books on sexuality, including *Rekindling Desire*, and the Psychology Today blog *The Paradox of Sex*

"Research is focusing increasingly on the impact of parenthood on couples' sexuality during the postpartum period. However, if you are seeking a book that looks at the impact of parenthood on couples from pregnancy through the 'empty nest' stage using an attachment-based perspective, this book is for you!"

—Peggy J. Kleinplatz, PhD, author of *Magnificent Sex*

"A necessary read for everyone moving from 'two' to 'three' to keep love secure and sex connected. Real examples make these important principles accessible for parents who want to build a safe, stable foundation so their children have a model for intimacy and strong relational skills to navigate the world."

—Laurie Watson, PhD, and George Faller, LMFT, hosts of the *Brave Love* podcast (formerly *Foreplay Radio*)

"*Parents in Love* is a deeply honest and essential glimpse into undercurrents of parenting, sexuality, and love. Rebecca Howard Eudy leads readers into territory that is rarely addressed but eminently necessary, particularly through a sex-positive framework. This book is an invaluable resource for parents and parents-to-be."

—Holly Richmond, PhD, author of *Reclaiming Pleasure: A Sex-Positive Guide for Moving Past Sexual Trauma and Living a Passionate Life*

"*Parents in Love* offers real hope for couples who thought passion was just another casualty of parenthood. This book doesn't ask exhausted parents to find more time—it shows them how to rebuild the connection that makes great sex possible again. Every couple needs this road map back to each other."

—Laurie Mintz, PhD, author of *A Tired Woman's Guide to Passionate Sex* and *Becoming Cliterate*

"This is the book parents everywhere have been waiting for. Rebecca Howard Eudy offers a powerful reminder that having children doesn't have to mean losing connection or passion. Through a blend of evidence-based theory, research, and reflective exercises, she normalizes the real struggles of parenthood while charting a hopeful path back to intimacy. Her tone is warm, relatable, and practical—making change feel not only worthwhile, but very possible. For any couple trying to find their way back to each other after kids, this is an absolute must-read."

—Isabelle Morley, PsyD, author of *They're Not Gaslighting You*

A Guide to Great Sex After Kids

PARENTS IN LOVE

REBECCA HOWARD EUDY, PhD, LMHC

PARENTS IN LOVE

Published by
PESI Publishing, Inc.
3839 White Ave
Eau Claire, WI 54703

Cover and interior design by Emily Dyer
Editing by Chelsea Thompson

ISBN 9781683738558 (print)
ISBN 9781683738565 (ePUB)
ISBN 9781683738572 (ePDF)

Printed in Canada.

PESI Publishing
pesipublishing.com

For Lee—my North Star

Table of Contents

Introduction

"I feel like he doesn't touch me anymore; he just gropes me," Maria says with a heavy sigh. "It's like my body became public property the moment we became parents. I know he wants me to want to have sex, and I feel terrible that I just don't. But I miss the romance we used to have."

"I don't mean to turn her off," says George. "I just want to touch her, you know? Her butt looks so good, and it's been so long since we had sex that it feels impossible to keep my hands to myself. I crave her touch; I feel desperate for it sometimes, and even though I know she doesn't respond well when I grope her, it feels like the only way I can get physical contact."

Maria and George are a married couple in their mid-30s with two kids, aged four and six. Like so many parents, their once-vibrant sex life hit a dry patch when their first child was born. They were sleep-deprived and exhausted from parenting, not to mention dealing with raging hormones, dirty diapers, and mountains of laundry, none of which was remotely sexy. Once the baby was finally asleep, they would fall into bed and, if they had any energy left, look at pictures of their kid together on their phones until they too fell asleep.

At first, they had faith that things would improve with time. However, as months blended into years and a second baby arrived, their sex life didn't bounce back. This is why they find themselves in my office looking for help.

Maria and George are caught in a negative sexual cycle. The more he asks for sex, either verbally or by groping her, the less Maria wants it. She feels annoyed and guilty, which shuts down her desire even further. When they do have sex, it fosters a connection between them that lingers, making their everyday interactions a little lighter. Still, there are times when Maria can't seem to shut off her brain to fully enjoy it. They need to change the narrative and get out of their negative cycle. This often entails the high-desire partner (in this case, George) taking the pressure off and collaborating with his partner to rekindle their sexual connection.

"Maria," I say, "Imagine this scenario: Instead of George's usual approach of groping you, picture him coming up to you in the kitchen. Instead of immediately grabbing your butt, he leans in close, his breath warm against your ear as he whispers, 'Your ass looks so good in those pants, I just want to put my hands on you.' And then (and this is the key), he simply walks away *without* touching you. How would that make you feel?"

"Oh wow," she says, flushing and smiling shyly at George, "Yeah, I think that would work."

What I suggested to Maria and George was rebuilding the flirtation, anticipation, and erotic charge between them—the very elements that make sexual encounters exciting and fulfilling. It's what fuels our yearning, lust, and desire. When their interactions shift from *wanting* to *having*, that spark, so present at the beginning of relationships, begins to fade. And with it, the desire that comes from waiting and wanting. So, is it any surprise that low desire is the most common issue that brings couples to therapy?

People are often fascinated by my work as a sex therapist. "Oh wow," they'll say, "you must hear some wild stuff!" The fact is that it is not nearly as sensational as people might think. Most of what clients share with me is about something very relatable: bad sex. I hear about people having it, not having it, having sex they don't want, or not getting enough of the sex they do want, and of course, all the relationship dynamics that come with such issues.

I also hear a lot about shame and anxiety around sex. Addressing shame and fear tends to be the main work of any therapist. For sex therapists, the content may be a little more "juicy" than some other topics. But sexuality is an integral part of the human experience, and as such, it spotlights our needs, desires, and vulnerabilities.

Still, due to shame and anxiety around their sexuality, many people are pretty desperate by the time they come to see me. Moreover, they will sometimes see me for months before mentioning the sexual problem, due to judgment and shame around what they should be doing, feeling, liking, wanting, or desiring in their sex life—whether partnered or solo.

Most often, I see couples like Maria and George, where one partner desires more frequent or varied sexual experiences than the other. In these situations, it's common for the partner with lower desire to genuinely want to want sex. This longing often stems from a mix of relational reasons, like wanting to nurture closeness with their partner, and personal motivations, such as a desire to feel more fully engaged in life and reconnect with a sense of vibrancy and joy both in and outside of the bedroom. However, despite their intentions, they often find themselves stuck, unable to bridge the gap between wanting to want sex and actually feeling desire. This disconnect can feel deeply frustrating and isolating for both themselves and their relationship.

One of the first and most important things I tell couples is that sex itself is not something anyone is entitled to. While sexuality is an integral part of being, no one has ever died from lack of sex; it is neither a basic need nor a human right. In other words, your partner does not owe you sex, nor do you owe it to them. In fact, to experience true desire, a person must feel safe to say no without consequences, that is, feelings of guilt or having to deal with an angry, sulky, sad, unhappy, or horny partner. When the partner with lower desire agrees to sex solely to dodge the relational strain that comes with saying no—what we might call *obligation sex*—it often worsens the cycle of low desire. This dynamic can inadvertently frame the lower-desire partner as "the problem" in the relationship, especially when the repeated disappointment of their partner centers the issue on them. Feeling like they are constantly falling short or getting it wrong creates a pressure cooker of guilt and resentment, which only dampens any authentic desire they might have had. Over time, this cycle breeds frustration and emotional distance for both partners, making it even harder to foster the connection and intimacy they both want.

Once we establish that sex is not an entitlement, I guide couples toward open and honest communication about their desires. We talk about what it means to be intimate and what they are both craving from each other, which often has nothing to do with the physical act of sex. For example, Maria expressed that she's turned off by the way George often expresses his sexual interest through grabs, pinches, and pokes. For her, this type of touch—sudden, quick, insistent—feels too similar to the way their children touch her. This similarity has caused her to experience his physical overtures as nonsexual, not to mention irritating.

"I'm just so touched out at the end of each day," explains Maria. "I just don't have anything else to give." This is a common refrain among parents, especially those who shoulder most of the caregiving work.

Interestingly, Maria's feeling of being "touched out" coincides with a deep sense of connection with her children. After a day full of hugs, kisses, cuddles, and loving gazes with her kids, her need for physical intimacy is beyond satisfied. As a result, George has little to offer that sounds more appealing to her than quiet alone time.

In many ways, the emotional experience of developing a deep attachment bond with a child mirrors the initial phase of a romantic relationship. The love and attachment between a parent and child are so powerful that they divert attention away from the romantic relationship. This shift in emotional focus, coupled with evolving roles and increased stressors, can lead to feelings of distance and disconnection within the romantic relationship, ultimately contributing to diminished sexual satisfaction.

I don't need to tell anyone reading this book that parenthood introduces many challenges, from sleepless nights and exhaustion to hormonal changes and the demands of caregiving. These challenges can strain even the most secure bonds, leaving partners isolated and unsupported. In the pages ahead, I'll explore the subtle yet profound ways in which the addition of children can disrupt the attachment between partners and how, if not intentionally addressed, this can continue long past the new-parenthood phase into the years of playdates, soccer practice, and teenage drama.

I'll also dispel the common misconception that the desire and erotic connection between partners will naturally reignite once the chaos of early parenthood subsides. The reality is that couples who reignite their sexual spark do so by taking purposeful steps to nurture it, even during challenging periods. They mutually decide to prioritize their relationship, including sex, and they actively work toward sustaining a robust emotional and sexual connection, despite the obstacles of spit-up, blowouts, tantrums, and sweet little ones literally shoving themselves between you at every turn.

Throughout this book, I'll weave narratives drawn from my own life and from my experience as a sex and relationship therapist. Six couples will guide us: Maria and George, Avery and Sam, Natalie and Henry, Leo and Amara, Mateo and Carrie, and Grace and Matthew. I will use their stories to illustrate the complexities of parenthood. I'll delve into their struggles and triumphs, shed light on common pitfalls, and demonstrate how they overcome challenges together. These stories don't directly represent any single client or couple, but they encapsulate recurring themes and experiences I regularly encounter.

While this book aims to include couples of all sexual orientations, genders, and racial and ethnic identities, it's essential to acknowledge that much of the research done on sexuality has been conducted within a heteronormative, white, cisgender framework. As a result, it often excludes the unique challenges faced by gender and racial minorities. This limitation in the field has received significant attention and is gradually changing, but as of publication, resources and research remain limited.

Nevertheless, the existing research, particularly around gender and sexual minorities, points to more similarities than differences across sexual orientations. Couples in committed relationships, regardless of orientation, tend to face very similar struggles in family life and committed relationships. One notable difference, however, is that while same-sex couples are just as likely to experience differences in desire, partners tend to struggle less with guilt and conflict around sex compared to heterosexual couples (Vowels et al., 2020). Same-sex and bisexual couples are more likely to navigate differences in sexual desire flexibly, perhaps leading to more satisfying arrangements for both partners (Nimbi et al., 2020; Vowels et al., 2020). For that reason, while we will address specific issues related to same-sex couples at various points, this book primarily deals with the challenges faced by heterosexual couples because research indicates they are the ones who struggle the most with sexuality after parenthood (Frederick et al., 2021; Vowels et al., 2020).

Similarly, while this book is written with parents in mind, many of the techniques and principles are just as relevant for couples without children, especially those navigating a difference in desire. The truth remains that all couples deserve to find solutions that work for them, fostering connection, communication, and mutual satisfaction. So, regardless of what kind of relationship and family you're in, you are welcome here!

How This Book Works

Love, sex, attachment, parenting, romance—they all come down to one thing: connection, including the fear of what happens when we lose it. As humans, we are wired for connection. When we feel disconnected, we often do seemingly irrational (sometimes counterproductive) things to regain connection with the people who matter most to us.

The tricky part is that couples can be deeply connected and still not feel the desire to have sex. Research has shown that while intimacy is essential, too much familiarity can actually dampen desire (Sims & Meana, 2010). Desire thrives on longing for something that feels just out of reach, so it's no surprise that finding the right balance between closeness and space is key. In one study, married women in their 30s shared that the very emotional intimacy and connection they valued in their relationships also contributed to a drop in sexual desire due to a lack of novelty and excitement (Sims & Meana, 2010). However, for some women, increased intimacy led to greater desire (Murray et al., 2012). These seemingly contradictory findings show there's no one-size-fits-all answer when it comes to love and desire. Every couple's dynamic is unique, which requires them to foster a balance of security and freedom.

I often use the term *vibrant connection* in referring to a close bond that achieves a couple's ideal balance between security and flexibility. Keeping the sexual spark alive in a marriage comes from nurturing this connection that honors the autonomy of each partner by maintaining individuality, intimacy, and room to breathe.

To achieve this vibrant connection, most people must undo years of conditioning and past experiences. To do that, we must focus on three simple but powerful steps:

1. **Notice:** The first step is developing awareness. This means paying attention to both our own feelings and the dynamics in our relationship. It's about recognizing patterns, emotions, and responses, both within ourselves and during conflict with our partners. By noticing these things, we become more present and attuned, which lays the foundation for genuine connection.

2. **Own:** Once we notice what's happening, the next step is to take responsibility for our part in the relationship dynamic. This involves owning our feelings, actions, and past experiences that shape how we engage. When we own our part, we move away

from blame and toward accountability, creating an environment of trust and growth.

3. **Connect:** Finally, with awareness and ownership, we can authentically connect. This step is about leaning into vulnerability and being open with our partners. Connection is the reward for the work we've done to notice and own our experiences, allowing us to cultivate intimacy and reignite desire in a secure and free relationship.

This three-step process creates a powerful feedback loop, where deeper intimacy and stronger desire grow from the balance of security and freedom in the relationship. But to make this work, it's essential to first recognize that *the only behavior you can truly control is your own.* Pointing out your partner's flaws or telling them what they need to change (and yes, I know how tempting that can be when it all seems so obvious) is a path that leads to frustration. Real transformation happens when you turn the focus inward, acknowledging your own patterns and working on those. That's when the magic starts to unfold.

This is especially hard because it's not a one-time fix or something you can check off a list. It's ongoing work that requires a daily commitment. It means creating new habits, letting go of old ones, and showing up consistently for yourself and your partner. The progress might feel slow at times, but it's those steady, small efforts that eventually lead to meaningful and lasting change. ♥

Part One

NOTICE

Chapter 1

Not as Easy as 1, 2, 3

From our very first date, I had an inkling my husband might be "the one." Of course, I barely admitted it to myself—I was far too busy wrestling with my fear of commitment and all things relationship-related. But by the time we'd had our third date in as many days, I found myself sitting in my apartment, asking my best friend, "How do you know when someone's *the one*?"

I can't remember what she said, but I'll never forget the look on her face. It was a quickly stifled mix of surprise and excitement, as if I'd just dropped the plot twist of the century. To her credit, she didn't mention that moment again for another three years—not until after our whirlwind elopement, triggered by a surprise pregnancy, which came just months after we bought a condo in the city. Moving in was a big milestone for us both, only slightly diluted by our third housemate. (Why let a perfectly good spare room go unrented?)

Fast-forward nine and a half months, and one housemate moved out to make room for another—a very messy, entirely inconsiderate, permanent one. In that brief timespan, we went from living separately to cohabitating to getting married while simultaneously preparing for a baby. To say it was overwhelming would be putting it mildly. We were both more in love and more out of our depth than ever before.

Our son, Gray, entered our lives like a nine-pound wrecking ball, bringing equal parts joy and chaos. As we fumbled through the early days of caring for him and figuring out how to co-parent (while still figuring out who was supposed to take out the trash), we'd exchange exhausted glances over his screams—"What does it *want*?" The mix of overwhelming joy and sheer helplessness that comes with new parenthood was unlike anything we could have prepared for.

Though we loved him fiercely, our relationship struggled to adjust. The demands of parenting stretched us in ways we hadn't anticipated, leaving us disconnected and trying to regain our footing as a couple.

For our first wedding anniversary, we planned to spend a weekend at Cape Cod. It was a trip we'd taken every year since we met, and a four-month-old wasn't going to stop us—or so we thought. Looking back, it's clear we were wildly overconfident. We were barely out of the driveway, car packed to the roof with luggage, baby gear, and our eight-year-old bulldog, Bo (who was neurotic during the best of times), when the screaming started.

Despite only being four months old, Gray had a well-established system: scream for 45 minutes straight, then maybe sleep. But if the car ride was less than 45 minutes, he'd just keep up the noise. I tried sitting in the back with him, thinking he just needed a little comfort. Big mistake. He took that as a challenge and cranked the screaming up a notch.

An hour in, just as we were getting acclimated to the soundtrack of his cries, disaster struck. A diaper blowout so massive, it reached *his hair*. Let's just say we needed to pull over for a full-scale cleanup operation. At that point, we had a real moment of reflection: "Should we just turn around?" But no, it was our anniversary! Besides, we were too far in to quit now.

Once our precious baby finally fell asleep, we sat in complete silence, both of us trying to bring our blood pressure out of the red zone—white noise blasting, too scared to even whisper, seriously questioning the wisdom of our choice to bring this show on the road when it was barely manageable in the safety and comfort of our own home. We communicated exclusively through panicked glances and shallow breathing for the rest of the drive.

Frazzled and exhausted, we finally made it to the hotel. It was nice enough, if you ignored the pack-and-play shoved in the corner. It turned out to be a waste of space, anyway; our little guy barely slept all night and eventually ended up in bed with us, ensuring that no one got any sleep. Meanwhile, the rain didn't let up for a second, so instead of a romantic night out, we found ourselves eating takeout in bed, with a wide-awake baby fussing beside us and the distinct smell of wet dog lingering in the air. The dog stared at us with a look that said, "Really? This is what we're doing?"

The highlight of the weekend wasn't the romantic dinner, the peaceful walks on the beach, or even the rare chance to reconnect after an undeniably wild year. Nope, the star of the show was Gray, rolling over for the very first time. Forget the dinner—we celebrated *that* moment like it was the pinnacle of the trip, and honestly, it kind of was. It made the entire chaotic weekend feel worth it.

Sort of.

Let's just say, we learned our lesson: no kids on anniversary trips ever again. That weekend was a crash course in balancing the needs of our new little family of three—or four, if you counted our neurotic dog and all *his* demands. Looking back now, we can laugh about it, but at the time, it was a hard adjustment. We hadn't quite found our new-parent rhythm yet, which meant our relationship took a bit of a back seat—our focus was 100 percent on the baby, all the time. On top of that, we were constantly thrown into situations that required quick decision-making, often under stressful and less-than-ideal circumstances (like in the middle of the night or on the side of the road with a screaming baby). Our lightly tested ability to make joint decisions was suddenly put under a glaring spotlight, and it became clear that our skills were amateur level, at best. The tension between trying to get it "right" for everyone while managing our own frustrations was real.

Now, with a bit of distance (and more sleep), we can see those moments for what they were: necessary growing pains. But in the thick of it, it was anything but easy.

Moving from "Me" to "We"

To truly grasp the weight of this shift in a couple's relationship, we need to rewind a bit to what many parents nostalgically refer to as the "good old days"—a time when there was energy and space to connect with each other while still tending to personal interests and needs. The tension between space and closeness is one of the most dynamic forces in a relationship. It's also one of the things that keeps desire alive (Ferreira et al., 2015). At its core, desire thrives on a balance of connection and individuality. This dance between togetherness and autonomy is often most pronounced during the transition from "me" to "we," as two individuals work to create a partnership without losing their own unique identities.

It's tempting to imagine this process as an effortless and romantic melding. After all, it's where most romantic movies end. But in reality, it's usually more complicated. Building a relationship where both partners feel seen, valued, and supported takes intentionality. It's about compromise, yes, but it's also about recognizing that maintaining your sense of self—your interests, friendships, and passions—makes you more vibrant and attractive to your partner. Desire isn't born from constant proximity; it grows in the tension between the known and the unknown, the familiar and the mysterious (Ferreira et al., 2014).

This balance is especially tricky because it asks for vulnerability and communication. It requires you to consider your partner's needs while still prioritizing your own, a task that can feel like walking a tightrope. Too much closeness and you risk losing the spark of individuality that first drew you to each other. Too much space and you can drift apart emotionally. The challenge lies in creating an ebb and flow—moments of deep connection interspersed with time apart to nurture your own growth.

From "We" to "Three"

This delicate balance between space and closeness becomes even more challenging—and often more critical—when life throws big changes your way. Few transitions highlight this tension as sharply as becoming parents. When the carefully constructed "we" expands to "three," the dynamics shift in ways no one can fully prepare for. The once-intentional dance between individuality and partnership is suddenly interrupted by the cries of a newborn and the unrelenting demands of caregiving. Time for yourself becomes a distant memory, and quality time with your partner is often reduced to exchanging logistic updates or collapsing in exhaustion.

It's no surprise that many couples feel their connection strain under the weight of parenthood, as the balance they worked so hard to build is challenged in ways they never imagined. In this new reality, both partners face significant sacrifices. The individual "me" identities and needs that once felt natural and fulfilling must now be carefully squeezed into the framework of a larger family unit. Personal hobbies, moments of solitude, and even the intimacy that once served as a cornerstone of the relationship can suddenly feel like luxuries you can't afford. What was once effortless now requires intention and planning, often against a backdrop of exhaustion and competing priorities. In navigating the delicate dance of maintaining personal and mutual identities while embracing the role of parents, partners need each other's support more than ever. Yet, the demands of parenthood can make it incredibly difficult to offer each other that support. Even the most well-prepared couples often find the transition to family life more taxing on their relationship than they anticipated (Lévesque et al., 2020).

Surgeon General's Warning: Parenting Is Hazardous to Your Health

In a 2024 advisory on parents' mental health, the US Surgeon General spoke out about what many parents have felt but haven't said out loud: Parenting stress has reached the level of public health crisis. Citing factors that range from division of household labor and financial challenges to worries over children's health, safety, and mental well-being in a rapidly shifting culture, as well as the growing recognition of parental isolation, burnout, and mental health conditions such as anxiety and depression, the advisory goes so far as to put parental stress in the same category as smoking and AIDS (US Department of Health and Human Services, 2024).

While this may be shocking, it's also validating. Modern parents face a unique pressure to invest more and more time, energy, and resources into nurturing their kids' lives, from academics and athletics to life skills and emotions. This approach, described by sociologist Dr. Sharon Hays (1996) as "intensive parenting," is intended to help children achieve the success their parents so deeply want for them. However, as shown by the surgeon general's warning, it often comes at the expense of parents' mental, emotional, and physical health.

The advisory stresses that parents need more support in creating healthy self-care habits and that the stigma around taking personal time needs to be challenged. It's essential for parents to recognize that taking care of themselves is not selfish—it's necessary for creating a balanced and healthy family life.

"We Can't Find Our Way Back"

Avery and Sam came to see me due to increased conflict, lack of connection, and a desire difference. They have been married for eight years and have two children, aged three and five. While both work full-time, Sam takes on more day-to-day parenting and household tasks because her work-from-home job is more flexible.

"We did pretty well in the beginning," says Avery. "We split the night feedings and diaper duty. I felt like we were really on the same team."

Sam nods in agreement before adding, "It got sticky once Greta was born. I think the second kid kind of broke us."

"That's when we stopped having time for each other or ourselves," Avery continues. "When it was just one, we would have little living room dates and make an effort to give each other breaks to work out or just be alone. It felt manageable. But once we added the second, it all went to hell."

"And now we can't find our way back," says Sam. "It's not just the physical exhaustion. It's the mental load—appointments, school activities, ensuring everyone is fed and clothed and where they need to be on time. It's relentless. I can't even think about spending time on our relationship, much less having sex. It feels like another thing on my to-do list, one that gets pushed pretty far down." She sighs. "I feel like I just need time for *me*. By the time the kids are in bed, all I want to do is collapse."

What Avery and Sam describe is a common experience for parents. Raising children is an all-consuming task; the time and energy that used to be available for nurturing the relationship are now consumed by the constant demands of feeding, changing, and entertaining a baby. It's only natural for parents to put the family's needs above all else. But over time, this neglect of individual and relationship needs can become a habit, one that creates a sense of isolation and resentment. Partners might feel like they're not being supported or understood, leading to arguments and further distance. Over time, the relationship can feel more like a co-parenting arrangement than a romantic partnership.

Even the best of relationships inevitably feel this way at times. There is simply not enough time to tend to all the needs at once. Ironically, the stronger the relationship is before kids, the easier it is to "ask" the relationship to wait indefinitely. Once the kids are a little older, once work settles down, once the house is organized and we finally start getting some sleep again, we'll find the time and energy to reinvest in the relationship. The problem is that the longer couples go without restoring their connection, the harder it is to find their way back.

It's Not Just You: The Baby Has Opinions Too

Some parents make it look easy. You know the ones—those unruffled friends and omniscient relatives who confidently dish out advice (solicited or otherwise) on sleep, feeding, and meeting developmental milestones. Maybe they have unlocked the secret to cruise-control parenting . . . or maybe their first baby just happened to be one of those mythical "easy babies."

Lee and I were not so lucky. Our first child had a gleefully dramatic temperament and an intense aversion to sleep. We tried everything: sleep training, consultants, blackout curtains, better blackout curtains, white-noise machines, dream feeds—you name it, we tried it. Nothing worked. It wasn't until our second child arrived and just slept, of his own free will, that we finally learned the secret: Temperament matters *a lot*!

Oddly enough, having a kid felt easier the second time around. After being humbled—okay, completely broken—by our first, we entered round two with zero illusions of control and a lot of flexibility. Meanwhile, those same friends who breezed through their first baby were completely blindsided when their second turned out to be a force of chaos.

The truth is that a child's temperament plays a huge role in how hard or easy parenting feels. Every couple eventually faces that moment when parenthood slaps them across the face with the undeniable truth that we're not in control here. It just doesn't hit everyone at the same time.

Navigating the Transition to Parenthood

The initial months of parenthood are a blur of diaper changes, feeding schedules, and trying to catch any bit of sleep. Couples can feel like they are constantly in survival mode, focusing on keeping their baby happy and healthy. Unsurprisingly, this intense focus on the baby often means parents—and let's be honest, it's usually moms—barely have time to meet their own basic needs, like getting enough sleep or eating regular meals. Forget luxuries like taking a shower, using the bathroom without an audience, or sipping a cup of coffee while it's still hot (instead of reheating it three times). And the relationship? It often gets pushed even further down the priority list.

I refer to this perinatal period as the "do no harm" phase of the parenting journey. The first one to three years of a child's life—essentially, until the baby is consistently sleeping and no longer breastfeeding—are a time when parents need to give themselves (and each other) plenty of compassion and patience. Understanding that *this phase is temporary* can help ease the pressure of unmet relational needs, allowing room for grace, understanding, and flexibility as the family adjusts. This time is all about not harming the relationship, recognizing the strain, and knowing this incredibly demanding period will pass.

Despite knowing this, couples often find it challenging to rekindle their spark after the baby starts sleeping through the night and things settle into the new normal. The disconnections formed during those early years can linger, making it difficult to shift focus back to the relationship.

"I remember those first few months," Avery says. "It was like we were on autopilot. We barely had time to talk, let alone connect. Our entire focus was on the baby and the toddler. We were just so consumed by trying to balance their needs."

Sam nods. "Yeah, and it was hard to see past the immediate. Everything felt urgent and exhausting. We kept telling ourselves it was just a phase, but it was tough."

The "Do No Harm" Agreement

The "do no harm" agreement is a suggested approach for couples to adopt during the challenging early days of parenthood. It serves as a framework to help partners navigate this transition with compassion and intentionality, recognizing that this phase may test their individual and collective limits. By embracing this agreement, couples commit to prioritizing their new family's needs while extending grace and support to each other, fostering a foundation of understanding and resilience during this transformative time.

As partners, we agree upon a "do no harm" approach during this transformative period. We acknowledge that this time may not showcase us at our best, understanding that we may not function optimally individually or as a couple.

We recognize that our focus must shift toward prioritizing the needs of our newborn and our new family unit over our own physical and sexual health, at least for the time being. This commitment is not permanent, but a temporary sacrifice where sleep may be in short supply and our emotional and physical reserves may be tested.

Throughout this period, we commit to extending an abundance of grace toward each other, understanding that we are navigating uncharted territory. We pledge to create a nurturing environment where we strive for patience and understanding with each other and with ourselves. We pledge to give and get grace for our shortcomings and misattunements as our relationship grows to make space for our child.

We vow to support each other through the emotional highs and lows, recognizing that miscommunications and cracks in our relationship may become pronounced when we are exhausted and overwhelmed. Yet, we also acknowledge the potential for experiencing a more profound love for each other than ever before.

In doing so, we aim to build a strong foundation for our family, ensuring that while this period is unique and challenging, it will also pass quickly. We commit to intentional moments of reconnection and understanding, knowing that our relationship's health and our family's well-being depend on mutual care and dedication.

Avery continues, "We used to have these little rituals, like having coffee together in the morning or watching a show before bed. But once the baby came, those moments disappeared for a while."

Sam adds, "I felt like I lost a part of myself. I was so consumed with being a mom that I forgot what it felt like just to be me."

Parenthood is a life-changing experience, for better and for worse. It brings immense joy, but it also introduces new challenges that can make relationships particularly vulnerable. As mentioned in the introduction, one significant factor is the intense emotional investment of parenthood. Falling in love with a baby is a seismic shift—it can be an incredibly enriching and fulfilling experience, but it also dramatically changes the dynamic between partners. The overwhelming love and attention given to the child can sometimes leave partners feeling neglected or overlooked, especially if their emotional needs for support and connection are unmet.

This shift can, in many ways, be likened to an affair. While the physical intimacy of parenting is different from sexual intimacy, it involves many of the same elements—loving gazes, skin-to-skin contact, affectionate touching—that trigger bonding hormones such as oxytocin and dopamine, the same hormones released during sex and romantic connection.

These hormones create feelings of deep love and satisfaction, driving a desire for more connection that can feel almost obsessive. Any new mom can relate to how all-consuming it is to care for a newborn—wondering constantly if they're safe, eating enough, and sleeping enough, or if you're doing it right. This obsession mirrors the early days of romantic relationships when you're constantly thinking about your new partner. This similarity suggests a crucial evolutionary link. Researchers now believe that romantic love may have adapted the bonding mechanisms initially used for mother-infant attachment to help partners form deep, lasting connections (Bode & Kushnick, 2021; Bode, 2023).

This comparison doesn't suggest loving your child is wrong. Quite the opposite—it's an essential part of parenting that often feels as natural as breathing. It does, however, illuminate how this dynamic can divert emotional energy away from the romantic relationship. While many couples find that having a child deepens their love for each other, it's common for one or both partners to experience a decreased interest in sex, which can trigger jealousy or feelings of rejection and loneliness, even in a loving relationship. Research bears this duality out, showing that marital stability increases as an effect of having children (Cowan & Cowan, 2000), but couples with children often report lower levels of happiness and relationship satisfaction (Hansson & Ahlborg, 2015; Doss et al., 2009).

This doesn't mean parents are necessarily less happy than nonparents. The key is distinguishing between *happiness*, which refers to short-term pleasure, contentment, and reduced stress, and *meaningfulness*, which is about long-term purpose, commitment, and working on something with deep personal value (Baumeister et al., 2013). Raising children often adds stress and reduces immediate pleasure while also bringing a profound sense of meaning and fulfillment. In other words, it pushes couples apart while also pulling them closer. As we so often say in therapy, two things can be true at once.

While we know how vital attachment is for both romantic relationships and early childhood development, there's surprisingly little research on how parents balance their romantic bond with the attachment they share with their children. This is an important area to explore. As parents, our deep love for our children often takes priority—out of both necessity and instinct. While this shift is a natural part of parenting, it can make it harder, but all the more essential, for couples to find ways to reconnect and nurture their romantic relationship amid the demands of family life.

Reconnection Doesn't Just Happen

After the "no harm" period, both partners need to make a conscious decision to prioritize their relationship again. Reconnecting as a couple requires intentional effort. It won't just happen on its own. At the same time, I know difficult it can feel to hear that. When children are involved, it often feels like you're forced to choose between two essential things.

Sam reflects, "Even after the kids started sleeping better, we forgot how to be a couple. Our entire world had shifted, and finding our way back to each other felt like an uphill battle."

"We had to relearn how to prioritize us," Avery says. "It wasn't easy and took time, but we knew it was important."

Our energy is finite, and most parents feel stretched to their limits. This feeling is especially pronounced in the United States, where most parents lack the social support they need. A study in 22 developed countries found that parents in the United States experience the most significant "happiness penalty" compared to nonparents (Glass et al., 2016), due mainly to the absence of family-friendly policies such as paid parental leave, affordable childcare, and flexible work schedules. In countries with better social policies, parents are often just as happy, if not happier, than nonparents.

While I wouldn't suggest that everything in life comes down to choice—any parent knows it's not that simple—choosing is still a vital part of the equation. Without the decision to prioritize each other, many aspects of the relationship can lose their power. Making a conscious choice to focus on your romantic relationship, including sex, if that is an aspect that is important to you and your partner, is critical to maintaining a strong and vibrant foundation for your family. Simply by choosing to read this book, you're already taking a step toward prioritizing your relationship. Even so, what I know from my work with couples and the research is this: Repeatedly choosing each other, even when it feels tough, is essential for creating the vibrant emotional and sexual connection couples long for (Vowels et al., 2024). It's a difficult task, but it's also vital for the health of your relationship and the strength of your family.

Reconnecting could include planning regular date nights or, if possible, taking a night or weekend away together. Of course, taking time away from the kids can be tough for parents with little family support, limited financial resources, or high-needs children. More than the setting or the timeframe, what truly matters is the intention and commitment behind the time spent together. It can be as simple as asking your child to wait while you finish a conversation with your partner or deliberately setting aside time to reconnect with each other emotionally and physically. The key is consciously making that connection a priority, no matter how small the gesture may seem.

It's crucial to acknowledge that reconnection can be tricky even when you make these deliberate efforts. Feelings of distance, hurt, or resentment don't magically disappear just because you decide to focus on your relationship again. If things feel a bit awkward or bumpy at first, that doesn't mean something is wrong—it's just part of healing and rebuilding connection. Think of each emotional roadblock as an ice cube that needs warmth and time to melt. In this situation, the warmth comes from intentional, conscious efforts to shift your relationship's dynamic.

The Power of Perspective

When couples come to see me, they're often surprised by how much attention I place on what's happening in their relationship right now, rather than immediately delving into the past. Whenever possible, I aim to catch the disconnection in the moment during therapy: "What just happened?" This focus on the present may seem counterintuitive, especially when so much of their hurt stems from unresolved events in the past. But here's the truth: True healing begins in the present.

Why? Because many couples are caught in a cycle of disconnection: a repeating pattern of reactive behaviors, misunderstandings, and emotional distance (Johnson, 2008; Real, 2022). These cycles keep them stuck, reinforcing the very pain they want to resolve. To begin healing, we must first address the present interactions that perpetuate these patterns. I often use the metaphor of a leaky faucet to illustrate this concept: You can't clean up the water (past hurts) if the leaky faucet (current cycle of disconnection) is still dripping and making a mess. To make progress, we need to first interrupt the reactive cycle. This means nurturing small, positive interactions—expressing appreciation, showing kindness, or being emotionally available, as well as approaching conflict with vulnerability rather than relying on protective moves that keep partners disconnected from each other. These efforts build warmth and trust, creating a buffer against the inevitable storms of family life.

A key part of breaking the negative cycle and fostering connection is something called *differentiation*. Also known as *perspective-taking*, it refers to holding on to your own feelings and experiences while also being able to consider your partner's perspective with empathy and curiosity. It's about moving from a reactive stance of blame or defense to a place where both partners can step back, recognize their own role in the dynamic, and truly see their partner's experience. This shift is crucial because cycles of disconnection thrive on rigid perspectives. When each partner feels misunderstood, invalidated, or unseen, their pain entrenches them in the belief that there is only one "right" way to see a situation. The truth, however, is that there are as many valid perspectives as there are people involved.

Differentiation also helps partners take things less personally. When you can truly see your partner as a separate individual, their reactions and behaviors stop feeling like a direct reflection of or attack on you. Instead, you can recognize their responses as being about them and their experience. This shift reduces reactivity and defensiveness, creating space for curiosity, compassion, and deeper connection.

For example, one partner might interpret emotional withdrawal as a lack of love, while the withdrawing partner may feel overwhelmed and powerless to meet their partner's needs. They are both right, and both have good reason to feel hurt and misunderstood. While each strives to have their perspective validated, each often unintentionally invalidates the other, pushing them further and further from the connection they both crave. Without perspective-taking, these narratives about the meaning of behaviors become locked in place, fueling the cycle. Differentiation allows each partner to step outside of this dynamic, soften their stance, and approach each other with greater compassion and curiosity. It's the antidote to the stuckness that keeps couples spinning in disconnection.

As couples learn to break their negative cycles, they begin to address past wounds from a place of safety and trust, rooted in their felt sense that things have genuinely changed between them in the present. Eventually, they gain the emotional distance needed to reframe those experiences. They might say something like "You used to ___, and that really made me feel ___, but I can see now that things are different." This perspective allows them to approach the past with greater empathy and less defensiveness, which then sets the stage for deeper healing. By focusing first on the present—nurturing trust, fostering safety, and practicing differentiation—couples create a solid foundation for a healthier, more resilient relationship, where they can truly understand, support, and grow with each other.

Balancing Competing Needs with Notice, Own, Connect

The transition to parenthood is rarely as smooth as we imagined. Balancing the competing needs of ourselves, our partners, and our children can feel like an impossible task—something, or someone, always seems to fall through the cracks. The push and pull between "me," "we," and "three" requires constant adjustment, communication, and patience, especially as the demands of parenting intensify. By using the Notice, Own, Connect framework, couples can navigate these challenges with greater clarity and intention, even during the most chaotic times.

NOTICE

The first step is to take a step back and observe how these dynamics are playing out in your life. Often, we get so caught up in the day-to-day demands that we lose sight of the bigger picture. By pausing to notice, you can begin to identify the areas where balance feels off.

Questions to ask yourself:

- Am I neglecting my own needs or sacrificing too much of myself for the family?
- Are there patterns of disconnection—like frequent arguments, irritability, or emotional withdrawal—that seem to keep us stuck?
- Do we prioritize time together as a couple?

Simply noticing these patterns, without judgment, is the first step toward creating change.

OWN

The next step is to own your part in the current dynamic. This doesn't mean blaming yourself, but it does mean taking responsibility for how you show up in the relationship and how your choices or behaviors might contribute to the imbalance.

Questions to ask yourself:

- Have I communicated my own needs clearly, or am I expecting my partner to read my mind?
- Are there unresolved emotions—like resentment, frustration, or exhaustion—that are shaping how I interact with my partner?
- Do I find it difficult to understand my partner's perspective during conflicts, or do I feel invalidated when their perspective differs from mine?

Owning your role creates space for both partners to step forward and say, "Here's what I can do differently." It's not about assigning fault—it's about building accountability and teamwork.

CONNECT

Finally, take intentional steps to reconnect with your partner. Connection doesn't have to be elaborate. It's the small, everyday efforts that matter most.

Questions to ask yourself:

- What small action can I take today to show my partner I value them?
- How can we carve out even a few minutes of uninterrupted time to connect?
- Can I try to focus on listening with curiosity and speaking with vulnerability next time we have a difference of perspective?

Connection might look like setting aside time to talk after the kids go to bed, sharing a laugh over something small, or simply offering a kind touch or reassuring word during a busy day. It's about showing up for each other in ways that remind you both that the relationship matters.

Balancing competing needs isn't about perfection. It's about constant microadjustments. The transition from "me" to "we" to "three" is messy, and that's okay. By using the Notice, Own, Connect framework, couples can start to identify where they're out of sync, take steps to realign, and build a stronger foundation for the challenges and joys ahead.

Remember, it's not about getting it right every time. It's about recognizing what truly matters and making intentional choices, over and over again, to nurture your relationship and family. ♥

Chapter 2

The Cycle of Disconnection

Couples often come to me wanting to talk about everything they fight about. Money, each other's parents, the kids, housework . . . the list goes on and on. Undeniably, specific issues that have led partners to feel discounted, misunderstood, or not in alignment make them emotionally primed for a difficult discussion or fight anytime these topics arise. It can feel like playing an endless game of whack-a-mole, trying to solve every issue as it comes up. However, the real problem lies beyond these specific issues. When couples come to see me, I'm less concerned with *what* these couples fight about and more focused on *how* they fight.

Every couple has a pattern to how their conflicts go. Typically, this pattern feeds on itself, repeating over and over, preventing the conflict from ever getting resolved and leaving the couple unable to reconnect. Dr. Sue Johnson (2008), the founder of emotionally focused therapy (EFT), clinically proven to be one of the most effective methods for working with couples, coined the term "the cycle" to describe this repetitive dynamic.

Let me say it again: *The content of your arguments is less important than the pattern your conflicts follow.* That sense of hopeless exhaustion or latent rage—"Here we are again; you're doing the same thing you did before, and I feel the same way I did before"—doesn't come from the actual issue you're fighting about. It's the cycle pulling you apart! (In fact, identifying that familiar feeling can be a tool that helps you recognize when the cycle is occurring.) Once both partners understand how their cycle works and how they both contribute to it, even the most challenging conflicts become more accessible to work through.

♥

Once deeply in love, Leo and Amara have drifted apart since the birth of their two-year-old daughter. Both have redirected their passion and desire away from each other and into other pursuits, she into mothering and he into work, leaving them disconnected and unable to find common ground. Without a shared focus, they struggle to see the qualities in each other that initially drew them together. The warmth and intimacy they once shared have faded, replaced by a sense of distance that has deepened with a decreased frequency of sexual intimacy. Their lack of sex and their difficulty in communicating have brought them into my office.

"I just want him to want to want me, and it feels hurtful that he doesn't," says Amara. "It's not just about sex, either. I feel like he avoids even talking to me at this point."

Amara's feelings of loneliness and rejection lead her to wonder whether something is wrong with Leo or herself. She wants to talk it through, but the more anxious and frustrated she feels, the more critical she becomes in how she seeks reassurance. This leads Leo to withdraw even further; silence and distance are his way of avoiding conflict. This, of course, deepens Amara's sense of rejection, anxiety, and frustration. She pushes harder, causing Leo to retreat further.

It doesn't help that Amara has seen the difference in how Leo interacts with her compared to how he acts at work. With his colleagues and employees, he comes across as engaged, energetic, and cheerful. Leo explains that his job is demanding but rewarding, and the admiration he feels within his workplace boosts his self-esteem, making it easy for him to engage with others.

"Amara is the only one who sees me so negatively," he says sadly. "Honestly, I don't even want to spend time with her anymore. She always seems mad at me. It's a lot easier to throw myself into work. At least there, I'm appreciated."

As with Leo and Amara, couples who are struggling often come to therapy believing that the solution lies in "fixing" their partner. Leo thinks that if Amara was less critical, he would feel more accepted, while Amara believes that if Leo was more affectionate, she'd feel less anxious. Both are "right," in that they both contribute to the cycle they are stuck in. Since this cycle is cocreated, it requires a collaborative solution.

In reality, both Amara and Leo want the same things: desire, understanding, the return of the connection they once had. Feeling safe with each other is what makes those things possible. Amara seeks verbal affirmation to feel safe, while for Leo, feeling safe comes from calm interactions. Both are trying to protect themselves, but their actions create the opposite result of what they want. If Amara felt more secure, her need for reassurance would decrease, and if Leo felt less overwhelmed by intense emotions, he would communicate more. Both could then find the connection they desire. The real enemy is not each other but instead the cycle they're stuck in.

Interestingly, their conflict is actually their longing for each other in disguise. Imagine if they could understand each other's actions for what they truly are: a bid for connection and an attempt to express the pain of feeling rejected and alone. If Leo responded to Amara's underlying need with support and warmth instead of defensiveness, she would likely feel less inclined to criticize and more secure in their relationship. Similarly, if Amara could recognize the underlying longing in Leo's desire to avoid conflict—his need to feel that he is valued and "enough" in this most important relationship—she might feel more able to express appreciation and create a calmer, more supportive environment that encourages Leo to participate more openly.

This sounds straightforward. The challenge is that both Leo and Amara have deep, unmet needs that keep them stuck in their cycle. Leo needs to understand that, while his silence may feel protective, it undermines Amara's sense of security. Small, consistent efforts to engage in conversation can gradually rebuild her confidence. Meanwhile, Amara needs to recognize that her anxiety-driven behaviors might overwhelm Leo, making him feel insecure and doubtful about saying the right thing, which leads to further silence and withdrawal. The key to breaking the cycle is mutual understanding of the emotions driving each other's behaviors.

Understanding this cycle is crucial because it helps frame the issue as a cocreated pattern rather than an insurmountable problem. By acknowledging each other's underlying needs, emotions, and action tendencies, both partners can start making changes to their part of the cycle and promote a more connected relationship.

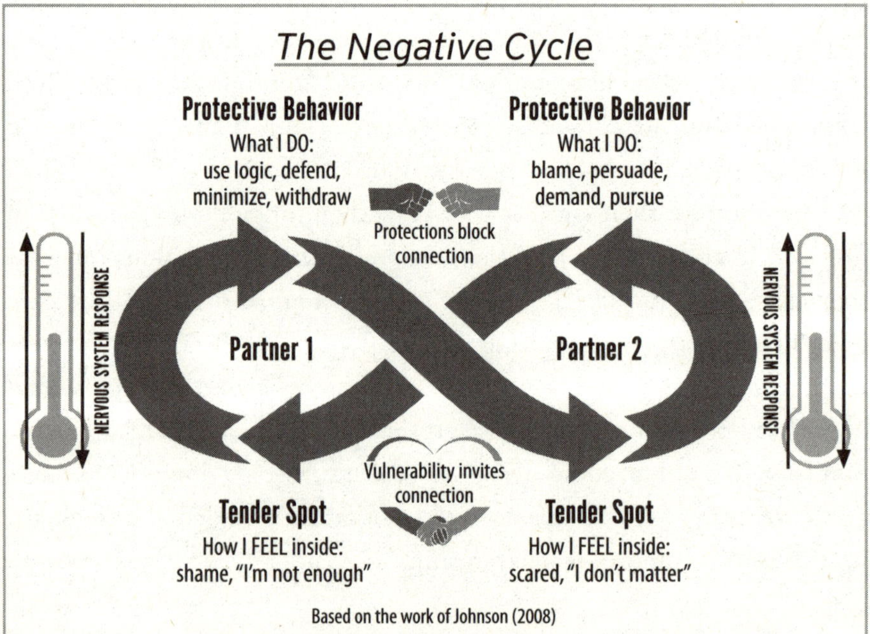

Types of Negative Cycles

Conflict is a normal and inevitable part of any relationship. It's a reflection of both partners' emotional investment and their desire to feel loved, respected, and secure. The challenge arises not from the presence of conflict (every relationship experiences it) but from how it's managed. Addressing how you handle conflict can lead to significant improvement in the relationship—something I've learned from personal as well as professional experience.

Most conflict tends to fall into predictable patterns or cycles. The three main types of negative cycles are *pursue/withdraw*, *pursue/pursue*, and *withdraw/withdraw*. Recognizing and understanding these dynamics is a crucial step toward breaking free from unhelpful patterns and fostering healthier communication and connection.

Pursue/Withdraw

The majority of couples' negative cycles follow a pursue/withdraw pattern most of the time. In it, one partner, typically driven by a need for reassurance or understanding, seeks to bridge the distance they feel by expressing concerns, asking questions, or even initiating sex. The withdrawer, overwhelmed by the emotional intensity of this outreach, disengages as a way of managing their discomfort or protecting the relationship from perceived harm. The pursuer interprets this withdrawal as disinterest or apathy, which heightens their anxiety and causes them to push harder. In response, the withdrawer retreats further.

Both partners are trying to protect the relationship in their own ways. The pursuer aims to resolve the conflict and reconnect, while the withdrawer seeks to reduce emotional tension and avoid damaging conflict. But as the cycle deepens, the pursuer starts feeling unloved and doubts their partner's commitment, while the withdrawer's anxiety about doing the wrong thing leads them to shut down even more.

Without intervention, the cycle can lead to frustration, resentment, and further emotional distance.

Interestingly, the difference in response often attracted them to each other in the first place. Pursuers are drawn to the calm, steady presence of withdrawers, while withdrawers appreciate the passion and drive of pursuers. However, in times of stress or conflict, partners can often be pushed apart by the same dynamic that used to draw them together.

To break free from the cycle, the pursuing partner must learn to manage their need for immediate reassurance, while the withdrawing partner must become more comfortable with emotional engagement. Over time, this will foster a healthier dynamic where both partners feel valued and safe to express their underlying needs and fears.

Variations on the Theme

While this cycle is the most common, the other types of negative cycles can often be mistaken for a highly escalated pursue/withdraw. For instance, a burned-out pursuer can look like a withdrawer, but their core attachment fears and insecurities are different. Conversely, a fed-up withdrawer can often have a quick fuse and become less conflict-avoidant out of desperation and despair.

Pursue/Pursue

While less common than the pursue/withdraw pattern, the pursue/pursue dynamic also significantly impacts relationships. In this pattern, both partners feel the need to address problems immediately and intensely, creating a simultaneous onslaught of heightened emotional engagement that each partner perceives as an attack by the other.

The pursue/pursue cycle often starts with both partners having a strong desire for connection and validation. Initially, this mutual pursuit might feel passionate and engaging. However, partners in these relationships tend to be very susceptible to signs of disconnection and respond by increasing their emotional engagement, using intense verbal communication to express their needs and frustrations.

Though this type of communication is intended to encourage the partner to engage emotionally, it can cause each person to see the other's efforts to connect as blaming and criticism. This results in escalating conflicts where both partners feel attacked and misunderstood, leading to intense and destructive arguments. Needless to say, the emotional intensity can be exhausting, leading to instability in the relationship if not addressed.

Withdraw/Withdraw

In the withdraw/withdraw cycle, both partners respond to conflict or emotional distress by retreating, resulting in minimal communication and engagement. These couples typically avoid conflict and emotionally charged conversations altogether, but while this may result in less "drama" in the relationship, it can also lead to significant emotional and physical disconnect.

This cycle often stems from a fear of conflict and a desire to protect oneself from emotional pain. Both partners may feel overwhelmed by the prospect of addressing issues; instead, conflict is avoided entirely, with both partners maintaining an emotional detachment, avoiding deep conversations and emotional expressions. As a result, they seldom argue but also rarely get close.

This mutual withdrawal creates a cold and distant atmosphere in the relationship, as well as a buildup of unresolved problems. Rather than addressing the problems directly, both partners default to avoidant positions, not counting on or trusting the other. Occasionally, they may have conflict when an emotionally raw spot is touched, but this is infrequent. Over time, the lack of emotional interaction can lead to significant emotional and physical disconnect, as neither partner is willing to initiate reconnection or resolution.

The Positive Cycle: Rupture and Repair

The cycle of *rupture and repair* is a natural and inevitable part of every relationship, even secure and healthy ones. No matter how strong the bond between two people might be, misunderstandings, disagreements, and moments of disconnection are bound to happen. These ruptures can range from minor miscommunications, like a snippy exchange, to more significant conflicts, such as a serious fight or betrayal of trust. While ruptures can feel destabilizing, for the most part, they are not inherently harmful. What matters most is how couples navigate the repair process afterward.

Repair is the process of addressing the rupture and restoring connection. It involves taking responsibility for one's role in the conflict, making amends, and working to understand each other's perspectives. Successful repair helps to rebuild trust and strengthen the emotional bond. It also creates resilience, showing both partners that their relationship can withstand conflict and grow stronger through it. In fact, research suggests that the way couples repair after a conflict is a better predictor of relationship success than the absence of conflict altogether (Gottman & Silver, 2015). Repair doesn't have to be elaborate. A heartfelt apology, a warm touch or smile, or acknowledging the need for space and then showing a willingness to revisit the conversation calmly can all be very effective.

Repair is crucial in all relationships, including those between parent and child. Children, like adults, experience moments of disconnection with their caregivers. These moments of misattunement are inevitable, but what matters is how parents respond. When parents model repair—acknowledging their mistakes, apologizing, and reconnecting—they teach children that it's okay to make mistakes and that relationships can endure conflict and remain safe. This modeling helps children learn emotional regulation, conflict resolution, and the ability to navigate challenging interactions. Repair in these moments helps lay the groundwork for children to build healthy relationships in adulthood.

One of my very favorite examples of a good repair was modeled by my children. While they were playing at a friend's house, a conflict over a toy hatchet resulted in serious hurt feelings and light physical injury. Once the initial anger and tears subsided, I—anxious to smooth things over—strongly encouraged my son to go and apologize. He resisted the forced apology march and confidently assured me, "Mom, we've got this."

About 10 minutes later, the group of kids came running by, laughing together as if nothing had happened. Being the repair enthusiast I am, I couldn't help but pull them aside to ask if they'd made amends. With big grins, they explained that they'd decided the hatchet was the root of all their problems, so they had ceremonially buried it. Yes, they literally *buried the hatchet.* Repair success! Kids: 1, Forced Apology March: 0.

Ultimately, the cycle of rupture and repair isn't just an inevitable part of relationships—it's a defining one. Each rupture offers an opportunity to build deeper trust, empathy, and intimacy. When we shift the focus from striving for perfection to prioritizing repair, families and couples create resilient bonds rooted in genuine connection.

Tender Places

Whether a fight starts over something seemingly trivial (like unloading the dishwasher or tone of voice) or something major (like the decision to have a baby or a serious parenting disagreement), the feeling of disconnection is what morphs it into something much bigger, something that encompasses not only the issue at hand but also past arguments, hurts, resentments, and critiques. Fights contribute to a negative emotional cycle less because of their content and more because the conflict touches on tender places, bringing up deeper emotional needs that are or have been unmet.

Sometimes, those unmet emotional needs are the result not of your present relationship but of past experiences or unresolved feelings. A *trigger* is an emotional reaction to something your partner says or does that activates wounds from the past. For example, if you had a parent who was critical and dismissive, you might find that anytime your partner seems to brush off your concerns, it triggers old feelings of being unimportant or unloved. This can lead to a strong emotional response that feels much bigger than the situation.

While your partner likely didn't install your sensitive buttons, they sure are good at pushing them! The more we care about someone, the easier it is for them to trigger us because their words and actions matter deeply to us. They have the power to affect us on a profound level. And when the reactions rooted in our past play out in our present relationships, the same event can result in entirely different emotional experiences for each partner. What your partner sees as an accidental, one-off offense, such as forgetting a commitment or responding tersely in a moment of stress, may activate an old feeling or fear you experienced in the past. On the basis of this old wound, you react with disproportionate intensity—lashing out, shutting down, becoming overly anxious or weepy. Your partner feels attacked or rejected by your reaction; it may even trigger their own past-wounds experiences. This can cause them to respond defensively, and before you know it, you're both caught in a downward spiral of negative interactions. No wonder couples often describe feeling helpless, confused, or alone in the middle of a fight. They are each having a completely different emotional experience that the other knows nothing about!

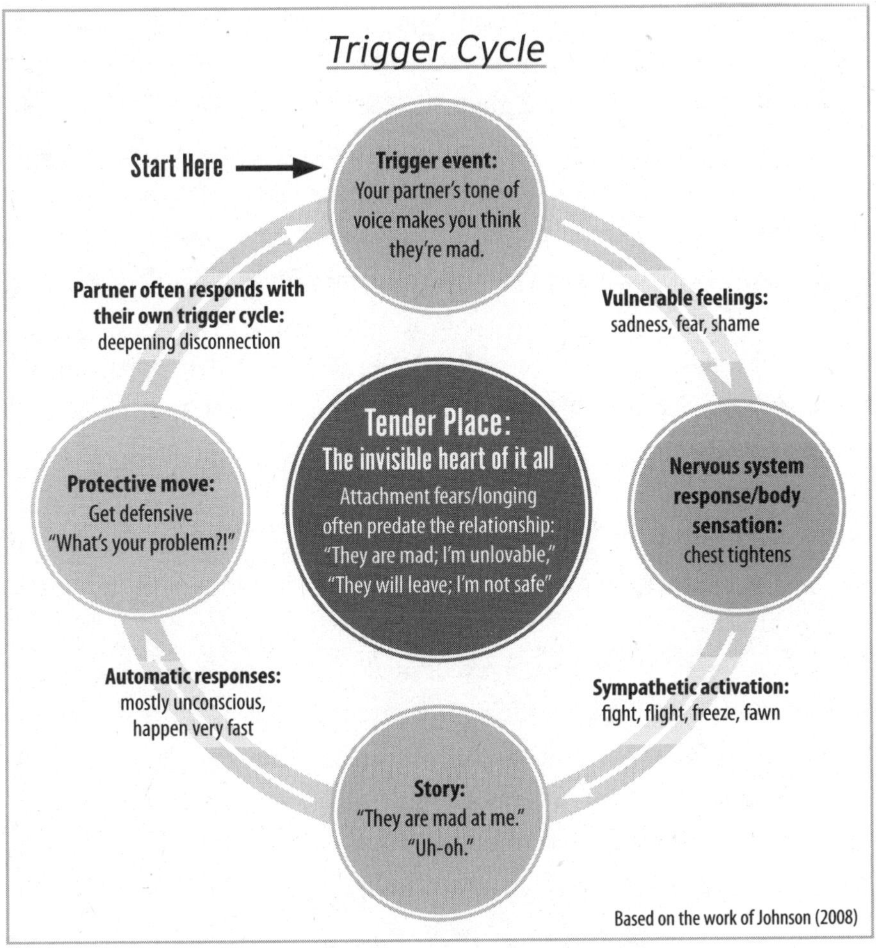

Healing the Negative Cycle

No matter which dynamic characterizes your conflicts, it's essential for each partner to recognize and work on their role in the negative cycle. You can't change your partner, and your work alone can't shift the dynamic between you. Couples must work together to identify their parts in the cycle and learn new moves.

For example, imagine a scenario where Amara, seeking to soothe her anxiety, tries to connect with Leo by talking about her feelings and encouraging him to share his own. Leo feels overwhelmed by this intensity and, hoping to help Amara (and himself) emotionally regulate, offers a minimal response and gives her space. This backfires: Amara only feels more anxiety, causing her to pursue connection even harder and with greater dysregulation. This, too, backfires: Leo pulls away further, scared that anything he says or does will make things worse.

To break this cycle, both partners must recognize what they fear and long for and what they do when they feel that way.

Amara might say, "I panic when I feel like I'm losing you. When I feel that way, I get really big and yell, hoping that you'll hear me and give me the closeness I want to feel from you."

Leo might say, "I feel like I've messed everything up even though I've been trying so hard to get it right. I worry I'll never be able to give you enough. It feels safer to shut down rather than risk doing the wrong thing."

This confession of deeper emotional needs can help Amara, the pursuer, understand that reducing her intensity and pressure can create a safer space for the withdrawer to engage. It can also help Leo, the withdrawer, realize that offering a little more engagement will calm Amara's anxiety, creating a more balanced emotional environment.

The Sexual Cycle

For many couples, the negative cycle plays out not only in their day-to-day interactions but also in their sexual intimacy. While one cycle may feel more dominant—like being emotionally connected but sexually distant, or having a satisfying sex life despite frequent emotional conflict—it's common for these patterns to overlap. Emotional and sexual intimacy are deeply connected, and struggles in one area often spill into the other, reinforcing disconnection.

The sexual cycle in a relationship shares all the features of the emotional cycle, but the content of the misattunement centers on how (and how often) a couple has sex, rather than how they communicate. Sex carries its own unique weight, often shaped by the heavy burden of expectations and shame, both of which add layers of complexity to the disconnection. These layers make sexual problems feel intensely personal and, at times, even harder to address than emotional conflict—largely because we often struggle to know *how* to talk about it.

♥

Natalie and Henry have been married for 15 years and recently sought help for their low-sex marriage. Despite this challenge, they are deeply connected as friends and co-parents. They share a strong emotional bond, communicate effectively in most areas, and work together seamlessly to care for their three-year-old twins. However, the gap in their sexual desire has become the primary source of strain in their relationship. While Henry has always had higher desire than Natalie, this difference didn't become a major issue until after the twins were born. The demands of parenting and the struggle to balance their many roles have amplified the disconnect, leaving them both eager to find a resolution.

"Henry thinks I'm withholding sex on purpose, but honestly, I can't remember the last time I had any thoughts of sex at all," says Natalie, adding matter-of-factly, "I think I could go the rest of my life and not miss it. The only thing I fantasize about these days is an empty hotel room where I'm all alone and don't have to see anyone."

The couple explains that they battled infertility for five years before finally conceiving through in vitro fertilization (IVF). During that period, Natalie became deeply involved in monitoring her ovulation cycle, making sure they had intercourse at least twice during her fertile window. She also followed a detailed post-sex routine to boost the chances of implantation. As a result, their sex life became entirely centered on conception, with all their previous foreplay activities falling by the wayside. Perhaps unsurprisingly, neither of them was very satisfied in these regimented encounters.

"Sex became almost clinical," explains Henry. "I felt like just a prop. I felt like my job was to show up hard and cum as quickly as possible. All the fun went out of it, and to be honest, after a while, neither of us felt like doing it when she wasn't ovulating because it felt like it had no point. I think that's where it started to go wrong for us."

Given the cost of childcare for two babies, Natalie left her job to stay home as the primary caregiver. She had long desired to have children and loves being a full-time mother, though of course she often finds it challenging and looks forward to her few hours of "time off" once the twins are in bed. Meanwhile, Henry began working longer hours to make up for the change in their income and the cost of kids. The more overworked and rejected Henry felt, the more he withdrew from childcare and household chores, partly due to exhaustion from his long workdays and partly to "punish" Natalie for withholding sex.

"It feels like our relationship has dwindled to the minutiae of work, kids, and chores," Henry says sadly. "I only ask for sex these days when I'm so lonely and desperate that I can't stand it anymore. But it doesn't work. She says she doesn't feel like it or she's too tired, and if I push it, we end up in a fight. I want her, but she doesn't seem to want me."

Natalie responds that she resents Henry's expectation that she be the caretaker of his sexual needs as well as of their children and the house. "Henry doesn't help around the house unless I ask—it feels like I'm managing him, not like we are working together. Honestly, it makes me feel less attracted to him. So when he asks for sex, it seems like just another chore. I feel like all he's interested in is sex, not *me*, you know?"

As you've probably noticed, a sexual negative cycle involves plenty of emotional issues: anxiety and disappointment, feelings of inadequacy or rejection, triggers from past relationships or long-held beliefs about sex. Discussions about sexual difficulties tend to be emotionally loaded and challenging to address, especially when unsuccessful attempts leave partners feeling vulnerable and unwilling to risk further embarrassment or hurt. This is further complicated by couples' unspoken expectations of what sex *should* look like in a marriage: who is supposed to initiate and how initiating should look, when and where are the "right" occasions for sex, what circumstances "should" turn someone on (or off), and of course, what is a "normal" frequency for sex to occur.

These expectations typically boil down to the idea of owing each other sex. This is a losing proposition on both sides. The more one person feels owed sex, the less patience and attunement they will have for what it takes to ignite the other person's desire. Meanwhile, the more pressure one partner feels to have sex, whether that pressure is actual or imaginary, the less desire they will feel. In both instances, it's more likely that sex will take place out of pity or obligation, which rarely feels satisfying for either partner.

Types of Sexual Cycles

As with emotional negative cycles, the most common type of sexual negative cycle is pursue/withdraw. In this dynamic, one partner seeks more frequent or intense sexual interactions, while the other partner feels overwhelmed by these advances or inadequate to satisfy them and withdraws in response. The more frustrated and disconnected the pursuer feels, the more they pursue, causing the withdrawer to feel more guilty and pressured, lessening their desire to have sex. This leaves pursuers feeling undesirable and rejected, while withdrawers often end up feeling inadequate and ashamed, as though there's something wrong with them.

It's worth noting that partners often swap roles between sexual and emotional cycles. The partner who is the emotional pursuer, constantly seeking verbal and emotional reassurance, becomes the sexual withdrawer, while the emotional withdrawer, who tends to avoid verbal or emotional confrontation, might take on the role of the sexual pursuer.

This is known as the *flip-flop cycle* or *crossover cycle*. In this dynamic, the emotional pursuer needs to feel emotionally connected before wanting to engage in sexual interactions, while the emotional withdrawer often feels safer expressing closeness through physical intimacy than through verbal exchanges.

In Natalie and Henry's cycle, Natalie is the *emotional pursuer* and *sexual withdrawer*, while Henry is the *emotional withdrawer* and *sexual pursuer*. Both partners believe they'd be more open and responsive if their preferred way of connecting occurred more frequently. This role reversal creates a complex dynamic. The emotional pursuer often feels that their emotional needs are overlooked, that sex is all their partner wants from them. Similarly, the sexual pursuer tends to feel unwanted or even criticized when their attempts to connect physically are met with rejection. This can lead each partner to withdraw in their own way, leaving them both feeling helplessly disconnected.

When I ask Natalie to think about what she wants from Henry, she answers, "It would be great if he could be more proactive with the kids and housework. But mostly, I want him to show interest in me outside the bedroom. My kids see me as just one thing, you know? I want him to see me as a whole person and show that he values me that way."

Henry is surprised. "I don't want you to feel like I don't value you as a person. I thought you were just mad at me. When I want sex, it's because I'm attracted to *all* of you—the same way I was before we got married."

"I get it . . . " Natalie reflects for a moment. "Maybe if it didn't feel so all or nothing . . . like if we could spend time kissing or cuddling without any expectation or pressure. If I knew that you were open to that, I think I'd be more open to seeing where it went."

As Natalie and Henry begin to understand that they are both longing for connection, expressing it differently helps them become more open to hearing each other's perspectives. Instead of assigning blame or expecting each other to change to fix the issues, they can work together to change their sexual cycle.

A Note on Gender

Men and women express their emotional and sexual needs based on cultural, societal, and personal influences. These expressions fundamentally concern the need for connection and closeness but are shaped differently for each gender.

For men, cultural norms often encourage stoicism and strength, leading them to express emotional needs through taking action, such as problem-solving, acts of service, and physical touch, rather than using words. In terms of sexual needs, men often use physical intimacy as a primary way to connect and express closeness.

Women have been socialized to be nurturing and empathetic, making them more comfortable communicating their feelings and needs though words, seeking verbal reassurance and validation from their partners. However, this same socialization can make it harder for women to fully embrace their sexual selves without shame. As a result, emotional connection can create a pathway where relational safety and trust pave the way for desire.

Synchronized Cycles

When the sexual and emotional cycles in a relationship align, with the same partner acting as either the pursuer or withdrawer in both contexts, it is often referred to as a *synchronized cycle*. In synchronized pursuit, one partner consistently seeks connection through both verbal reassurance and physical intimacy; they are proactive in trying to engage their partner emotionally and sexually. Synchronized withdrawal occurs when one partner, often feeling overwhelmed by demands for connection, tends to distance themselves from emotional conversations and sexual interactions to protect themselves from the stress of potential conflict or emotional exposure.

This is the case for Leo and Amara. Though they rarely have sex anymore, neither has been unfaithful; instead, Leo masturbates to porn regularly (mostly for stress relief, he says), while Amara says that she wants to have sex with Leo, but her desire for "solo sex" has all but dried up.

"I want to have sex with him, but I want him to initiate—I want him to show desire for me," says Amara. "I bring it up occasionally, but I'm so angry at this point it always leads to a fight. And the less we have sex, the more I find myself getting annoyed with little things around the house and micromanaging him, which I know he hates."

"I feel like I can't do anything right," Leo says again. "She wants me to want her, and I do, but when she initiates sex, I just feel pressured, and then I don't want to have sex, even if I did before. I feel resentful that she thinks there's something wrong with me, but to be honest, I worry about that sometimes, too. There's no way I want to hop in bed when I feel that way."

Underneath all these cycles are deep longings for security, love, and connection. In other words, it's all rooted in past and present *attachment*—that is, the way we experience emotional bonds with those close to us. Research shows that our childhood experiences of attachment with caregivers set the pattern for how we manage stress, regulate emotions, and connect with others later in life (Girme et al., 2020). This can explain why we often find ourselves stuck in the same kinds of relationships over and over again, even when we know they're not working for us.

It also explains why certain situations trigger the same responses over and over again, no matter how many times we've thought through them and resolved to do better. Even with conscious intentions to do things differently, our responses often come automatically, before we even have a chance to think through them. This is because our nervous system—the network of nerves and cells that acts as the body's command center, regulating everything from our stress responses to our emotional reactions—is shaped by past experiences.

By understanding more about our early attachment experiences, we can identify the deep needs that trigger the automatic responses fueling our negative cycle. Difficult as it can be, couples are drawn closer together when they express their underlying needs and fears. This leads to more understanding and open communication, empowering us to break free from old cycles and create healthier, more fulfilling connections.

Differentiation and the Negative Cycle

When we're stuck in a negative cycle, it's usually because we're caught up in our feelings of hurt and attachment injuries. Our partner is also stuck on their island with their feelings. Being intently focused on our own emotions makes it hard to hear what the other person is feeling; if anything, hearing them share their viewpoint often makes us feel invalidated.

This is where differentiation becomes helpful. As we learned in the last chapter, differentiation means considering a situation from a different point of view than your own. When we see our partner as a separate person with their own valid perspective, rather than as someone responsible for our feelings, we can understand their perspective without feeling threatened by it. This understanding helps us move past the negative cycle.

It's counterintuitive, but the more deeply we care about a relationship, the harder it can be to shift our perspective or fully consider our partner's. The closeness and trust that draw us into a committed relationship often lead us to subconsciously assume that our partner knows us so well that they'll always understand how we feel, what we need, and what we want in any given situation, and act accordingly. In a sense, we see them as infallible, much like how children view their parents in early life.

Attachment theory sheds light on this dynamic as well. In adulthood, our bond with a partner often takes the place of the attachment we formed with caregivers in childhood. Just as children rely on parents to intuitively understand their needs, even when those needs are unspoken or unclear, we often expect our partners to do the same. We may look to them for emotional safety, reassurance, and consistency, believing they'll instinctively prioritize our well-being, even at the expense of their own needs.

On a rational level, we understand that our partner is human—imperfect and entitled to their own feelings and perspectives. But on an emotional level, those early attachment instincts persist. We rely on this unspoken expectation as a foundation for trust and security in the relationship. Letting go of that can feel unsettling because it challenges the very sense of safety we depend on. Recognizing this dynamic is key to building healthier, more balanced connections in which both partners feel understood and supported without the impossible expectation of mind-reading or perfection.

When our partner is careless with our feelings or doesn't show up as we hoped, it's easy to read their actions as being intended to hurt us. After all, they know us better than anybody—how could such a targeted hurt be an accident? In the same way, when a partner expresses their perspective about something we've done, it can feel like a criticism of our own perspective. Instead of validating them (as we'd want them to do for us), we often focus on defending our intentions instead.

In my experience of working with couples, it is very rare for partners to intentionally hurt each other. Most partners hurt and frustrate each other as a result of feeling deeply hurt and frustrated themselves. Assuming positive intentions on both sides frees us to understand and validate our partner's feelings. When we can do this, it breaks the negative cycle and begins to restore connection, in and out of the bedroom.

Blame the Cycle, Not Each Other

Couples often view problems linearly: If one partner changes a specific behavior, everything will improve. Drawing this line in the sand may seem like a way to simplify the issue, but it really just sets both partners up for a stalemate where each feels unseen, invalidated, or unsupported by the other. You're no longer fighting about the dishes or the last time you had sex—you're fighting over whose perspective is right or whose needs are being ignored.

Instead of figuring out who is ultimately to blame for the disconnection, the solution is to *blame the cycle*. The real enemy in the relationship is the negative conflict pattern you've cocreated. Recognizing the cycle and working to change the roles you play in it allows you to move toward a more understanding and supportive relationship in which you can see each other's needs, validate each other's perspectives, and respond to each other's feelings with compassion instead of frustration.

Breaking the Cycle with Notice, Own, Connect

Breaking free from cycles of disconnection requires intentional effort, but the Notice, Own, Connect framework provides a practical roadmap. By identifying the cycle, taking responsibility for your part, and leaning into more vulnerable ways of connecting, you can disrupt harmful patterns and build a healthier, more secure relationship dynamic.

NOTICE

The first step is to notice when the cycle is playing out. This means pausing to observe the patterns that arise during moments of conflict or emotional distance. Are you falling into a familiar dynamic of one partner pursuing while the other withdraws? Are unresolved past hurts driving your current reactions? Take a moment to name the emotions you're feeling—frustration, loneliness, fear of rejection—and recognize that your partner might be caught in their own emotional loop as well. Noticing helps you step back from the heat of the moment, allowing you to see the cycle as the problem, not your partner.

Questions to ask yourself:

- What vulnerable emotions, fears, and longings are under my reactions?
- How do I interpret my partner's behavior, and is that interpretation fueling my feelings?
- What do I feel when we get stuck in the same predictable pattern?

OWN

Next, own your role in the cycle. While it's tempting to focus on your partner's actions, meaningful change begins when you examine how your own responses contribute to the dynamic. Reflect on the ways you might protect yourself when you feel hurt or disconnected. Are you shutting down, becoming defensive, or lashing out? Owning your role isn't about assigning blame; it's about acknowledging how your actions, even unintentionally, may perpetuate the cycle. Taking responsibility for your part empowers you to make choices that foster connection rather than reinforce disconnection.

Questions to ask yourself:

- How do I typically respond when I feel hurt or vulnerable?
- What might my partner experience when I react this way?
- How can I take maximum responsibility for my part in the cycle?

CONNECT

Finally, replace protective moves with vulnerable ones. This is the most challenging step, as it requires stepping outside of your comfort zone and trying new ways of interacting. If your default is to withdraw, it might mean expressing your feelings instead of retreating. If you tend to pursue, it might mean softening your approach rather than escalating. For instance, instead of saying, "You never care about what I need," try "I'm afraid I don't matter to you." Vulnerable moves signal to your partner that you're not attacking or pulling away—rather, you're inviting them into connection.

Questions to ask yourself:

- How can I share my feelings with vulnerability, not blame?
- What is my typical tendency in conflict—do I pursue or withdraw? What kind of different approach could I try to move toward connection?
- How can I view my partner's behavior through the lens of their vulnerable emotions, fears, and longings, using my new understanding to foster empathy and connection?

Breaking the cycle of disconnection takes patience and practice. Vulnerable new moves may feel awkward or even risky at first, especially if they challenge ingrained habits. But over time, they create a new pattern of responding to each other with empathy, curiosity, and care. This foundation of safety and trust allows both partners to feel seen and valued, even during moments of conflict.

Breaking the cycle isn't about eliminating conflict or fixing everything overnight. It's about engaging in a way that prioritizes understanding over defensiveness, and, most importantly, giving yourselves and each other lots of grace. You're both learning something new, and it won't feel natural or easy right away. By practicing these new approaches, you're stepping out of old patterns and creating a relationship where connection feels authentic, lasting, and secure. ♥

Chapter 3

A Crash Course on Attachment

Every person has a deep longing for closeness and connection, a secure home base, and a safe person. No one is an island. This vulnerability—the need for others—can feel incredibly difficult, especially when the attachment suffers a rupture from conflict, disappointment, or disconnection.

In relationships, this rupture is inevitable. Whether it stems from the imperfections of parenting or the natural missteps between two imperfect humans, we will inevitably miss each other at times. Expecting perfection in our relationships is unreasonable and unrealistic. The goal for a healthy relationship is not to avoid disconnection entirely but rather to develop the skills to repair and reconnect when disconnection occurs.

We may know this rationally, but it becomes especially hard to navigate when we as parents are working on two essential attachment tasks at once, often having to choose which relationship gets neglected. The monumental task of raising a tiny human is, by necessity, all-consuming. In that all-consuming role, the romantic relationship often has to wait . . . and wait. While this neglect is usually benign, it often leads to a paring down of our interactions to only what feels necessary.

The elements vital to sexual and romantic connection—romance, eroticism, flirting—seem like a luxury, if not a distraction, when we're in the throes of late-night feedings, after-school shuttling, or teenage melodrama. But when these elements become casualties of the paring down of parenthood, it can lead to a sense that your partner is not there for you or, worse, that they don't care to be. These attachment injuries further deepen the reconnection challenge.

Mateo and Carrie, a couple in their mid-30s, have been together for eight years and married for five. They shared a deep bond and a plethora of adventures before the arrival of their son dramatically altered their lives. Today, the challenges of parenthood have created a rift in their once solid relationship that seems to grow wider with each passing day.

Neither Mateo nor Carrie had fully anticipated the whirlwind of changes in store for them. The sleepless nights, constant demands, and relentless responsibilities left them both physically and emotionally drained. Carrie's experience with postpartum depression brought overwhelming feelings of sadness and anxiety that made it difficult for her to connect with Mateo and even their son at times. Meanwhile, Mateo's insomnia, triggered by the stress and unpredictability of their new routine, left him perpetually exhausted, irritable, and anxious. Their communication, once the cornerstone of their relationship, began to falter under the weight of these new challenges. Minor misunderstandings quickly escalated into arguments, and moments of intimacy became rare as they both struggled to navigate their new roles. The laughter and spontaneous adventures they once shared were replaced by a routine that felt more like a series of obligations than a partnership.

Carrie felt deeply unsupported during those tumultuous months after their son's birth. Her requests for help seemed to go unheard, and she was left feeling isolated and alone in her struggles. The memories of those difficult times continue to haunt her, casting a shadow over their relationship and clouding her thoughts about the possibility of expanding their family.

"I'm still angry with Mateo," says Carrie. "I'm really trying to move past it, but I was struggling so much after our son was born, and he just wasn't there. It felt like he was only concerned about himself, and I felt so alone." In particular, she recalls long hours spent rocking and nursing their son while Mateo was relaxing or sleeping. "Mateo said he couldn't soothe him, but what he didn't see was that I couldn't soothe him either! I just held him while he screamed and tried everything to calm him—Mateo could have done that as well as I could. He just wasn't willing to." Crying, she continues, "Now, when I try to think about having another child or even having sex with him, all I can think about is how terrible I felt for those months. It's a block for me."

Mateo, meanwhile, grapples with feelings of guilt and inadequacy. He is profoundly apologetic for not being there for Carrie when she needed him the most, saying, "I don't even recognize that guy. I know I wasn't there for her, but it doesn't seem like me." Yet despite his regret, his battles with insomnia still make it challenging for him to be fully present. Protective of his sleep and overwhelmed by the demands of fatherhood, Mateo finds himself retreating into himself, unaware of the damage it is causing to their relationship.

"I don't know what to say when she is so sad and angry," he says. "I feel so bad, but I can't change the mistake I made in the past. Even now, I don't know if I could do anything differently. It's made me doubt myself."

Carrie knows Mateo feels terrible, but she cannot move forward. "I just don't know if I can ever trust him again. He let me down, and I never thought he would. Everyone else has let me down, too, but I thought he was my safe person," she says. "I want to get over it, but I can't seem to."

The rupture of their relationship, prolonged over the long postpartum months, has caused a significant attachment injury for both of them. The sense of safety and trust crucial for a healthy relationship has been compromised, and they don't know how to fix it.

How We Develop Attachment Styles

As we learned in the last chapter, attachment (the emotional bonds we form with those closest to us) plays a critical role in how we perceive intimacy, independence, and trust as adults. Understanding our attachment style gives us insight into our present relationship patterns, particularly how we approach closeness and navigate connections.

Early attachment experiences directly influence a child's nervous system, which governs how they react to stress and connection. When caregivers are consistent and soothing, they teach a child's nervous system to recognize safety and return to a calm, connected state after moments of stress. This ability to self-soothe becomes essential for managing emotions and building resilience. However, if caregiving is unpredictable or inconsistent, a child's nervous system may stay on high alert or become overly shut down, making it harder to regulate emotions and form secure relationships later in life.

Secure attachment develops when caregivers are responsive and consistent, creating a strong foundation for trust and emotional security that encourages the nervous system to develop a healthy balance. This balance is what helps children grow into adults who can confidently explore the world, manage challenges, and build meaningful connections with others. Securely attached adults tend to be comfortable with both intimacy and independence in romantic relationships.

Secure early attachment develops the crucial skill of emotional regulation, which allows us to effectively manage stress and intense emotions. This ability to self-soothe is an essential element in healthy relationship dynamics, allowing partners to navigate challenges without becoming overwhelmed. Overall, securely attached individuals typically have an easier time setting boundaries, communicating their needs, and maintaining a healthy balance between closeness and autonomy, which supports more fulfilling and resilient relationships.

In contrast, inconsistent or unresponsive caregiving can lead to insecure attachment patterns. The following sections will discuss the three most common styles of insecure attachment.

Anxious attachment can result in a heightened stress response, leading to clinginess and fear of abandonment. Those with anxious attachment styles—shaped by unresponsive or inconsistent caregiving—may find their insecurities magnified in romantic relationships. They often seek frequent reassurance and validation from their partners, driven by a fear of abandonment and rejection. This can result in clingy or dependent behaviors and heightened anxiety. Their internal working model, formed by early inconsistent caregiving, makes them hyperalert to perceived threats in the relationship, often leading to frequent conflicts or emotional distress.

Pursuing behavior is commonly linked to anxious attachment, but even individuals with generally secure attachment can exhibit these tendencies when feeling insecure or disconnected in their relationship. Pursuing often stems from a deep desire for reassurance, connection, or closeness—and the fear that these longings will go unfulfilled. Understanding this pattern is crucial because it allows us to connect with the underlying attachment needs and longings driving these behaviors.

Here are some reflective questions to help you determine if you lean toward anxious attachment:

- Do small changes in my partner's behavior, like them being quieter or distracted, make me feel anxious or insecure?
- Do I tend to escalate conflicts or express my feelings in ways that push for immediate reassurance or resolution?
- Do I feel panicked or overwhelmed if a conflict isn't resolved quickly or if my partner needs space to process?
- Do I sometimes neglect my own needs, interests, or boundaries in an effort to keep the peace or gain approval?

Avoidant attachment may cause the nervous system to downregulate emotional responses, resulting in emotional withdrawal and excessive self-reliance. Individuals with avoidant attachment styles—often shaped by early experiences with inconsistent or intrusive caregiving, perhaps due to parenting challenges or a mismatch in temperament—tend to prioritize independence and self-reliance. These individuals may struggle to rely on others, frequently keeping emotional distance in relationships to protect themselves from vulnerability. In romantic relationships, they might avoid emotional intimacy, appear distant or disengaged, and downplay the significance of the relationship.

Withdrawers in relationships often exhibit avoidant strategies, pulling away rather than engaging emotionally. As with pursuers and anxious attachment, it's important to remember that not all withdrawers have an avoidant attachment from childhood; they may just employ an avoidant strategy in their current relationship. This behavior is typically driven by a desire to maintain peace, avoid conflict, or safeguard the relationship.

Here are some reflective questions to help you determine if you lean toward avoidant attachment:

- Do I avoid sharing feelings or needs with my partner because it feels easier to handle things on my own?
- Do I find myself pulling away or withdrawing during conflicts instead of engaging in conversation or repair?
- Do I ever feel overwhelmed by my partner's emotions or needs?
- When faced with emotional conflict, do I tend to retreat into work, hobbies, or distractions?

Disorganized attachment in adulthood is the most rare type of insecure attachment and stems from early experiences of abuse or neglect with caregivers, leading to conflicting and painful emotions about relationships. Adults with this attachment style may deeply desire closeness but simultaneously fear it, creating push-pull dynamics in their interactions.

This can manifest as erratic or contradictory behavior, chaotic and high-conflict relationships, difficulty trusting others, and a tendency to oscillate between clinging to and withdrawing from partners. These patterns are rooted in unresolved trauma or loss, leaving the individual struggling to regulate emotions and navigate intimacy in a deeply painful way.

In relationships, disorganized attachment can lead to heightened anxiety, difficulty managing conflict, and a fear of abandonment or rejection. These individuals may view relationships as a source of both comfort and danger, making it hard to establish secure, stable connections. Most often, people with disorganized attachment relate to the emotional experience of anxious attachment—feeling a frantic need for closeness only to push their partner away once they feel too close, driven by fears of both abandonment and intimacy (Menanno, 2023; Beeney et al., 2017).

Here are some reflective questions to help you determine if you lean toward disorganized attachment:

- Did I find myself saying "yes" to most of the anxious attachment questions?
- Do my relationships often feel chaotic and intense, with frequent conflict and drama?
- Do my emotions feel overwhelming or stronger than what others seem to experience?
- Do my feelings for and about my partner shift quickly, often swinging between extremes?

Healing from any of these insecure attachment styles often involves therapy or intentional work to build self-awareness, process past trauma, and cultivate healthier emotional regulation and communication skills. Over time, with consistent and supportive relationships, individuals with insecure attachment can move toward greater security and trust.

All of these early attachment experiences create *internal working models*—mental frameworks that consist of beliefs, expectations, and emotional responses regarding oneself and others. Secure attachment fosters positive internal working models, in which we view ourselves as worthy of love and others as trustworthy. Insecure attachment, however, often leads to negative models, with individuals perceiving themselves as unworthy or others as unreliable. The internal working model is the mechanism by which childhood attachment styles extend into adulthood, causing familiar patterns to be triggered in intimate relationships.

There are two things worth noting here. The first is that having a secure attachment style doesn't guarantee perfect relationships. Even those with secure attachments develop protective strategies, such as defensiveness, criticism, or withdrawal, and face challenges due to attachment injuries in their intimate relationships as adults. Even two people who enter a relationship with a secure attachment style need to work to create a secure relationship. After all, being human—and in a relationship with another imperfect human—can be hard work!

The second is that our attachment styles are not set in stone. Therapy, self-awareness, and positive relationship experiences can help individuals develop a healthier internal working model that leads to a more secure attachment style, which in turn leads to healthier and more fulfilling intimate relationships.

Breaking the Cycle: How Self-Awareness Supports Secure Attachment in Kids

Research shows that parents who are aware of their own attachment patterns and can reflect on their child's thoughts and feelings are better equipped to support secure attachment in their children. By increasing self-awareness and working to understand your relational patterns, you're not only strengthening your connection with your partner but also promoting your child's emotional security and well-being (Sümer et al., 2024).

Protective Strategies

Protective strategies are automatic behaviors that we develop in childhood to safeguard our attachments and shield our tender feelings. These strategies often arise as coping mechanisms that helped us navigate emotional pain or uncertainty with caregivers. While they serve a purpose in childhood, these strategies frequently carry over into adulthood, showing up in our relationships as instinctive reactions to feeling hurt, scared, or simply vulnerable. These responses aren't usually deliberate but rather are ingrained patterns that shape how we handle emotional challenges with those we care about most. They include:

Pursuing

When one partner feels emotionally disconnected, they pursue connection though criticism, complaints, or even anger. Beneath these actions are feelings of fear, loneliness, or insecurity about the relationship. While their intent is to reestablish closeness, their approach can feel overwhelming, causing their partner to pull away. This unintended consequence deepens the disconnect they're trying so hard to repair.

Withdrawing

Some people respond to emotional distress by withdrawing or shutting down. This behavior is often rooted in fear of rejection or a need to avoid feeling overwhelmed. While withdrawing provides a sense of safety for them, it can leave their partner feeling anxious, abandoned, and more likely to pursue them, fueling a cycle where both partners feel misunderstood and stuck.

Defensiveness

When one partner feels attacked or misunderstood, defensiveness can be a way to protect their sense of self. Beneath this response is often fear of failure, shame, or inadequacy. While defensiveness aims to shield against hurt, it can prevent accountability and empathy, leaving the other partner feeling invalidated and escalating the conflict further.

Overfunctioning or People-Pleasing

Some people cope with conflict or tension by people-pleasing, agreeing to plans or tasks they don't want to avoid upsetting their partner. Beneath this strategy lies fear of rejection or abandonment, as well as a deep need for harmony. While the people-pleaser hopes to maintain peace, their compliance often leaves their own needs unmet, leading to feelings of resentment or invisibility. This, in turn, creates emotional distance instead of the closeness they desire.

Anger or Explosiveness

Anger often serves as a "safe" mask for deeper emotions such as fear, sadness, hurt, or shame. People may raise their voice, slam doors, or display other intense behaviors to feel heard or regain a sense of control. Beneath these reactions lies a deeper emotional need, such as seeking validation, safety, or connection. However, the intensity of their response can unintentionally push their partner away or activate their partner's own protective strategies, leading to further disconnection.

Overthinking or "Fixing"

Some people respond to emotional challenges by overthinking or trying to fix the problem. Instead of addressing the emotional need, they default to offering solutions to ease anxiety or feel helpful. Beneath this strategy lies discomfort with vulnerability or a need to regain control. Unfortunately, this approach can make their partner feel dismissed or unseen, creating emotional distance instead of connection.

Oftentimes, we see each other's protective strategies very differently while we're still in the "just us two" phase. The focus is on tending to each other's emotional needs, and the relative ease of two adults coexisting can give us a false sense that we've got love, partnership, and communication figured out. But once baby makes three, and our dependence on each other deepens through the creation of a family, we discover our partner's (and our own) secret strategies. Protective strategies tend to get more pronounced in times of stress, which makes parenting a prime opportunity for these behaviors to emerge, often to our own surprise.

These strategies are essential to identify in yourself because *they are the behaviors your partner sees.* Behavior is communication, but when we're in the midst of a protective strategy, it's like we suddenly start speaking different languages. The actions we take aren't usually accurate representations of how we feel toward that person, and, in fact, they may send the opposite message! Making holistic assumptions about our partner's intent based on their protective strategies is a surefire way to deepen our own attachment injuries.

By identifying our own protective strategies and recognizing the underlying emotions or attachment needs that drive them, we can replace these defensive behaviors with more vulnerable and emotionally open interactions, strengthening our bond. That's why it's so important to focus on yourself when applying this information. It can be tempting to analyze your partner's behaviors, but the real work starts with turning the mirror inward. By understanding and addressing your own patterns, you're focusing on the one thing you can truly change: yourself.

Attachment and Parenting

Attachment styles play a crucial role in relationship dynamics after a child is born. The bond between parent and child is critical—it shapes the next generation—but it can also shake up the connection between romantic partners. The new demands of caring for an infant leave little time and energy to nurture your relationship. Sleep deprivation and constant caregiving can make it challenging to find moments together. This lack of connection can exacerbate hurts and misattunements and create a breeding ground for misunderstandings and conflicts.

In Mateo and Carrie's case, the birth of their son highlighted their latent attachment styles. Mateo, who tends toward avoidant attachment, found himself overwhelmed and anxious, struggling with insomnia and the demands of work and fatherhood. His instinct to withdraw left Carrie feeling unsupported and alone during a time when she craved connection and reassurance. Carrie's anxious attachment style made her more sensitive to Mateo's absence, interpreting it as a lack of care and commitment.

"I've always tended to retreat when I feel stressed or scared," says Mateo. "It's almost as if I don't realize I'm doing it. After the baby was born, I felt completely overwhelmed and anxious. I've always struggled with insomnia, and it only made my anxiety worse. Work was incredibly stressful, and he would cry constantly. I felt I was failing everyone I cared about. Carrie was always upset, but I couldn't seem to help her, no matter how hard I tried."

When Mateo feels stressed or overwhelmed, he tends to shut down to protect himself from feelings of shame and inadequacy. While Carrie observed withdrawal as a lack of care, Mateo's internal emotional experience was quite the opposite: He cared so much that his inability to fix the situation overwhelmed him, leading to the shutdown. Although Mateo and Carrie had a securely attached relationship when it was just the two of them, having a child brought out their latent attachment tendencies and made it difficult for them to communicate. When it became too challenging for Mateo, he retreated into the safety of his head, leaving Carrie feeling alone at her most vulnerable. However, his retreat was not because he didn't care, but rather because of his deep desire to get everything right and the feeling that he was failing. In other words, he shut down out of a fear of making things worse because he cared so much. Unfortunately, Carrie didn't see it that way.

Good-Enough Parenting

Parenting is undoubtedly one of life's most rewarding yet challenging experiences. From the moment a child enters our lives, we are tasked with the immense responsibility of nurturing, guiding, and supporting them through every stage of development. However, the pressure to be perfect parents can often feel overwhelming, despite our best intentions. In today's society, where social media showcases curated images of flawless families and parenting advice inundates us from every angle, the expectation to excel in every aspect of parenting can be daunting.

Yet, perfection in parenting is unattainable. Children don't come with a manual. Every child is unique, requiring different approaches and strategies. Mistakes are inevitable, and the journey of parenthood is filled with moments of uncertainty, doubt, and trial and error. Balancing the needs of our children with our own, as well as other responsibilities and challenges life throws our way, often necessitates compromise and flexibility.

The relentless pursuit of perfection can damage parents' mental and emotional well-being, leading to worry, guilt, resentment, and shame when we inevitably fall short of unrealistic expectations. However, what if we challenged the notion of perfection and embraced the concept of good-enough parenting?

In the 1950s, renowned British pediatrician and psychoanalyst Dr. Donald Winnicott (1971) observed the intricate dynamics between mothers and babies and proposed that parents need not strive for perfection in meeting their children's needs. Instead, he suggested that allowing for some degree of imperfection and gradual detachment as children grow more independent is beneficial for their development.

Winnicott's research revealed that meeting a child's needs most of the time and focusing on repair when they can't is sufficient to foster happiness and secure attachment. This approach acknowledges the inevitability of parental imperfection and highlights the importance of allowing children to experience autonomy and resilience-building challenges. By relinquishing the pressure to be flawless parents and embracing the concept of good-enough parenting, we can create a nurturing environment where children thrive without driving us to distraction!

"I thought he didn't care," says Carrie. "He would just go to sleep or go to work and leave me with the baby. I know he said he couldn't soothe him, but it felt the same way to me! I couldn't soothe him either, and I felt like such a failure. But I had no choice to leave. I was so stuck." She cries, "Stuck and alone."

When Carrie is going through a difficult time, she craves connection and feels anxious (but not surprised) when it's not there. She's felt unsupported in the past in her relationships and wishes that her partner would simply be present with her. When he withdraws, she feels like he doesn't care, which makes her feel even more abandoned and lonely—which fits into her experience in past relationships. She's left feeling foolish for believing that Mateo could be different, further blocking connection.

Understanding each other's attachment styles can help partners offer the proper support and avoid misinterpreting each other's actions. For example, Mateo's retreat was not a sign of indifference but a coping mechanism driven by his feelings of inadequacy and overwhelm. Similarly, Carrie's need for reassurance was not meant to be a burden and was instead a reflection of her desire for connection and support.

Building Security with Notice, Own, Connect

The foundation of any strong relationship is secure attachment, but achieving and maintaining it takes effort. Attachment styles shape how we seek connection, handle conflict, and rebuild trust. While these patterns are often rooted in childhood, adult relationships offer a chance to grow and create greater security.

The transition to parenthood, while deepening commitment and attachment, also introduces inevitable challenges. With sleepless nights, shifting roles, and heightened emotions, this life change can expose hidden fears and tendencies, increasing the likelihood of misattunements or disconnections. Navigating these moments with the Notice, Own, Connect framework in mind can really help.

NOTICE

First, take a moment to reflect on how you respond during moments of disconnection or conflict in your relationship. Do you find yourself seeking reassurance by pursuing your partner, or do you withdraw to avoid potential conflict? Understanding these patterns is the first step to shifting them.

Questions to ask yourself:

- What are my protective moves? Do I get critical, demanding, or clingy? Do I shut down, retreat, or go into people-pleasing or "fix it" mode?
- What are the feelings underneath the feelings?
- How does my behavior affect my partner's response? Does it bring us closer or create more distance?

By recognizing these tendencies, you can begin to see how they influence your interactions. This awareness empowers you to choose new responses that address the underlying fears and longings driving your behavior, paving the way for deeper connection and understanding with your partner.

OWN

This step is about acknowledging and taking responsibility for your feelings and behaviors without judgment. It's an opportunity to get honest about what you truly need and how your actions—intended to protect you—might actually backfire, negatively impacting your partner and the relationship, ultimately getting you *less* of what you really want.

Questions to ask yourself:

- What am I truly needing or longing for when I pull out a protective move?
- How do my protective strategies—like people-pleasing, criticizing, or avoiding—affect my partner and our dynamic?
- What fears, insecurities, or past experiences might be shaping my responses in the present moment? When else have I felt like this?

Owning your role in the dynamic isn't about taking all the blame—it's about taking responsibility for how you show up and being willing to try new approaches, even when they feel uncomfortable or risky. This self-awareness paves the way for more intentional, compassionate interactions and deeper connection.

CONNECT

Replace protective strategies with honest, open communication, even if it feels uncomfortable at first—these are your new moves!

Questions to ask yourself:

- How can I share my need for connection and express my fears in a more open and vulnerable way?
- What do I understand about my partner's feelings under their protections, and how can I respond to them with care?
- How can I ask for connection without falling into old patterns of protection?

Connection deepens when both partners create a safe space to share their feelings by approaching conflict with vulnerability. This allows them to meet each other with empathy. Practice softening your tone, pausing to truly listen without judgment, or simply staying present and engaged in the moment. Over time, these small, intentional efforts build trust and intimacy, changing old patterns and making space for new moves.

Secure attachment isn't about avoiding conflict or achieving flawless communication—it's mostly about knowing how to repair after moments of disconnection. By practicing Notice, Own, Connect, you create a clear road map to better understand yourself and your partner, strengthening trust, emotional intimacy, and resilience. This work not only nurtures your relationship but also lays a solid foundation for the family you're building together, paving the way for a love that is both secure and lasting. ♥

Chapter 4

The Nervous System

The attachment system described in the previous chapter ensures that we bond and connect with others, shaping how we seek safety, closeness, and connection in relationships. But attachment doesn't operate in isolation—it relies on the nervous system to power and guide it. The nervous system is a complex network of nerves and cells that controls many bodily functions, including how we instinctively respond to experiences, manage stress, and foster connection.

Think of attachment like a garden—it represents the love, trust, and connection we cultivate in our relationships. The nervous system is the irrigation system, providing the essential water that nourishes the plants and keeps the garden thriving. When the irrigation system is working well (a regulated nervous system), the garden flourishes, even through occasional dry spells or storms. Flowers bloom, roots deepen, and the garden becomes a source of safety and joy.

However, when the irrigation system is malfunctioning—whether it's flooding the plants (overactivation) or failing to provide enough water (shutdown)—the garden struggles. Plants wilt, weeds take over, and it becomes harder to nurture the connection and growth we desire. A dysregulated nervous system can make it difficult to respond to relational challenges, leading to overreacting, shutting down, or feeling disconnected.

Much like an irrigation system, regulation isn't a static state. Just as a garden requires ongoing adjustments to watering to meet its needs, the nervous system at its best can move fluidly through various states. Having a well-regulated system doesn't mean being in a constant state of calm or contentment. While feeling secure and happy is undeniably more pleasant than experiencing dysregulated states like anger, sadness, or frustration, regulation is an active process rather than a fixed goal. It's something we do, not something we have.

Instead of striving for perpetual calm, imagine the nervous system like riding a bike: It's meant to stay in motion, constantly adjusting to maintain balance. True regulation is about increasing the nervous system's flexibility, allowing it to move smoothly through different emotional states. This adaptability is the true measure of a healthy, regulated system, enabling us to navigate ups and downs while maintaining the balance we're designed for.

Coregulation: A Real-Life Superpower

Did you know that emotional connection is a powerful survival tool? Crafted over millions of years of evolution, it's the glue that holds us together, whether it's a mother soothing her baby, the support of a partnership, or the collective strength of a community. Connection doesn't just help us survive; it allows us to thrive. At the heart of this connection lies *coregulation*, the shared emotional rhythm wherein we mirror, respond to, and stabilize one another's emotional states.

When we feel safe and cared for by someone close to us, our bodies respond by releasing bonding hormones like dopamine and oxytocin. These little chemical messengers make us feel warm, connected, and secure, literally wiring us for connection. It's not just emotional, it's biological. Coregulation is a nervous system tool that helps us build strong, secure attachments and keeps relationships thriving, thus increasing our chances of survival.

But here's the flip side: When we feel disconnected from someone we love, our nervous system freaks out a little. It treats the disconnection like a threat, the same way it would handle physical danger. Suddenly, the brain dials down rational thinking, problem-solving, and the ability to connect emotionally, and instead kicks into survival mode with quick, instinctive reactions. Helpful in a crisis? Absolutely. During an argument with your partner? Not so much.

This ability to co-regulate is deeply rooted in our biology, driven by subconscious processes that help us detect safety or danger in our environment. Understanding these processes helps shed light on relationship patterns that at times feel out of our control.

Neuroception: Our Internal Surveillance System

"Are you mad at me?" Carrie asks anxiously. It's morning, and Mateo has just come downstairs. He's feeling overwhelmed with the day ahead and didn't sleep well. His mind is already fast-forwarding to all the work waiting for him at the office.

"No," he says tersely, not making eye contact as he grabs a cup of coffee.

"Well, you seem mad," Carrie replies, feeling a knot of anxiety tighten in her stomach. She's sure that something is off, and her mind begins racing through all the reasons he might be mad at her.

"I'm not mad," Mateo repeats, his shoulders tensing.

"I got up early to make breakfast so you could sleep in. The least you could do is be civil to me," Carrie says, her voice wavering with hurt.

"It would be nice if I were allowed to be in a bad mood without you jumping all over me for it," Mateo growls, slamming his coffee cup on the counter.

♥

How many times have you said (or heard) in an argument, "It's not *what* you said; it's *how* you said it!"

As cliché as it is, this statement is entirely accurate. The nervous system is extraordinarily sensitive, constantly scanning our environment for danger. Dr. Stephen Porges introduced the term *neuroception* in his groundbreaking polyvagal theory to describe the nervous system's ability to detect subtle cues of threat or safety: fleeting facial expressions, changes in tone of voice, a brief touch, or even just a general vibe coming from a person or situation. Our nervous systems are keenly attuned to these cues, shaping our emotional and physiological responses in real time, for better and for worse. For instance, a gentle smile or a reassuring touch can convey safety and calm, while a tense posture or a sharp tone can trigger feelings of anxiety and unease.

During a disagreement, our nervous system uses neuroception to pick up on a partner's furrowed brow, crossed arms, or raised voice as threats. These perceived threats can trigger our sympathetic nervous system, leading to a fight, flight, or freeze response. Instead of addressing the issue calmly and rationally, we may become defensive, withdrawn, or immobilized.

When we come into contact with a regulated nervous system, especially that of someone we love, we receive signals of safety and respond in kind, easily using all our faculties to express ourselves the way we want to. Conversely, when we encounter a dysregulated nervous system, we instinctively perceive that whatever caused that dysregulation may also threaten our safety, and often respond unconsciously with anger, anxiety, or fear. In other words, co-dysregulation!

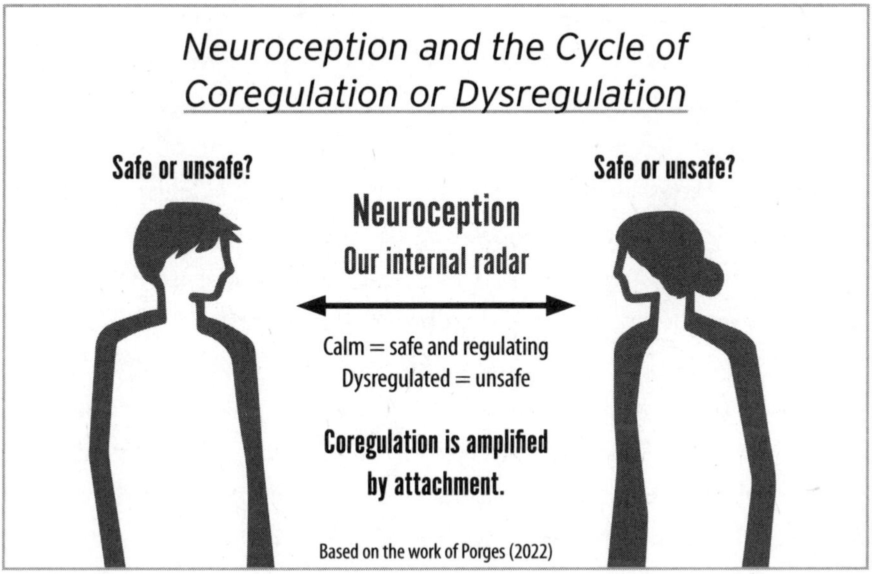

The interaction between Mateo and Carrie above is an example of neuroception, but also of coregulation. While coregulation is most often used in reference to a soothing interaction where one person's calm energy down-regulates another person's stress and emotional activation, it can work in the other direction as well, heightening each other's arousal and triggering survival reactions instead of calming and reassuring each other.

When Mateo entered the kitchen, Carrie's nervous system registered subtle cues that Mateo was dysregulated. While her neuroception was accurate—he was, in fact, anxious about the day ahead and suffering from lack of sleep—she inaccurately interpreted these "danger" cues to mean that he was mad at *her*. As a pursuer in the relationship, she reached for connection and understanding by asking if he was angry at her.

In response, Mateo's already dysregulated nervous system picked up on danger signals from Carrie's dysregulated response and activated his self-protective withdrawal. Feeling hurt and rejected, Carrie escalated her efforts to connect, while Mateo, feeling attacked and misunderstood, snapped at her. Their nervous systems were co-regulating by amplifying their distress. The more heightened their nervous system responses became, the less ability they had to perceive each other accurately, let alone listen or understand. Driven by their brains' threat responses, both resorted to protective strategies that only drove them further apart.

Our nervous systems are finely tuned to detect hints of unpredictable behavior, often leading us to react even before we realize what we might be reacting to. I live near a city where it's common to encounter people on the street or subway who are suffering from mental illness. Anytime I hear someone start yelling or acting unpredictably near me, I feel myself go on high alert, my nervous system screaming, *Danger! Danger! Run, hide, be safe!* Having started my career working with people with severe mental illness, I understand on a rational level that these individuals are very unlikely to pose a real threat to my safety. However, my clinical knowledge and lived experience do little to quiet the automatic response of my body.

This reaction is only heightened when you perceive that your partner is dysregulated. Unlike encountering a stranger yelling on the train, you're much more likely to take your partner's dysregulation personally. Perceiving a threat from someone we love, trust, and depend on is deeply confusing to the nervous system—the person we look to for safety is making us feel unsafe. This confusion only intensifies the survival reaction, cutting off our access to rational thinking, problem-solving, and relational capacity. Unable to fully engage in calm, thoughtful communication, we respond more like a distressed child, lashing out in fear-fueled aggression, tearfully begging for reassurance, or withdrawing in shame and resentment.

Porges's polyvagal theory gives us a fresh perspective on how our nervous system responds to stress. It helps reframe our reactions and those of others not as personal shortcomings but as natural, built-in responses from our bodies guided by the vagus nerve, a kind of superhighway connecting the brain and body that plays a huge role in how we sense and respond to safety or danger. To understand this better, let's explore the concept of the polyvagal ladder and how it maps out these responses.

Polyvagal Ladder

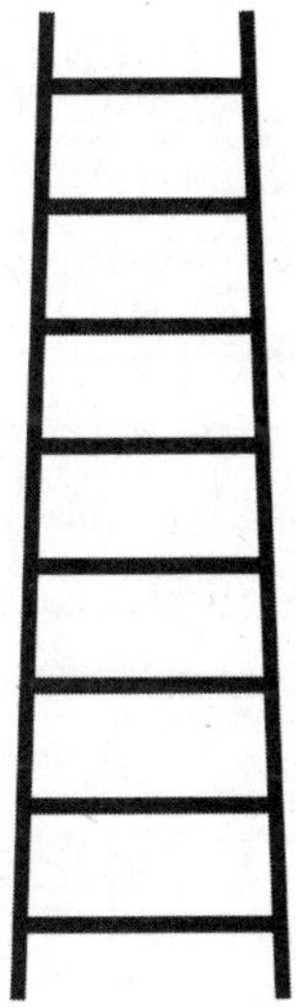

Ventral Vagal
Safe and social
Feelings: calm, connected, clear thinking, social

Sympathetic Nervous System
Fight, flight, freeze, or fawn
Feelings: alert, tense, anxious, defensive, scared

Dorsal Vagal
Shutdown
Feelings: disconnected, collapsed, frozen

Based on the work of Porges (2022)

Ventral Vagal State (Safe and Social)

In this state, you feel calm, relaxed, and fully at ease, allowing you to connect with others easily. Think of a time when you were with a close friend, sharing a laugh or having a meaningful conversation, and you felt completely comfortable. Your body wasn't tense, your mind wasn't anxious, and you were able to enjoy the moment. In this state, your body is telling you, "I'm safe," so your heart rate is calm, your breathing is steady, and your muscles are relaxed. Because you're not on alert, your brain can focus on connecting with others instead of protecting yourself.

In this state, you're open to making eye contact, smiling, and being emotionally available. You feel good, safe, and understood, making it easier to share your thoughts and feelings and to truly listen to others. It's the opposite of feeling anxious or stressed, where your body is tense and your mind is scattered. The safe and social state lets you feel grounded and present, making it the ideal state for building relationships and communicating. Your body and mind feel safe, allowing you to connect deeply with others, which is why it's so important for healthy relationships.

When you feel this kind of safety, your body and mind work together to support connection and collaboration, even during moments of conflict. Instead of reacting defensively or shutting down, you're able to approach disagreements with curiosity and compassion. This state allows you to navigate conflict more effectively by expressing your needs clearly, hearing your partner's perspective, and working together to find solutions. It creates a foundation for trust and emotional safety, which are crucial for resolving challenges and strengthening the relationship.

Sympathetic Nervous System State (Fight, Flight, Freeze, or Fawn)

When the nervous system detects danger, it activates the fight-or-flight response of the sympathetic nervous system. In a relationship conflict, this survival strategy usually shows up as either confrontational behavior (fighting) or avoidance (fleeing). However, there are two less familiar responses: freezing and fawning. The freeze response involves becoming immobilized while remaining highly alert, like hitting a pause button in the face of overwhelming threat. Unlike shutdown (the dorsal vagal state, described below), freezing traps energy in the body, poised to act if the situation shifts. Finally, the fawn response is a strategy of appeasing the perceived threat to ensure safety and avoid conflict. Imagine a puppy showing his belly to a much bigger dog in order to avoid a fight he cannot win. All four reactions—fight, flight, freeze, and fawn—are adaptive survival mechanisms automatically triggered by the nervous system when it perceives a threat, whether real or imagined.

These responses are designed to prepare the body for immediate action. Adrenaline is released, heart rate increases, energy surges, and resources are redirected away from nonessential functions like digestion. Simultaneously, access to the prefrontal cortex—the part of the brain responsible for rational thinking, impulse control, decision-making, and emotional regulation—is reduced. This shift prioritizes quick, instinctive reactions over logical analysis, which was critical for our ancestors when faced with life-and-death threats like escaping a saber-toothed tiger. While this response is incredibly effective in true emergencies, it can sometimes work against us in modern, non-life-threatening situations, such as a misunderstanding with our partner.

The sympathetic nervous system state isn't just about responding to threats. It plays a crucial role in providing the energy and focus needed for everyday life. In a controlled state, it helps us stay productive, tackle challenges, and push through demanding tasks, like completing a big to-do list or powering through an intense workout. It sharpens problem-solving skills and allows for quick, effective responses in critical moments, such as avoiding an accident or catching a falling object. Even in nonemergency situations, like giving a presentation or competing in sports, the sympathetic system fuels the alertness and drive necessary to perform at our best.

The key to resilience and well-being lies in our ability to move flexibly between activation and recovery. This balance allows the brain and body to provide energy when needed and restore calm and stability afterward. When regulated, the sympathetic nervous system not only supports survival but also empowers us to thrive, meeting life's demands while maintaining emotional and physical health.

In modern life, our nervous system can react to things like a negative social media post, a stressful thought, or even a partner's tone of voice in the same way it would to an actual physical threat, like facing a wild animal. These everyday stressors trigger the same fight-or-flight response, even though there's no real danger that requires immediate action. This mismatch between modern stressors and our ancient survival instincts can lead to heightened anxiety and stress because our bodies overreact to things that don't need a physical response.

When this happens, stress hormones such as adrenaline and cortisol build up in our system. These hormones are meant to give us a burst of energy to fight or flee—making us stronger, faster, and more alert—but in today's world, there's often no physical outlet for this energy. When not burned off, these stress hormones hang around and cause unpleasant physical symptoms including digestive issues (because the brain shuts down digestion to save energy when facing a threat), trouble thinking clearly, emotional overwhelm, dizziness, feeling hot or cold, a racing heart, or even blurred vision.

Dorsal Vagal State (Shutdown)

When we're overwhelmed by stress or fear to the point that neither fight nor flight feels possible, our nervous systems activates the dorsal vagal response, effectively hitting the off button. In this state, you might feel numb, disconnected, or frozen, as if your body is shutting down to protect itself from emotional or physical overload. This response, often described as the "freeze" or "shutdown" state, is a survival mechanism designed to conserve energy and shield you from further harm when escape and defense feel impossible. While this state can feel distressing or disempowering, it's important to understand that it's the nervous system's way of keeping you safe.

The dorsal vagal response isn't inherently bad. In a balanced and regulated nervous system, this pathway also plays a critical role in restorative processes. It supports the body's rest-and-digest functions, allowing for recovery, healing, and moments of stillness. For example, it helps us relax after a meal, enjoy deep sleep, or find calm during quiet reflection. The key is flexibility: When we can move fluidly in and out of this state, the dorsal vagal response supports balance and resilience, helping us recharge and feel grounded.

Problems arise when the dorsal vagal system becomes dysregulated, trapping someone in prolonged shutdown or disconnection. This can happen in response to chronic stress or trauma, where the nervous system gets stuck in defensive mode. By understanding the dual nature of the dorsal vagal response—as both a protective mechanism and a source of restoration—we can begin to recognize when we're out of balance and work toward cultivating a nervous system that supports both safety and well-being.

An example of how this commonly shows up in day-to-day life is doomscrolling: the endless intake of bad news or social media when life feels overwhelming. You're not really engaging with the content; instead, it becomes a way of checking out. Your mind is on autopilot, your body is conserving energy, and you feel emotionally distant. This is a typical shutdown response to feeling powerless or stressed. Instead of reacting with high energy or running from the problem, your body shuts down to cope with everything feeling like *too much*.

In modern life, especially as a parent, this shutdown response can be pretty common. When juggling kids, work, and the never-ending list of responsibilities, it's easy to feel emotionally drained and slip into this state. You might feel like you're there physically but not fully present—detached from your emotions, your family, and yourself. It's your body's way of saying, "I can't handle this right now, so I'm pulling back to protect you."

This state isn't a failure. It's your body's natural survival mode kicking in to help you cope. The key is to recognize it and not be hard on yourself. Sometimes, you just need to slow down and recharge. While it might feel frustrating, it's important to acknowledge that your body is trying to manage overload. The goal is to gently reconnect, whether that means taking a break, asking for support, or slowly finding ways to reengage with the people and things that matter to you.

Moving Out of Stuckness

To move from the shutdown state (dorsal vagal) back into the safe and social state (ventral vagal), your body needs to pass through the sympathetic state first. The sympathetic state is where your body reactivates, building energy and bringing you out of that numb, checked-out feeling. However, this activation can feel tough, especially when you're already feeling disconnected or drained.

The key is to find ways to gently activate your system without overwhelming it. Activities like talking, laughing, or connecting with someone you trust can help stimulate the sympathetic state in a positive way, allowing you to move toward feeling more engaged and alive. Even just a small conversation or shared joke can begin to lift you out of that low-energy place.

For others, more physical activation might be necessary, like vigorous exercise or progressive muscle relaxation. Exercise gets your heart pumping and activates your system in a controlled way, helping to shake off that feeling of being stuck. Progressive muscle relaxation, where you tense and then relax different muscle groups, can also help to gently bring your body back online. By engaging your muscles, you signal to your body that it's safe to wake up and reengage.

Moving through the sympathetic state can feel like shaking off a heavy blanket. At first, it's hard to find the energy, but as you activate your system—whether through social interaction or physical movement—you gradually work your way back to the safe and social state, where connection, calm, and ease are possible again. It's about finding that balance of reactivation without pushing too hard, allowing your body to transition through these states at its own pace.

Regulate Your System with a Thermal Reset

This exercise is inspired by the benefits of cold plunges and saunas, but it's easy to do at home using your shower. Alternating between cold and hot water helps train your nervous system to shift smoothly between states, building resilience and promoting balance. It's perfect for moments when you feel stuck, overwhelmed, or in need of a reset.

1. **Set up your space.**
   - Make sure you are in a safe space where you will be undisturbed for 2 to 10 minutes (longer if you plan to soak in a warm bath). Have a towel and cozy clothes nearby for after the exercise.
2. **Start with cold water.**
   - Begin by immersing yourself in cold water—either under the shower or by submerging your hands or face in a cold tub.
   - Stay in the cold for 30 seconds to 2 minutes, depending on what feels manageable.
   - Focus on slow, deep breathing to calm your initial reaction to the cold. Notice the energy and alertness it brings.
3. **Transition to hot water.**
   - Switch to warm or hot water, letting the heat relax your body.
   - Spend 2 to 5 minutes soaking in the warmth or standing under the shower, focusing on the comfort and soothing sensation.
   - Take deep breaths, focusing on extending your exhale—for example, inhale for a count of 4 and exhale for a count of 8.
4. **Repeat the cycle.**
   - Alternate between cold and hot water two or three times, focusing on your breathing. Spend more time on the warm phase if you want to end on a relaxed note.
   - Pay attention to how your body feels as you transition between the two states.
5. **End on your preference.**
   - If you want to feel energized, finish with a short burst of cold water.
   - If you're seeking relaxation, end with warm water.

Benefits:

- Builds nervous system flexibility, helping you shift more easily between stress and calm.
- Improves circulation and reduces muscle tension.
- Boosts vagal tone, supporting emotional regulation and resilience.

How Coregulation Moves Us Up or Down the Ladder

The negative cycles in relationships, as discussed in chapter 2, are often both a result of and a trigger for moving into sympathetic activation. Conflict leads to heightened arousal (for example, shouting, crying, withdrawal, shutdown), which erodes trust and sets the stage for disconnection. Prolonged periods of disconnection erode trust further, setting the stage for conflict and more heightened arousal in reaction not only to this conflict but to the one (or many) that came before. Over time, this creates a negative feedback loop in which every conflict, no matter how trivial, instantly puts both partners back in the same dysregulated states, keeping the couple locked in their negative cycle.

What makes it more tricky is that in the early stages of the relationship, our partner is usually the one we rely on for positive coregulation. Even when the relationship is challenged by conflict, the overall state of safety and connection we experience with them makes our nervous system resilient enough to access the calmness and empathy needed for coregulation. But when the nervous system is chronically overtasked, as it so often is throughout parenthood, we're effectively living with one foot on the next rung of the ladder—it only takes a slight stressor to move one or both of us upward into a state of heightened arousal and defensive reactions. And if one partner reacts to conflict with anger or fear, it can easily amplify the other partner's stress response, leading to negative coregulation that escalates the conflict. If all of this is determined by individuals' unconscious perceptions and automatic reactions, how can couples break their negative cycle? The solution is the same as the problem: We do it by working with our nervous system to help it become more flexible. This is something each partner can work on individually.

Developing Awareness

The first step in building a more resilient nervous system is recognizing your default response to dysregulation. When you feel stressed or experience conflict, do you go to fight, flight, freeze, or fawn? (Hint: It's likely to be a process of two or more steps, for example, first withdraw to avoid conflict, then eventually snap.) Identifying this pattern helps you develop awareness in the moment. By understanding your own responses, you can begin to notice when your neuroception senses a threat or old hurts are triggered. This recognition is critical to creating change. It allows you to create a small space between your reaction and the action that instinctively follows. It's in this space that transformation begins.

Intentionally Shifting Your State

What you do within that small space can be transformative. Something as simple as taking a deep breath or acknowledging that you need a moment to process will give your nervous system a chance to regulate before you react. Depending on the intensity of your state, you might use grounding techniques, such as focusing on your breath, feeling your feet on the ground, or using sensory experiences (such as holding a comforting object), to help you move out of a fight, flight, fawn, or freeze response. For some people, it might help to reconnect with your partner nonverbally—for example, holding hands or simply moving closer to them—while others may need physical space to regulate before trying once again to communicate over the conflict.

Nervous System Regulation Hacks

Down-Regulation: Calming Your Nervous System

- Deep, slow breathing (exhales longer than inhales)
- Humming, singing, chanting, or breathing techniques (e.g., box breathing, belly breathing)
- Spending time in nature
- Sitting on the ground to signal safety to your nervous system
- Gentle stretching or yoga (e.g., child's pose, downward dog)
- Walking or slow movement to soothe your system
- Rhythmic motion (e.g., rocking, swaying, swinging)
- Physical contact like hugs or snuggling a pet

Up-Regulation: Energizing Your Nervous System

- Vigorous exercise (running, dancing, jumping, shaking body)
- Progressive muscle relaxation
- Cold water therapy (splash face, use a cold pack, or take a cold shower)
- Laughing to release tension
- Socializing or trying something new to spark energy
- Contrast therapy (alternate cold and warm water)
- Physical contact like hugs or connecting with pets

These quick, accessible tools can help you work with your nervous system to release stress and return to balance. Experiment to find what works best for you!

Returning to Calm and Connection

Once you know what works for you in moments of distress, it's just a matter of practicing it. Given how quickly our nervous systems can sense and respond to threats, you may not even become aware of what's happening until the conflict is well underway. It may feel awkward or even counterintuitive to say "I'm getting dysregulated—I need a few minutes to process" in the middle of a fight. With time, though, you'll find it easier to notice when you're dysregulated and take steps to bring yourself back into balance and resume the interaction feeling more calm, thoughtful, and connected. And trust me, any initial awkwardness is worth working through to achieve a restored connection and a stronger relationship.

Identifying Your "Home Away from Home"

In moments of stress or conflict, our nervous systems often default to familiar protective sympathetic states—what Deb Dana (2021), a leading expert in the field of polyvagal research, so aptly calls our "home away from home." These are the states we've unconsciously practiced over time, including fight, flight, freeze, or fawn. While these responses may feel automatic, they're deeply rooted in our nervous system's attempts to protect us. Identifying your default state is the first step toward creating change and moving back into connection.

For me, fight is my go-to home away from home. When I feel myself getting angry, defensive, or combative, I know I've slipped into that familiar response. My work is to step away, take a few deep breaths, and focus on regulating my nervous system—bringing my rational brain back online before I reengage. When I can do this (which is easier some days than others), I can return to the situation with empathy and clarity, rather than reacting out of defensiveness and self-protection.

For someone whose home away from home is shutdown or withdrawal, the challenge looks different. Their work involves pushing through the instinct to retreat into silence or emotional distance. It might mean taking a deep breath and making the effort to let their partner know how they feel, even when staying present feels uncomfortable or vulnerable.

Recognizing your home away from home isn't about judging your reactions—it's about understanding your nervous system's patterns. When you become aware of your go-to responses, you can start to shift out of the default reactions that often kick in automatically, even when they're not helpful or necessary. With awareness comes the power to choose a different response, opening the door to the possibility of deeper connection.

Building the Path "Home"

The practices you use in the moment of stress or conflict are an important part of developing nervous system resilience. Regular self-care practices can help your system return more quickly and easily to a calm ventral vagal state. In addition, you can use life's everyday challenges as opportunities to practice moving down the ladder. When you feel frazzled or "touched out" after a long day with the kids (that is, in a sympathetic/dorsal mixed state), engaging in activating yet grounding activities like taking a walk outside, exercising, connecting with a friend, or alternating between hot and cold water in a shower can be highly effective. Pairing these practices with intentional breathing—especially focusing on a lengthened exhale—can further help to regulate your nervous system and bring you back to balance.

In moments of high activation, such as dealing with a stressful work situation, arguing with your partner, or managing your toddler's twelfth tantrum of the day, your sympathetic system may be in overdrive. Here, calming activities like deep breathing, sitting on the ground, going

The Diving Reflex: A Shortcut to Regulation

All air-breathing vertebrates have a built-in survival mechanism called the *diving reflex*, which activates when cold water touches the face. This reflex engages the ventral vagal pathway, signaling safety and promoting a state of calm regulation. This ventral vagal activation slows the heart rate, reduces oxygen demand, and redirects blood flow toward the heart, brain, and other vital organs, supporting a state of physiological calm and safety. This is why the classic advice to splash some cold water on your face actually works: It's a quick way to signal safety to your nervous system and disrupt patterns of dysregulation.

The diving reflex is a powerful and accessible tool for state shifting, offering a way to anchor back into a regulated nervous system state during moments of stress or overwhelm.

Simulating the Dive Reflex

Even without full submersion, you can activate the dive reflex to calm your nervous system and regulate stress. Here's how:

Splash cold water on your face.

- Focus on your forehead, eyes, and cheeks.
- Use noticeably cold (but not painful) water.

Apply a cold compress or ice pack.

- Place it on your forehead, eyes, cheeks, and back of neck.
- Breathe deeply while holding it in place.

Hold cold water in your mouth.

- Take a sip of ice-cold water and hold it in your mouth.
- Focus on slow, steady breathing.

Take a cold shower.

- Let cold water run over your face, neck, and upper chest.
- Focus on calm, steady breathing.

outside, or even letting yourself have a good cry can help release the tension and bring you back to balance. Recognizing where you are on the nervous system ladder allows you to choose the most supportive tools for the moment, helping you move toward greater connection and calm.

Everyone's nervous system responds differently, so it's essential to build a personal tool kit of strategies that work for you. While techniques such as deep breathing, progressive muscle relaxation, and yoga are widely supported by research, you may find that other activities—like painting, journaling, or dancing—are just as effective in helping you feel grounded (Jerath et al., 2006; Khoury et al., 2013; Pascoe et al., 2017). Some people find solitude and quiet practices helpful, while others thrive with more active, social, or creative outlets.

It's also important to have a range of tools to suit your current state and circumstances. For instance, gentle yoga might feel perfect on one day, while a vigorous run or screaming into a pillow might be what your body needs on another. Experimenting with different approaches not only helps you discover what works best for your system but also strengthens your ability to tune in to yourself, recognize your nervous system state, and respond to your needs with care and intention.

The key is consistency and curiosity—creating space for practices that help you return "home" and feel connected, no matter what your day throws your way.

The Magic of Mixed States

Your nervous system sends danger signals for a reason—that's its job! Somewhere along the line, it learned what causes you the most pain, worry, or danger and developed quick responses to protect you from these experiences. Befriending your nervous system means recognizing your state and your sensitivities without shame and working with them rather than fighting against them.

Reducing Stress to Support Regulation

Managing stress isn't just about self-care—it's also about examining the overall stress load in your life. Chronic stress keeps your nervous system in a constant state of activation, making you more reactive to even small challenges. To reduce this load and improve your ability to regulate, consider such strategies as:

- **Addressing mental load:** Everyday responsibilities like planning, organizing, and juggling domestic tasks can significantly increase stress and create an imbalance in a relationship. Dividing these responsibilities more equally ensures that both partners share the burden, creating space for each to breathe, recharge, and feel supported.
- **Allowing transitions:** Give yourself time to shift between tasks or environments, rather than expecting yourself to jump seamlessly from one role to another. (This is especially important when trying to make time to be sexual.)
- **Incorporating mindfulness practices:** Techniques such as deep breathing, meditation, or simply taking a mindful pause can help calm your nervous system.

Small adjustments in your day-to-day stressors can lead to big improvements in your emotional and physical well-being.

Of course, working with your nervous system is just that: work. Understanding your triggers and disarming them requires a lot of conscious attention, communication, and patience—things that are in short supply for most parents. Avoidance can sometimes feel like a valid short-term strategy, as it keeps you from facing overwhelming responses. However, relying solely on avoidance leaves your nervous system primed for activation even when you're consciously trying to engage in the safety of your current relationship.

Trauma and the Nervous System

While self-care strategies can be helpful for shifting your state, they don't always work for everyone or in every situation. You might find that your nervous system reacts intensely to seemingly small triggers, leaving you in a funk that no amount of yoga or journaling can break you out of. This is especially true if your sensitivity stems from deeper wounds, such as unresolved trauma. Trauma affects how your nervous system processes threats, sometimes keeping it in a state of heightened alertness that can feel disproportionate to your current situation.

Trauma deeply impacts the nervous system, often leading to heightened sensitivity and exaggerated responses to perceived threats. In the aftermath of trauma, the nervous system remains on high alert, scanning for danger, which can make even minor stressors trigger a fight-or-flight response. This hypervigilance can blur the line between actual danger and safe situations, leaving individuals feeling anxious and reactive, even in everyday life.

In some cases, trauma can also cause the nervous system to shut down, triggering a dorsal vagal response. This happens when the body perceives a threat as inescapable, leading to feelings of numbness, detachment, and hopelessness. Individuals may find it hard to engage with others or enjoy activities they once loved.

These responses are the nervous system's way of protecting us, even though they can sometimes feel overwhelming. Healing involves recognizing these patterns and taking steps to retrain the nervous system through support, mindfulness, and activities that promote safety and relaxation. Over time, with self-compassion and patience, the nervous system can regain balance, helping us to respond more appropriately to current situations and fostering well-being.

If you suspect or know that your heightened sensitivity is linked to past trauma, working with an individual trauma therapist can be an essential step. A therapist can help you disarm those deeper triggers, so you can engage with your partner on the terms of your present relationship—not on the terms of past wounds. This deeper work allows you to create space for connection and growth, unburdened by the weight of outside scars.

A better strategy is to work toward developing *nervous system resilience*. Think of this as a powerful association of safety, like a child's security blanket. Resilience empowers us to manage stress and hardship more productively, improves our ability to problem-solve even under pressure, and, perhaps most importantly, lets us keep enjoying life even in the midst of hardship.

The great news, especially for couples, is that a particularly effective way of building nervous system resilience is to participate in *mixed-state activities*. A mixed state is the blending of different nervous system responses, creating nuanced physiological and emotional responses that help us navigate the complexities of daily life.

For the purposes of this chapter, we will focus on two main mixed states. The play state combines the grounded security of the ventral vagal system with the energy of the sympathetic system. This allows individuals to feel safe while engaging in activities that are lively and exciting. Similarly, the intimacy state blends the calm and connection of ventral vagal activation with the stillness and restfulness of the dorsal vagal state, creating an environment for deep emotional connection in activities such as snuggling, meditating, or sharing vulnerable moments.

Mixed states provide a way to experience safety and excitement or security and vulnerability at the same time. They are crucial in relationships, allowing partners to balance independence with closeness and risk with safety. By intentionally restoring playfulness and enriching intimacy, couples can not only strengthen nervous system resilience but also deepen their emotional connection, allowing them to support each other's nervous systems in moving more quickly into regulation when they are challenged by conflict.

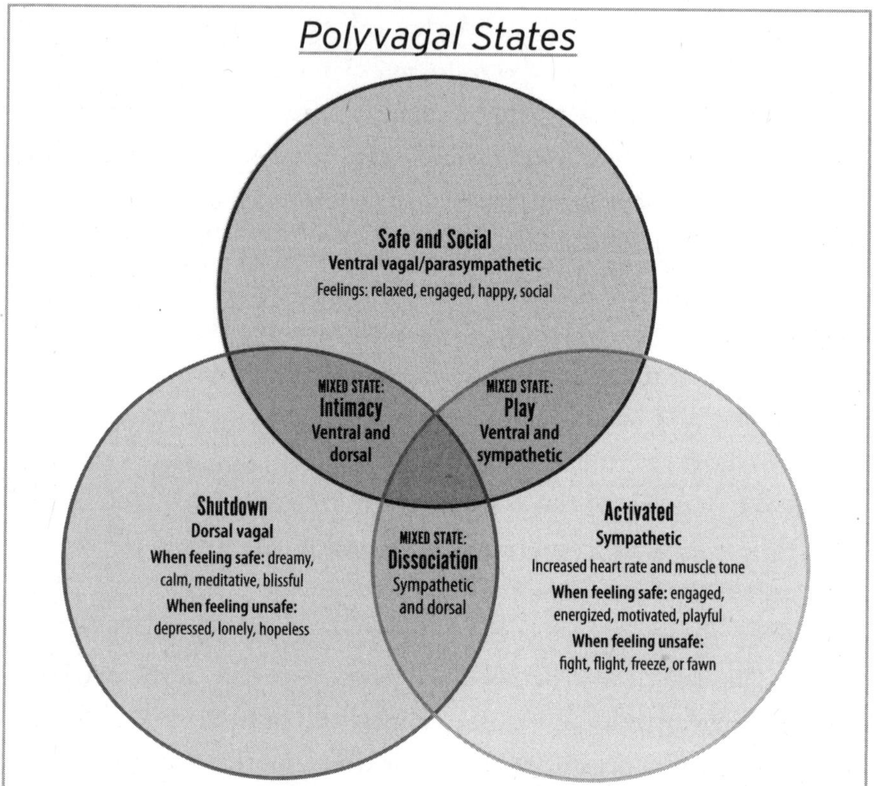

Adapted from *3 Key Principles of The Polyvagal Theory*, by the Polyvagal Institute (https://www.polyvagalinstitute.org/whatispolyvagaltheory).

Play: The Antidote to Routine and Disconnection

Many couples reminisce about how they used to have fun together or lament how long it's been since they felt the flirty vibe that characterized their relationship before kids entered the picture. From the perspective of polyvagal theory, this fun, flirty energy is known as the *play state*, a mixed state that combines ventral vagal and sympathetic states. In play state, the body benefits from the calm and security of the ventral vagal state while tapping into the energizing effects of the sympathetic state. Kids slip into this state easily and often; it's easy to observe in how our little ones manage to be both relaxed and energetic at the same time. Many people find it more difficult to access this playful state in adulthood, feeling as though we don't have the time or believing that being silly and playful is inappropriate or out of place for adults.

But cultivating play offers a powerful channel for couples to simultaneously restore connection and express their individual autonomy. From playing cards or a board game with your partner to going on an adventurous date to turning dinner prep time into a spontaneous kitchen dance party, play activities blend our senses of security and excitement, independence and connection. Even something as simple as lighthearted banter with your partner can engage this mixed state—the ventral vagal state helps you feel connected and understood, while the sympathetic state energy makes the experience lively and exhilarating.

Another important aspect of this hybrid state is its engagement of the *vagal brake*, the vagus nerve's ability to suppress elevated heart rate and other stress responses. While the sympathetic state provides energy and excitement, the vagal brake keeps this activation in check, ensuring we stay within our window of tolerance.

We see the vagal brake at work in the mixed state of play, where excitement (sympathetic state) is balanced by calm and connection (ventral vagal state). However, when the vagal brake fails, excitement can escalate unchecked, leading to the familiar parental prediction "This is going to end in tears." Without regulation, playful energy can quickly tip into chaos, resulting in accidents, frustration, or emotional meltdowns. Flexible vagal brakes are essential for us to modulate our energy levels before this type of failure occurs, so that we can stay engaged and responsive without tipping into panic or shutting down.

When we strengthen the vagal brake through practices such as physical play or safe social connection, we increase our ability to remain in our window of tolerance—the state where we can think clearly, make thoughtful decisions, and maintain emotional balance. This flexibility is critical not only for managing acute stress but also for building resilience over time. It ensures that even when life feels chaotic or demanding, we can return to a sense of safety and stability, which enables us to respond to challenges with greater ease and confidence.

Unsurprisingly, one of the most appealing benefits of cultivating the play state is its impact on a couple's sex life. After all, what is sex but adult play? The more comfortable partners become in this mixed state, the easier it is to approach sex not as an entitlement or a chore, but instead as an outlet for excitement, creativity, even adventure. The activation of the sympathetic state helps each partner be open to the other person's desires and fantasies, while the grounded security of the ventral vagal state empowers them to assert their own (and maintain any important boundaries without guilt). This opens the door for couples to indulge pleasure and explore desires in a mutually satisfying way.

Cultivating play helps partners reconnect emotionally, restores a sense of individuality within the partnership, and lays the groundwork for a more satisfying sex life. Play shifts the focus from solving problems to enjoying each other's company, which strengthens the bond without the weight of obligation or pressure.

Intimacy: The Anchor of Safety and Trust

The mixed state of intimacy combines the calm and security of the ventral vagal state with the silence and rest of the dorsal vagal state, resulting in a state of quiet, peaceful, profoundly connected closeness. You can recognize this state in various scenarios: a parent snuggling their baby, a long hug between friends, the contemplative comfort of petting an animal, or even the feeling of transcendence that comes in quiet meditation or prayer. In all these situations, the common thread is the absence of fear, a stillness in the body, and a loving, intimate connection with another.

In the context of sexual activity, this mixed state creates an environment where both partners feel secure and at ease. The social safety of the ventral vagal state allows partners to feel emotionally grounded and open to each other, while the restful, inward-focused effect of the dorsal vagal state helps partners feel a tranquil sense of meditative presence. The result is a space where vulnerability and trust can flourish, emotional bonds are strengthened, and a sense of unity and oneness is felt.

When partners approach sexual activity from this mixed state, they experience deep attunement to each other's needs and responses, opening the door to a transcendent level of physical pleasure in which their emotional connection feels as significant and satisfying as the act of sex itself. Connecting from the state of intimacy is immensely helpful in overcoming sexual challenges and for healing any trauma or anxiety related to sexual activity. It provides a haven where partners can rebuild trust and comfort with each other, paving the way for healthier and more enjoyable sexual experiences in the future.

Intimacy is a beautiful counterbalance to play. Where play brings energy, intimacy offers stillness. Together, they create a rhythm that allows couples to feel deeply connected in all areas of their relationship. Intimacy fosters trust and security, making it easier to explore vulnerability—not just sexually but emotionally as well.

Cultivating the Mixed State of Intimacy

1. **Start with a nervous system check-in.**
   Take a moment to check in with yourself and your partner. Are either of you feeling stressed, anxious, or a little disconnected? If so, try a regulating technique detailed in this chapter—like deep breathing, a quick hot or cold shower, gentle touch, or grounding exercises—to settle your nervous systems. A well-regulated state is the foundation for connection and intimacy.

2. **Slow down and come into the present.**
   Pause and intentionally tune into each other. This might look like sharing a simple moment—talking about your day, holding hands, or enjoying a lingering hug while focusing on your breathing. Slowing down together creates calm and connection, which naturally opens the door to deeper intimacy.

3. **Use gentle touch.**
   Start with pleasurable, nondemanding touch that feels good. You could run your fingers lightly along your partner's arm, rub their shoulders, or simply rest your hand on their leg with just the right pressure. This kind of touch sends signals of safety and trust, gently laying the groundwork for connection. This can be done with or without clothes.

4. **Connect skin-to-skin.**
   Skin-to-skin contact is like hitting the fast-forward button for all the bonding, feel-good hormones. Oxytocin floods in, stress hormones including cortisol drop, and your nervous systems sync up in that calm, connected ventral vagal state. It's coregulation magic, helping you feel instantly safer, closer, and more attuned to each other.

5. **Move together.**
   Find a shared rhythm that feels good for both of you—whether it's dancing, rocking, swaying, or something more intimate. Pair your movement with deep, intentional breathing to sync up your nervous systems. These rhythmic, shared actions deepen your sense of connection and unity.

6. **Incorporate eye contact.**
   Maintain a soft, open gaze as you look at each other. Eye contact is a simple yet powerful way to build safety and connection, helping you both feel seen, valued, and fully present.

7. **Build emotional and physical synchrony.**
   As your connection deepens, let your touch, breathing, or movement naturally fall into sync. This kind of emotional and physical harmony amplifies intimacy and keeps you fully attuned to each other.

Looking for Glimmers

If you're in a situation with your partner that feels untenable, this slow, steady process of cultivating change may seem like the opposite of what you're looking for. After months or years of living through your exhausting negative cycle, you want something to change *now*. In fact, it's quite likely that the transformative something you're seeking is already there. It's just a matter of learning to notice it.

We've talked already about the power of triggers to instantly shift us into a state of heightened arousal and dysregulation. But there's another kind of micro-moment shift that can instantly push us into a state of security and regulation. Nervous system expert and trauma therapist Deb Dana (2018) refers to these moments as *glimmers*.

Where triggers activate our awareness of possible threats and arouse our instincts for self-protection, glimmers activate our sense of safety, calm, and even awe. The spark of human warmth you feel when sharing a smile with a cashier, the glow of wonder that comes from looking up into a lofty tree canopy or a gazing at a glorious sunset, the melting gratitude that flows through you when a friend sends a thoughtful text just when you needed it—all these glimmer experiences offer a pervasive feeling of security. Just as triggers send a mind-body message that you are in danger from some generalized, unknown source, glimmers send a mind-body message that you are surrounded by universal protection and care.

Triggers and Glimmers

Same system, different signal

Triggers send signals of threat— tension, shutdown, or fight/flight.

Triggers: Moments that spark stress, fear, or disconnection. A sharp tone, a certain look, or an old wound getting poked.

Glimmers send signals of safety— ease, connection, and warmth

Glimmers: Small moments of warmth, safety, and connection. A soft smile, a kind touch, or sunlight hitting just right.

Based on the work of Dana (2018)

Giving attention to triggers comes naturally to our threat-sensitive nervous system. Learning to intentionally focus attention on glimmers is crucial to befriending and ultimately rewiring our nervous systems. While partnering as parents indeed brings miscommunication, failed expectations, and emotional ups and downs, it also brings many occasions of connection, affection, support, and wonder over the magic of watching your child grow (and each other growing as parents). When we're awash in stress, frustration, and conflict, we tend to overlook these moments. Training ourselves to notice these glimmers and savor them unlocks their benefits for our nervous system and our relationships. For instance, you might pause and let a small moment of warmth or safety sink in, or you can keep track of your glimmers daily in a journal. The more you notice glimmers, the more your brain learns to seek them. Over time, glimmers help rewire your system toward ease, connection, and resilience.

Building Resilience Means Restoring Connection

In our busy modern world, many of us find ourselves lingering in a single state (usually the dysregulated version), whether it be a state of high stress (sympathetic fight or flight) or shutdown (dorsal vagal). Our problems with dysregulation are the result not of the state itself, but rather of getting stuck there. A well-regulated nervous system constantly moves up and down the vagal ladder, shifting and regulating our state to suit each situation we find ourselves in.

Consider how it works when you ride a bike. You don't hop on the seat and balance in place before moving forward. Rather, you move forward by remaining in a constant state of balancing. In the same way, nervous system regulation is an active state of continuous change, correction, and adaptation.

Noticing and befriending our nervous system empowers us to take charge of regulating it in challenging moments and, over time, to cultivate the appropriate state for different situations, from preparing for a job presentation to getting some sleep between late-night feedings to, yes, having sex with your partner. This nervous system development is, first and foremost, a personal responsibility. While we can ask for support in co-regulating, the work is ultimately our own. However, as each partner develops the ability to regulate their own nervous system, they improve their ability to co-regulate together. This is a vital milestone on the way back to restored sexual connection.

A great example is my friend Sofia, who explained to her husband, Tyler, that on days when they plan to have sex, she needs him to be the one in charge of the kids' bedtime routine. Her own work on nervous system regulation helped her realize that bedtime leaves her feeling touched out, exhausted, and shut down—the opposite of sexual arousal. Even if she felt receptive to sex earlier in the day, the demands of bedtime push her into a dorsal vagal state where sex feels impossible.

Sofia told Tyler that because their sexual connection is a priority for her, she needs to opt out of the bedtime routine in order to get into the right headspace for pleasure, play, and connection.

Sofia's work on her own ability to regulate allowed her to communicate clearly to Tyler about how they could work together on prioritizing their sexual connection. It gave Tyler insight into the source of their past sexual struggles—it wasn't anything he was doing wrong, but rather her nervous system needing support to foster intimacy rather than pushing through exhaustion to "force" a feeling of desire. With this knowledge, it was an easy yes to take over the bedtime routine on nights when they want to have sex, so that Sofia has time and space to unwind from the chaos of the day and shift into a state of emotional presence and physical connection.

Another part of building resilience as a couple is recognizing and supporting each other's regulation needs, even when those needs differ. Of course, when both partners are dysregulated in a conflict, it's not always possible for them to show up for each other the way each one would like. What they can do, however, is tune in to their own nervous system state while respecting their partner's regulation needs.

For example, I often crave coregulation when I'm upset—I want a hug or reconnection right away to help me reregulate. My husband, in contrast, needs time and both emotional and physical space to regulate. These differing needs can put us at odds, but it helps to remember that your partner isn't responsible for fixing your dysregulation. For me, this means I can ask for a hug, and if he can't give it to me in that moment, it's hard—but it's my work to respect that boundary. Learning to navigate these differences with care and mutual respect strengthens a couple's ability to remain connected, even in conflict.

Whether it's through coregulation in a moment of stress or building moments of mixed-state activity into their lives, couples who work on mutually developing nervous system resilience create a foundation of safe connection that helps them regulate even during conflict. Building resilience together allows couples to approach disagreements with less reactivity, maintaining their connection instead of deepening disconnection. Over time, this work does more than just help them recover more quickly from stress; it restores and deepens connection in a world that often pulls couples apart.

Befriending Your Nervous System with Notice, Own, Connect

This chapter explored how your nervous system influences your responses to stress, connection, and intimacy. By understanding how your nervous system interacts with your attachment patterns, you lay the groundwork for transforming the way you show up in your relationship. Your body's natural survival responses—fight, flight, freeze, or fawn—are designed to protect you but can sometimes interrupt connection and intensify negative cycles. Learning to tune into the cues your nervous system is sending and work *with* your state rather than ignoring or fighting against it is the first step toward breaking these patterns and creating a foundation of safety and trust.

NOTICE

Your nervous system is constantly scanning for safety or danger, often before you're consciously aware of it. By tuning into your physical sensations, emotional responses, and triggers, you can recognize when you're moving into dysregulation or shifting into connection. Identifying both the triggers that push you into stress and the glimmers that ground you in safety helps you regain awareness of your patterns.

Questions to ask yourself:

- What physical sensations do I notice in my body when I feel stressed, disconnected, or overwhelmed?
- What is my default response when I feel dysregulated (for example, withdrawing, criticizing, shutting down)?
- What small moments of joy or connection (glimmers) have I experienced today that made me feel calm, safe, or grounded?

OWN

Your nervous system's responses aren't your fault, but they are your responsibility. Owning your role means understanding how your automatic reactions impact your connection with your partner. Whether you tend to withdraw, lash out, or shut down, becoming aware of these protective moves allows you to pause and choose a different response. It also empowers you to identify tools and practices that help you self-regulate, moving you back into a state of calm and connection.

Questions to ask yourself:

- How can I put some space between the trigger and my default response?
- How might my response be contributing to disconnection with my partner?
- What can I do to regulate myself so I can respond instead of react?

CONNECT

Once you've given yourself permission to step back and regulate your nervous system when needed, it becomes much easier to genuinely connect with your partner. This means replacing automatic protective moves with more vulnerable choices, such as checking in on the feelings beneath the surface, taking ownership of your emotions without blame or shame, asking for what you need, and validating your partner's experience, even when it's different from your own. These intentional actions strengthen your bond and create a foundation for deeper intimacy, trust, and resilience.

Questions to ask yourself:

- When I feel calm and grounded, how can I initiate connection?
- How can we co-regulate as a couple? What actions help us both feel safe and connected?
- What do I enjoy doing with my partner that helps us access the mixed states of play and intimacy?

Your nervous system is central to how you experience and respond to the world, including your relationships. By asking yourself these guiding questions, you can develop a more flexible, resilient nervous system that supports both your personal well-being and your partnership. Whether through playful connection, moments of shared intimacy, or simply pausing to regulate in the midst of conflict, these practices help you restore safety and connection—inside and out. ♥

Part Two

OWN

Chapter 5

The Red Herring of Desire

When couples have high sexual satisfaction, it makes up 15 to 20 percent of their overall relationship satisfaction. However, when sexual satisfaction is low, it accounts for a whopping 50 to 70 percent of their overall satisfaction with their partner (Metz & McCarthy, 2011). Unsurprising, then, that low desire and a mismatch of desire (known clinically as *desire discrepancy*) are among the most common concerns that bring couples into therapy (Vowels et al., 2020; Galizia et al., 2023).

Parents in particular often face difficulties in maintaining a satisfying sex life (Hansson & Ahlborg, 2015). Research indicates that they frequently report lower sexual satisfaction, reduced sexual frequency, and diminished sexual desire after having kids (Rosen et al., 2021). This struggle likely stems from the challenge of balancing personal needs with the demands of both partner and children. While caring for others and prioritizing their well-being is central to all close relationships, adding children, who are notoriously needy, to the mix can really limit a couple's ability to nurture their sexual connection.

The extent to which parents prioritize family needs over their own can greatly impact their sexual relationship. When partners make each other a priority, it can enhance sexual satisfaction, particularly when both value their intimate connection. However, focusing more on the kids—driving them to activities, helping with homework, arranging playdates, and so on—can reduce opportunities for intimacy or lower sexual desire (Vowels et al., 2024).

Now, I don't need to tell parents this—it's pretty much common sense. But what are we supposed to do? Neglect our kids, stop driving them to soccer, let them fail school, and just free-range it so we can hop into bed?

Kind of, yes.

When partners feel like they're truly focusing on each other, it leads to higher levels of sexual satisfaction and desire, even if they're not having sex more often. Simply knowing that their relationship matters can make them feel more connected and attracted to each other despite the busy demands of family life. This means parents can have less frequent sex and still feel satisfied, as long as both feel like they make each other a priority (Vowels et al., 2024; Rosen et al., 2021). Ultimately, it comes down to desire—when couples recognize that their relationship and sex life are important, they can be content with less frequent intimacy. What really matters is feeling wanted.

♥

Maria and George's relationship started out long distance, with months between visits. Going that long without seeing each other definitely had its challenges, but their reunions tended to make the long wait feel worth it.

"I would fantasize about seeing him again," Maria shares. "I'd buy new lingerie and wear it on the plane. It made me feel like a completely different person, like this sexy alter ego."

George remembers it just as vividly. "God, I couldn't wait to see her. She'd step off the plane, and we'd go straight to my place and have sex. It was always so hot."

Their friends learned not to expect either George or Martha to return calls or texts whenever one was visiting the other. "They assumed we were having sex all the time . . . and we were." Maria sighs. "But that wasn't real life—it was a break from real life."

Once they committed to living together, things shifted. Within weeks of George moving in, Maria was unexpectedly laid off from her job. Between not feeling good about herself and seeing him every day, her desire seemed to dry up.

"I loved having him close—he's my best friend, you know? But I didn't feel like having sex all the time. I was more interested in the comfort of having him there. It felt so good to snuggle on the couch at night and have him to lean on during the ups and downs of looking for a new job."

George nods. "It was hard for me because she's my best friend, too, and I want to be there for her in the ways she needs . . . but I still want to have sex with her all the time. For me, those feelings feed into each other. It's hard not to feel rejected when she doesn't seem to feel the same way."

"Things never really rebounded after we moved in together," Maria admits. "We got married and had kids pretty quickly after that, and that made sex even less appealing to me. I can hardly remember that person who used to wear sexy lingerie on the plane."

The research is clear: Desire discrepancy is the norm rather than the exception in long-term relationships (Herbenick et al., 2014). It can certainly cause both partners frustration, disconnection, and suffering, but it doesn't mean that something is wrong. Trying to change the low-desire partner, as many couples do, oversimplifies the issue and can perpetuate feelings of blame and guilt that only drive couples further apart. The key factor in restoring sexual connection isn't about meeting a quota of encounters in the bedroom—it's about fostering open communication and reawakening desire and building anticipation outside the bedroom.

The First Thing to Take Off Is the Pressure

If readers take away only one thing from this book, let it be this: *Taking the pressure off having sex is essential for increasing desire.* Approaching sex with expectations or treating it like a task can create performance anxiety and a sense of obligation, which stifle spontaneity and make the experience more perfunctory. These interactions aren't satisfying for either partner, even the one with the higher desire. In contrast, when the pressure is reduced, desire has the space to develop naturally. When both partners feel free from rigid expectations around sex, be it frequency or style, curiosity and anticipation bloom, leading to more fulfilling and enjoyable sexual experiences.

It can't be denied that the task of reducing the pressure falls largely on the higher-desire partner. This can be hard for them to accept, especially if they've suffered feelings of neglect, rejection, or insecurity. And when the lower-desire partner shows little or no interest in sex at all, the higher-desire partner may fear that being less persistent could mean that sex disappears altogether. For the higher-desire partner to feel safe releasing pressure, the lower-desire partner needs to express genuine commitment to preserving sexuality in the relationship. In other words, both must commit to working on the issue together.

There's a big difference between genuinely reducing pressure with the goal of fostering intimacy and simply waiting with arms crossed to see how long it takes the lower-desire partner to initiate sex. If the waiting is tainted with underlying resentment or anger, the effort will be wasted; the low-desire partner will sense the pressure even without anything being explicitly said. Likewise, there's a difference between paying lip service to addressing desire discrepancies and genuinely committing to making it a priority in the relationship. Expressing a desire to fix the issue without taking concrete steps can leave the other partner feeling even more rejected. Restoring connection involves taking action, whether seeking help from a therapist or coach, reading this book together, or engaging in open and honest discussions about intimacy (Galizia et al., 2023).

Desire Discrepancy

Despite their challenges in the bedroom, Maria and George remained good friends and saw each other as supportive domestic partners. What brought them to therapy, more than anything, was their genuine desire not to hurt each other. This is actually quite common. Many partners with desire discrepancy begin addressing the issue for the sake of the relationship, rather than from a personal drive for more or better sex. Maria's starting point was wanting George not to feel bad, not wanting sex herself. While George understood that she was starting where she could, it was difficult for him to accept. He longed for her to genuinely want sex with him, not just to avoid hurting his feelings.

For decades, a lot of attention has been given to understanding what inhibits individuals' (and particularly women's) interest in sex rather than examining the broader context in which sexual desire arises or diminishes. Recently, there's been a shift toward focusing on the quality and pleasure derived from sexual experiences as a foundation for desire. Rather than judging a given couple's situation by an oversimplified view of what sexuality "should" be, concepts such as "sex worth having" (Kleinplatz & Ménard, 2020) and "pleasure is the measure" (Nagoski, 2015) provide better guidance in understanding the factors that contribute to low sexual desire and finding solutions that work for both partners.

The Gender Divide

Research clearly shows that men and women experience parenting and sexual desire differently. Across both heterosexual and same-sex relationships, the needs of each gender tend to follow consistent patterns, making it challenging to untangle social influences from biological differences (Vowels et al., 2020; Gonzalez-Rivas & Peterson, 2020; Holmberg et al., 2010). And while there is considerable variability in sex drive across genders and throughout an individual's lifespan, research consistently shows that men generally express higher levels of sexual interest than women. Men tend to fantasize more about sex, report stronger desire, masturbate more frequently, initiate sexual activity more often, and exhibit different attitudes and behaviors related to sexuality. The lower desire in heterosexual women is shaped by a combination of factors, including unequal divisions of labor, rigid caregiving roles, lack of emotional intimacy, and societal expectations around sexual initiation, alongside hormonal influences. In short, women's sexual desire is more heavily influenced by the stresses of parenting and relationship dynamics, while men's desire tends to remain more stable over time (Frankenbach et al., 2022; Sims & Meana, 2010; Baumeister et al., 2001).

Research also notes a difference in the way desire arises between men and women. Before the early 2000s, understanding of desire was primarily spontaneous desire—the kind that just appears out of nowhere, like when you suddenly feel in the mood for sex without any specific reason. Studies by sex therapist Dr. Rosemary Basson (2000) significantly shifted the established understanding with the concept of spontaneous versus responsive desire.

Spontaneous desire refers to sexual interest that arises suddenly and without any specific external trigger. People with spontaneous desire typically don't need much to spark their interest—the mood just hits out of nowhere. *Responsive desire*, on the other hand, develops in reaction to external stimuli or context. This could be anything from a suggestive look or accidental brush of the fingers to a slow dance to your favorite song or even specific physical touch that builds arousal before desire fully kicks in. People with more responsive desire typically need something to "get them in the mood" before they feel interested in sexual engagement.

While everyone can experience both spontaneous and responsive desire, most people notice they experience one type more frequently. Both forms of desire are normal and valid ways of experiencing sexual interest. Many couples, particularly in long-term relationships, experience responsive desire more often than spontaneous. Often, the same couples fall into the trap of comparing their current experience to the early days of their relationship, when spontaneous desire seemed more common. But is this truly accurate, or is it a story they've both been telling themselves?

"She was always ready to have sex," George recalls wistfully. "I barely had to look at her, and she'd jump me. I miss that."

I remind him of what Maria said earlier about their long periods of being apart, how they spent so much time thinking about and longing for each other. I also remind Maria of her story about picking out lingerie and wearing it on the plane. Their time apart provided a perfect opportunity for both of them to stoke desire for each other. In other words, the desire they felt once they reunited was a lot more responsive than spontaneous desire.

Still, it's true that George experiences desire more suddenly and intensely than Maria. This is common in men, as testosterone plays a significant role in fueling spontaneous desire. George struggles to understand why Maria needs so much "buildup" to feel the same way he effortlessly feels for her. Maria feels like there is something wrong with her for not experiencing immediate desire the way George does. This self-doubt often turns into resentment, especially when she feels pressured or misunderstood in their intimacy.

Maria's feelings are far from unusual. The traditional model of the human sexual response cycle—desire, arousal, orgasm, resolution—developed by Dr. William Masters and Virginia Johnson (1966) tends to align more closely with male sexuality. It does tend to fit women's experiences at the beginning of a relationship or during casual sexual encounters, but in long-term relationships, especially with the added distractions and fatigue of parenthood, women's sexual experiences often diverge significantly from this traditional model.

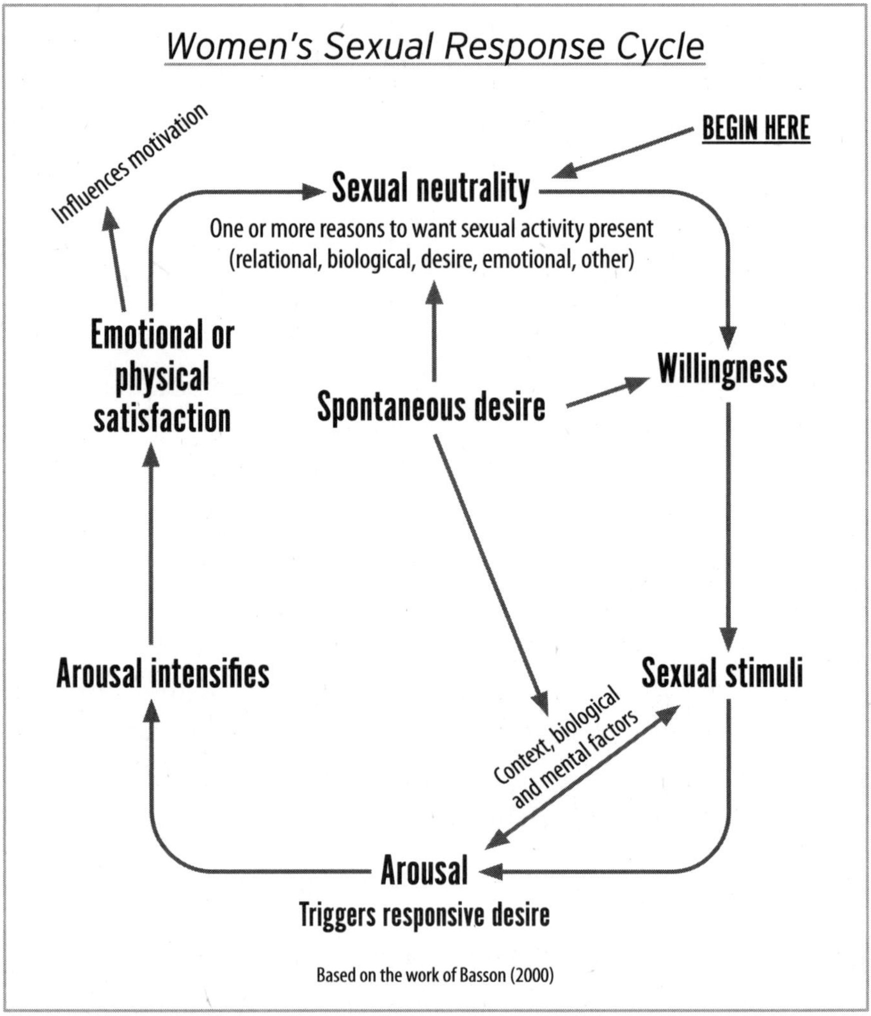

In long-term relationships, many women begin sexual encounters from a place of neutrality: They aren't actively desiring sex, but they aren't opposed to it, either. Perhaps a better word than *neutrality* would be *openness*. Given that women naturally have lower levels of testosterone, it makes sense that their desire often emerges after they begin engaging in sexual activity. This responsive desire is fueled by contextual stimuli such as emotional connection, feeling appreciated or supported, or craving closeness. For Maria, this means that desire isn't missing—it just follows a different path, one that requires understanding and patience.

But could it also be linked to imagination or excitement? Thrilling experiences, romantic settings, or novel situations—like planning a surprise, sharing an adventure, or even enjoying the freedom of "vacation sex"—can act as powerful turn-ons. The novelty and lowered stress of a vacation, for example, often create a perfect storm for desire, tapping into excitement, relaxation, and the feeling of escape from daily responsibilities. These stimuli can spark desire in women and men alike. Importantly, novelty doesn't have to be constant or dramatic to have an impact. In fact, many couples find they get a lot of mileage out of just a little novelty: a change of scenery, a new experience, or simply breaking from routine can reignite desire.

The difference between types of desire is commonly misunderstood by the spontaneous-desire partner, who might initiate sex with physical touch. This can be jarring for the partner with responsive desire, whose struggle to shift gears from open to ready can create tension between them.

A friend recently shared a particularly telling example with me: Her husband's go-to move for initiating sex is poking her with his erect penis.

"It's not that I don't like his dick," she said, "but what am I supposed to do with it at seven a.m. in the middle of the kitchen? Am I supposed to drop everything and fall to my knees right there? I don't really get the point."

"Does it turn you on?" I asked.

"I mean, kind of?" she answered, with a facial expression that said quite the opposite. "I mean, I'm glad he's turned on by me, but what happened to the romance? I feel like I should at least get a kiss on the neck or something first. It's not that I'm not open to sex, but a penis poke just doesn't do it for me. I'm stuck between playing along while feeling a little resentful or being honest and making him feel rejected."

Let me emphasize that starting from a place of neutrality is just as normal as a spontaneous feeling of desire. Regardless of gender, people experience a mix of both spontaneous and responsive desire. Sometimes, you're ready for sex without much prompting, and other times, it takes the right context or stimuli to feel desire building. Both patterns are healthy and can coexist within the same relationship. Understanding how they work together can help couples navigate desire differences in their relationship.

Normal Isn't Just One Thing

It's worth noting that variations in sexual desire are natural and expected in all long-term relationships due to the diversity of human sexuality. While there are biological differences between men and women when it comes to sex drive and desire, there is a broad spectrum of normal across genders, and differences in sex drive are just as likely to affect same-sex couples as they are heterosexual couples. However, research shows that heterosexual couples tend to experience more distress, guilt, shame, and conflict around these differences (Vowels et al., 2020). Something about the traditional expectations of a heteronormative relationship seems to intensify feelings of inadequacy or disappointment when those differences arise.

Arousal Versus Desire

This leads us to another important duality in sexual connection: arousal versus desire. Desire is the mental feeling of wanting sex, while arousal refers to the body's physical response.

In the traditional model of sexual response, desire comes first and leads to arousal. For some people, particularly for those who experience spontaneous desire, this model is accurate. Sexual interest sparks unexpectedly, and the body rapidly responds with physical arousal, often in the form of lubrication or an erection.

Two Forms of Desire

Spontaneous Desire **Responsive Desire**

But for people whose desire is more responsive, the process works in the opposite way. They need to feel physically aroused before the mental desire for sex kicks in. And where does the physical turn-on typically come from? You guessed it: external stimuli, such as a romantic setting, playful touch, or such positive relational factors as empathy, support, or simply a feeling of closeness. Sometimes, it's about a willingness to engage in a sexual encounter just to see where it leads, while other times, novelty and mystery serve as powerful turn-ons, sparking curiosity and excitement. The emotional and mental factors that so many spontaneous-desire-oriented people access without knowing it—the "buildup," as George called it in the last story—are actually the tinder that spark the fire of desire.

♥

After spending the week since their last session reflecting on what contributes to their sexual desire (or lack thereof), Natalie and Henry have some insights to share.

Natalie begins, "I think I've worked out why I'm always so shut down when it comes to sex, even when I feel like I miss him and want to reconnect. It's because when we're finally alone at the end of the day, my brain is still going a hundred miles an hour. I've got this never-ending list of things to do—the kids' schedules, groceries we're out of, what needs to be cleaned, appointments to make. It's not just the physical exhaustion—it's that my mind is constantly running. Even when I try to relax, I think about what's left to do tomorrow or what I forgot today."

Henry jumps in, "You know I'm always ready to help, though! All you have to do is ask me."

"I appreciate that," Natalie answers, "but honestly, that's just one more thing for me to think about, you know? Deciding what to delegate to you, and explaining it, and making sure it's done right . . . " She stops, seeing his hurt expression. "No offense, but if you haven't done it a thousand times like I have, you don't know exactly how it needs to be done. If I have to micromanage you or redo it myself, then it's not really helping." She takes a deep breath. "I appreciate that you want to help, but I need more than help. I need to know that you can actually take some of these responsibilities as your own, where I don't have to think about them at all."

Henry is quiet, considering what Natalie has said. "So you're saying that if I took over some of the responsibilities at the end of the day, you could turn off that running list in your head?"

Natalie nods. "I really think so, yes. A lot of time, when you initiate, I'm still in 'mom mode' and trying to suddenly shift gears for sexy time feels like too much pressure. If I had time to reset for a little while, I think I could be open to connecting."

Henry leans forward, his expression serious. "I hear you. Let's figure out which things I can take over so you have the time to turn off that mental list."

♥

Natalie and Henry's conversation is a great illustration of something known as the *dual control model of sexual response*. Developed by Dr. Erick Janssen and Dr. John Bancroft (2006), and popularized by Dr. Emily Nagoski (2015) in her book *Come as You Are*, the dual control model describes sexual arousal as a balance between sexual excitement and sexual inhibition. This balance is influenced by a wide range of factors, and each person's sensitivity to these factors varies.

To understand this model, compare sexual arousal to driving a car. Sexual excitement is the car's gas pedal—this can be anything that gets you in the mood, including physical touch, flirting, feeling emotionally connected, foreplay, whatever sparks desire for you. Sexual inhibition, meanwhile, is the brake—everything that stops you from getting aroused, including stress, body image concerns, unresolved relationship issues, or intrusive thoughts.

For some people, the gas pedal is very sensitive, meaning sexual cues quickly turn them on. Others may have a more sensitive brake, where minor distractions or stressors can quickly dampen the mood. These systems aren't fixed in place—they're influenced by such factors as stress, the state of your relationship, and your surroundings. For example, someone might have very sensitive brakes at home, where intrusive thoughts about laundry or packing school lunches interfere with desire. But on vacation, those brakes ease off and the person finds their gas pedal much more accessible.

Sexual reconnection asks partners to recognize that both systems need to work in harmony. If you're feeling stuck, it's probably not just a matter of pushing the gas pedal harder; instead, the "fix" comes from learning what triggers your brake and what can help release it. In other words, knowing what turns you off is just as important as knowing what turns you on. Much of desire discrepancy comes down to the simple matter of working to understand each other's brakes and gas pedals.

In Natalie's case, her brakes are highly sensitive, largely due to the mental load of managing household and parenting responsibilities. She longs for intimacy with Henry, but her gas pedal can't help them move forward when the endless to-do list of motherhood has its foot on the brakes. Henry, meanwhile, has a more sensitive gas pedal. It's not that he doesn't experience stress or feel overwhelmed at times. It just doesn't affect his sex drive as strongly as it does Natalie's. If anything, when Henry is stressed, it tends to increase his sex drive; he seeks the distraction and comfort that sex provides. For Natalie, however, relaxation is required to release the brakes and press the gas pedal.

It's important to remember that everyone has a unique balance of gas pedal and brakes. While it's helpful to identify what turns someone on or off, it's just as crucial to understand that these factors don't impact everyone the same way. For instance, even if Natalie and Henry shared similar triggers for arousal and inhibition, their experiences might still differ significantly because of how intensely they are affected by those factors. One person's brakes may hit harder, or their gas pedal may be more responsive, even with the same stimuli. So, in other words, even if a couple has similar lists of brakes and gas pedals, their experiences may still be very different because of how strongly they're affected by them. Someone with a sensitive brake might find that even when their gas pedal is pressed, it can be easily counteracted by minor distractions: Feeling too cold or having a fleeting thought can slam on the brakes, halting any arousal they may be feeling. Someone with a more sensitive gas pedal might be less affected by these distractions because their desire and arousal are strong enough to overpower any brakes that come into play. Understanding this balance helps explain why people react so differently in similar situations and why a one-size-fits-all approach doesn't work when it comes to sexual desire.

Find Your Gas Pedal and Brake Sensitivity

Instructions: This quiz will give you a clearer idea of whether your gas pedal or brake is more sensitive and how that impacts your sexual desire and arousal. For each statement that follows, rate how much you agree on a scale of 1 to 5, where:

- 1 = Strongly Disagree
- 2 = Disagree
- 3 = Neutral
- 4 = Agree
- 5 = Strongly Agree

Section 1: Gas Pedal Sensitivity (Sexual Excitation)

____ I feel sexually aroused quickly when my partner touches me in a way I enjoy.

____ I get turned on when I have an emotionally close moment with my partner.

____ Seeing my partner in an intimate setting (like getting ready for bed) often triggers sexual thoughts.

____ I enjoy thinking about sex and can get aroused just by imagining an intimate moment.

____ When I feel attractive or confident about my body, I tend to feel more sexual desire.

____ Taking time to relax (for example, a vacation, massage, or good sleep) helps increase my sexual desire.

____ Flirty or suggestive comments from my partner make me feel more sexually excited.

Section 2: Brake Sensitivity (Sexual Inhibition)

___ If I'm feeling stressed or anxious, it's hard for me to get in the mood for sex.

___ When overwhelmed by tasks or responsibilities, I find it difficult to focus on intimacy.

___ Feeling insecure about my body makes me less interested in being sexual.

___ If I hear a distracting sound or think about something unrelated to sex, it quickly kills my arousal.

___ I need a clean, quiet, and comfortable environment to feel sexually interested.

___ When I'm upset with my partner, it's hard for me to feel sexually aroused.

___ If I'm tired or physically uncomfortable, it's difficult for me to want sex, even if I was initially in the mood.

Scoring

Gas Pedal Sensitivity: Add up your scores from section 1: ________________
Brake Sensitivity: Add up your scores from section 2: ____________________

Interpretation

Gas Pedal (Excitation)

30 to 35 points: You have a highly sensitive gas pedal, meaning sexual stimuli quickly turn you on. You likely find it easy to get aroused in the right circumstances.

20 to 29 points: You have a moderately sensitive gas pedal. You can get turned on, but it might take certain conditions, like feeling emotionally connected or relaxed.

Below 20 points: Your gas pedal isn't very sensitive. You may need a lot of stimulation or very specific conditions to feel aroused.

Brake (Inhibition)

30 to 35 points: You have a highly sensitive brake, meaning minor distractions or stressors can quickly reduce arousal. Your inhibition system plays a vital role in regulating your desire.

20 to 29 points: You have a moderately sensitive brake. You can be thrown off by distractions or stress, but you can also manage it if the environment and circumstances are right.

Below 20 points: Your brake isn't very sensitive. You're able to stay focused on sexual desire even when stressed or when there are distractions around you.

Reflection

- What are the common factors that trigger your gas pedal? How can you create more of those conditions in your life?
- What are the biggest brakes for you? How can you reduce these distractions or stressors to create a more relaxed and intimate environment?
- If your partner took the quiz, compare your results with theirs. Do you notice any differences? How might this help you understand your relationship dynamic around sex?

When the Signs Point to Yes but the Answer Is Still No

Sometimes a person's body may show signs of arousal even if they don't feel mentally or emotionally aroused. In other words, their body might respond physically—like an erection or lubrication—while they don't actually *feel* desire or want sex. This disconnect is a normal, involuntary response and doesn't necessarily mean they are interested in or consenting to sexual activity. Conversely, it's also completely normal for someone to feel desire, fully consent, and be enthusiastic about a sexual encounter, yet not have their body physically reflect that. For example, during perimenopause and menopause, women can be aroused without experiencing physical signs like wetness. Similarly, men may feel arousal and desire but not achieve an erection.

Arousal nonconcordance refers to the mismatch between physical signs of arousal and the subjective experience of sexual desire. Research shows that for women and those with vulvas, there can be as little as 10 percent overlap between physical arousal and sexual desire (Nagoski, 2015). For men and those with penises, the overlap is higher, around 50 percent, meaning their physical responses tend to align more closely with their mental and emotional arousal (Nagoski, 2015; Chivers et al., 2010).

While many people without a history of trauma experience arousal nonconcordance for various reasons, trauma can significantly intensify this disconnect between a person's emotional desires and their body's physical responses. Trauma often disrupts the link between mental and physical arousal, making it more challenging for survivors to align their emotional readiness with their body's reactions. This makes it especially important to seek clear communication and consent throughout every sexual encounter to build safety and trust. Many survivors experience arousal nonconcordance during sexual trauma, often leading to feelings of doubt, shame, and confusion because their body's physical response didn't align with their emotional experience.

While sexual violence against women is tragically common and widely discussed, many men—especially young men—also experience nonconsensual sexual encounters. If a man experiences an erection or even orgasm during an unwanted encounter, he may not see himself as a survivor. However, if the encounter was uninvited and lacked consent, it can still lead to trauma, regardless of his body's physical response. Understanding that physical arousal does not equal consent is crucial in addressing and healing from these experiences.

In long-term relationships, sexual encounters might happen for reasons beyond immediate physical desire, often related to the desire to connect or positive relational factors. Understanding arousal nonconcordance can help couples approach these moments with empathy, ensuring ongoing consent and clear communication.

Trauma and Sexual Response

Trauma, particularly sexual or relational trauma, can significantly affect the balance between the gas pedal and the brake. For those who've experienced trauma, the brake can become extremely sensitive, making it easy for arousal to shut down in response to triggers that may seem minor or unrelated. The brain learns to associate certain cues—like touch, environments, or even specific words—with danger, causing the body to hit the brakes to protect itself.

In some cases, trauma may also dampen the gas pedal, making it difficult to feel desire or arousal, even in a safe, loving relationship. The hypervigilance that often accompanies trauma—constant scanning for threats—makes it hard to relax and allow natural arousal to emerge. On the flip side, trauma can sometimes make the gas pedal more sensitive, leading to increased sexual activity as a coping mechanism to regain control or seek comfort.

Healing from trauma often involves learning to feel safe again, both emotionally and physically, so survivors can feel a concordance between their desire and response. Because much trauma occurs in relational contexts, healing often needs to happen in supportive relationships. A skilled therapist can help guide this process, offering a safe space to rebuild trust and restore a healthy relationship with oneself and others.

What If I *Want* to Want to Have Sex, But I Just Don't?

Wanting to be sexual is a standard and valid place to begin, especially when you've decided together that maintaining a sexual connection is a priority for your relationship. It's common for people to feel this way—knowing that sex or physical closeness can strengthen their bond but not necessarily experiencing the desire in the moment. This starting point reflects a deep awareness of and care for the relationship, acknowledging the importance of intimacy, even if the natural urge to engage isn't there yet. The key is recognizing that desire often fluctuates and doesn't always align perfectly with emotional or intellectual intentions.

The experience of wanting to want can stem from various factors—stress, fatigue, emotional disconnect, or even hormonal changes. When life is busy, especially in relationships that involve children, careers, and other responsibilities, the energy or inclination to be sexual can take a back seat. What's important to remember is that desire isn't always spontaneous. In fact, it is more common for it to be responsive in long-term relationships, meaning it may need nurturing or specific conditions to develop.

A big part of navigating this feeling is normalizing that figuring out how to cultivate desire may not always feel natural or easy. This may involve making intentional efforts to create space for closeness or, conversely, space for individual needs, even if it doesn't immediately lead to sex. Small moments of physical affection, emotional connection, or shared experiences can help build a foundation where desire might grow. It's also about understanding that wanting to be sexual doesn't have to be forced—it can be explored slowly, with patience and understanding of your own body and needs.

Communicating openly with your partner is also essential. Letting them know that you care deeply about the relationship and value intimacy but that your current drive might not match theirs helps create a shared understanding. It can also relieve any pressure you might put on yourself to perform in a certain way. When both partners are on the same page, it's easier to work together to find a balance that honors your needs.

Exploring Desire with Notice, Own, Connect

Desire discrepancy is a common challenge in long-term relationships, but it's important to understand that it's the norm, not a sign that something is fundamentally wrong. Female desire is often misunderstood. Women are more likely to develop responsive desire, often starting sexual encounters from a place of neutrality. Addressing desire discrepancies effectively requires a holistic, pleasure-centered approach that considers both partners' needs, rather than focusing solely on the low-desire partner. While low sexual satisfaction can have a significant impact on overall relationship happiness, open communication and mutual understanding can help reduce tension and strengthen intimacy. By recognizing the differences between desire and arousal, and normalizing experiences such as arousal nonconcordance, couples can approach their sex lives with curiosity, compassion, and the tools to foster deeper connection.

NOTICE

The first step in addressing desire is noticing what's happening in your relationship and within yourself. Desire is influenced by numerous factors, including stress, mental load, body image, and relational dynamics. Identifying your own patterns of desire—whether spontaneous, responsive, or somewhere in between—can help you recognize where shifts might be needed.

Questions to ask yourself:

- What patterns of desire or arousal do I notice in myself? Do I experience desire spontaneously, or does it tend to be responsive?
- What are my biggest brakes (stress, exhaustion, mental load)?
- What gas pedals increase my desire (romance, relaxation, fantasy, novelty, emotional connection)?
- How does my current relationship dynamic impact my experience of desire and arousal?

OWN

Owning your role in the dynamic of desire discrepancy means taking responsibility for your own experiences and responses. While you can't control your partner's feelings or actions, you can reflect on how your feelings, behaviors, expectations, or unspoken assumptions contribute to the challenges. This might mean advocating for your needs, addressing unresolved feelings, or exploring ways to support your partner without creating pressure.

Questions to ask yourself:

- How do I typically respond when my partner initiates or doesn't initiate being sexual?
- Am I holding on to any frustrations or expectations?
- What steps can I take to address my own brakes or enhance my gas pedals?

CONNECT

Connection starts with open, nonjudgmental conversations about sex and intimacy. By sharing your observations and needs, while listening to your partner's perspective, you can build mutual understanding. Moving toward connection also involves taking intentional steps to create an environment that supports both partners' desire—whether through reducing stress, introducing novelty, or prioritizing quality time.

Questions to ask yourself:

- How can I communicate my needs and preferences in a way that feels inviting rather than critical?
- What small steps can I take today to make being sexual feel more accessible—for myself or my partner?
- How can we work together to prioritize our connection, even amid busy family life?

It is essential to shift the narrative around desire discrepancy from a source of conflict, blame, and shame to an opportunity for deeper understanding and connection. By exploring each other's gas pedals and brakes, nurturing responsive desire, and intentionally creating moments of closeness, the tools in this chapter offer a path toward a more fulfilling, connected, and compassionate sexual relationship. ♥

Chapter 6

Gender Myths

Much of this book focuses on heterosexual couples because research shows that this group often experiences the most relationship pain and disruption due to desire differences, especially when parenthood enters the picture. In this chapter, I want to focus on gender roles and norms in the traditional sense, that is, the expectations placed on all of us based on our assigned sex at birth. While this isn't exclusively for heterosexual couples, cisgender dynamics are often the least critically examined when it comes to gender roles. Questions like *What was I taught about gender?* and *What actually fits for me today?* are less likely to get asked because, for many cisgender folks, identifying as "man" or "woman" often feels like a comfortable fit. But without a critical look at some of the cultural expectations tied to gender, what do we miss? What limiting or harmful expectations might we be playing out without even realizing it?

These unexamined norms can shape not just how we see ourselves, but also how we relate to our partners, and can subtly impact everything from desire to how we navigate parenting and intimacy. By not questioning these roles, we may unintentionally reinforce patterns that aren't serving us or our relationships.

Gender Roles in the Bedroom

Maria and George originally came to see me because of a significant difference in their sexual desire. George wants sex regularly, while Maria doesn't feel the same level of desire. George is consumed by thoughts of sex, constantly planning ways to initiate and tracking her responses. At one point, he even stopped initiating altogether, hoping to see a shift from Maria. His disappointment when she didn't start initiating sex made him even more frustrated.

"What hurts the most," George explains, "is that she doesn't even notice. I want her all the time, but it's like she doesn't care how long it's been since we've had sex. I could tell you the exact days and minutes, but it's not on her mind."

Maria nods. "He's right," she admits. "I don't think about sex. I only know it's been a long time once he starts getting grumpy, and we fight about it. But beyond that, it's the furthest thing from my mind."

George feels increasingly frustrated and disconnected due to the lack of sexual intimacy in his marriage. While he deeply values the emotional closeness he and Maria share, he often feels that the absence of physical intimacy creates an unspoken gap between them. For George, this deprivation is not just about the act of sex—it's about feeling desired, validated, and connected on a deeper level. As a devoted father and loving partner, he finds himself conflicted: He cherishes their emotional bond but can't ignore the growing sense of loneliness and rejection that comes from their mismatched desires. This issue, which they both acknowledge as the biggest challenge in their relationship, leaves George feeling stuck, questioning how they can bridge the gap while maintaining the emotional closeness they both treasure.

In the last chapter, we mainly discussed the nuances of responsive desire and the struggle that both partners may feel with this new view of what normal desire looks like. Now we need to dive into why many men I see in my clinical practice feel such an intense *need* for sex. There's a cultural narrative that suggests men just naturally have a higher sex drive than women and that it's "normal" for men to feel an almost primal urge for sex. While studies have shown that men do tend to have a consistently higher sex drive compared to women, we need to go deeper: Why do many men feel like they need sex as urgently as they need air, food, or water (Frankenbach et al., 2022)? Why do they often feel so deeply deprived when they don't get the sex they want?

The answer isn't as simple as biology. Yes, hormones and physical desire play a role, but for many men, conditioned from birth to be strong and stoic, sex is one of the few ways they know how to connect. Sex fulfills not just their physical needs but their emotional needs as well. It offers validation, comfort, and reassurance that they are valued in the relationship and that their partner finds them desirable. No wonder it feels like an essential need rather than just a desire. (I want to be clear that this is not the case for all men, nor only for men; however, in my work with heterosexual couples, I more frequently see this pattern with men than with women.)

The way men and women often approach sex is deeply influenced by cultural narratives about how it's acceptable for each gender to express their needs and vulnerabilities. For women, on the one hand, societal messages often encourage suppressing sexuality and desire, portraying them as less central to a woman's identity or even as something to be downplayed. This can lead women to see sex as contingent upon other emotional needs—comfort, validation, safety, and support—being met before they can fully embrace or even recognize their own desire.

For men, on the other hand, cultural norms tend to stigmatize emotional vulnerability, portraying it as "unmanly" to express needs for comfort, reassurance, or connection. As a result, men may suppress these emotional needs and instead channel them through physical intimacy, where cultural messaging has long affirmed that it's acceptable for men to seek connection. Sex becomes one of the few socially sanctioned avenues for expressing vulnerability and receiving emotional validation, making it feel essential rather than optional.

While the origins of these dynamics are complex, they likely stem from a nuanced interplay of biological hardwiring and generations of societal expectations. What is clear, however, is that when freed from these expectations, men and women alike are capable of viewing sex as a way to meet multiple needs, emotional and physical. Unfortunately, cultural scripts often constrain this ability. When women suppress their sexuality, they may miss opportunities to experience sex as a source of emotional connection or validation. Likewise, when men suppress their emotional needs, they may miss chances to cultivate intimacy in ways that extend beyond the sexual realm.

By recognizing how these cultural narratives influence our perspectives, couples can begin to shift their dynamics. Women can feel empowered to embrace their desire as a valid and multifaceted part of their identity, and men can feel safer expressing emotional needs in ways that aren't solely tied to sex. This mutual understanding can help partners bridge the gap between their different approaches to intimacy, creating a more balanced and fulfilling relationship for both.

Male Myths

For men, societal narratives revolve around dominance, strength, and control, discouraging vulnerability and emotional expression. Boys are raised to believe they must be physically and emotionally tough. They are conditioned from an early age to suppress emotions such as sadness, fear, and vulnerability, learning instead to replace them with a narrow range that includes angry, proud, happy, and horny. Over time, this emotional suppression becomes second nature. The cost is significant. While appearing strong on the outside, many men feel disconnected on the inside—cut off from their emotions, their partners, and even themselves.

This limited emotional landscape, shaped during childhood, significantly affects relationships as many men struggle to express and communicate complex feelings. Unlike girls, who often receive more acceptance, coaching, and practice in emotional regulation and social interaction, boys are frequently left without the same guidance, told "boys will be boys" or to "be a man." Ironically, research shows that boys actually need more support in these areas.

On average, important sections of boys' brains—particularly the right brain, which governs emotional regulation, social connection, and nonverbal communication—are about one month behind girls' in development at birth. This makes boys not only more vulnerable but also less capable of regulating their emotions effectively. This developmental gap, combined with societal expectations to suppress vulnerability, means that boys actually need more coaching and nurturing but often get less. This does not set men up well to process and express the complex emotions that intimate relationships entail (Kraemer, 2000; Schore, 2017).

While society is increasingly expecting men to be emotionally available and more active participants in both their relationships and their children's upbringing—sharing domestic duties and emotional support—the conditioning and expectations around invulnerability, and the expectation of traditionally male tasks of protecting and providing, are deeply ingrained in both men and women. This makes it difficult to unlearn those patterns and leads many modern men to feel as though they can't get anything right.

Men are left balancing two worlds: providing financially and being emotionally engaged partners and fathers. The weight of these expectations, combined with the lack of practice expressing feelings and asking for help and emotional support, can lead to burnout, anxiety, and even a sense of failure if they feel they can't meet both demands. It creates an internal conflict where men feel the pressure to do it all without learning the emotional tools to navigate that tension, further complicating their relationships and their own well-being.

Being desired touches something deeper for everyone, not just men. It affirms self-worth, boosts confidence, and fosters a sense of being alive, sexy, and special. For men, however, societal norms that discourage vulnerability often make sex the only accessible channel for soothing emotional wounds like inadequacy, loneliness, or rejection—feelings they may struggle to articulate openly. While this dynamic is understandable, relying on sex as the primary avenue to meet these needs can create pressure and lead to misunderstandings in the relationship, leaving both partners feeling unseen or disconnected.

Regardless of gender, these needs are also driven by the belief that sex is part of the "deal" in a relationship and that it's an expected component of partnership. When partners don't express the same level of desire, it's easy for sexual pursuers to feel let down, as though their partner is not holding up their end of the deal—or that there is something fundamentally wrong with their partner or, worse, with themselves. A lack of sexual interest from a partner can be deeply felt as a personal rejection or evidence of failure. This leads to a negative sexual cycle of frustration and disappointment in the relationship.

The pressure on men to perform sexually also compounds this issue. Men are often taught to equate their masculinity with their ability to deliver mind-blowing sexual experiences, leaving little room for emotional nuance. In the bedroom, men are often expected to perform on demand, going from flaccid to fully erect instantly. Their sexual prowess is commonly measured by three main factors: their ability to achieve and maintain an erection (ideally for a long time), the size of their penis (where bigger is considered better), and their ability to make their partner orgasm, ideally multiple times, though penetrative sex with their "big, hard cock." The underlying message is clear: If a man can leave his partner breathless and fully satisfied after the best sex of their life, he's "won" in the bedroom—validating his worth.

Remember, pride is one of the few emotions that men are culturally "allowed" to express, so as Emily Nagoski (2024) so aptly puts it, "winning" in the bedroom often helps soothe more vulnerable, less socially accepted emotions such as sadness, rejection, unworthiness, self-doubt, and loneliness. These feelings are frequently viewed as unmanly or unacceptable to express openly, making sex an outlet where men can affirm their masculinity and make it worthwhile to be close to their partner.

This constant pressure sets men up to measure their masculinity through their sexual performance, creating unrealistic expectations on both sides. For men, the pressure to perform can lead to anxiety, self-doubt, and feelings of inadequacy if they fall short of these ideals. For their partners, it can create a sense of obligation or emotional distance when sex becomes more about hitting benchmarks than fostering genuine connection and intimacy.

Female Myths

For women, societal conditioning is equally restrictive but takes a different form. Girls are taught to be nurturing, giving, and emotionally available, often at the expense of their own needs. They are expected to take on emotional labor from an early age, managing the emotions of those around them: friends and family, and later, children and romantic partners. Society emphasizes the attractiveness of such traits as kindness, humility, and agreeability while discouraging anger or assertiveness, making it harder for women to express their own needs openly.

In leadership roles, women walk a fine line between being assertive and being "likable." Too much confidence can lead to being labeled bossy, while too little seems weak. Modern women are encouraged to succeed, but only in ways that align with traditional gender norms: being ambitious but nurturing, confident but modest. This creates a double bind where success often feels contingent on societal approval, forcing women to navigate a narrow path to avoid criticism. On top of this, they are judged for their appearance—expected to look good, but not too good, while meeting these other demands. To paraphrase the quote about legendary ballroom dancer Ginger Rogers, it's like doing the same work as men, but backward and in heels.

The patriarchal system also sexualizes women, emphasizing their appearance and role in pleasing others. Women are conditioned to mold themselves to fit ever-changing standards of beauty—whether by dieting, exercising, or altering their appearance through plastic surgery—often at the expense of their emotional and physical well-being. This pressure to conform can leave women disconnected from their own sense of self.

In the realm of sexuality, patriarchy conditions women to prioritize a partner's needs over their own. Women are expected to want sex, but not too much (slut, whore), nor too little (prude, cocktease). They are also expected to enjoy the type of sex deemed "normal" (penetrative), orgasm easily, and do so in a way that protects their partner's feelings. Historical patriarchal norms often position women as passive participants in sex, responsible for fulfilling their partner's desires rather than expressing their own.

This pressure to be physically attractive and sexually available while remaining modest and not "too sexual" creates a confusing and restrictive framework. As a result, women may feel disconnected from their bodies and desires, struggling to assert their own needs or experiment sexually. This often leads to dissatisfaction or feelings of objectification.

These gendered expectations place a heavy burden on both men and women, limiting their ability to experience the full spectrum of human emotions. For men, the inability to express vulnerability leads to emotional isolation. For women, the pressure to be nurturing and self-sacrificing can lead to burnout, resentment, and a loss of identity. Recognizing and challenging these patterns creates space for everyone to engage more fully and authentically in their relationships and their sexuality.

What Happens When Traditional Gender Roles Are Reversed

While cultural norms paint men as the sexual pursuers in heterosexual relationships, it's actually very common for women to be the ones seeking more frequent sex. This dynamic can be particularly challenging because it flies in the face of traditional gender roles. Because the cultural narrative paints men as the ones who are "supposed" to have the higher sex drive, a woman who finds herself asking for more sex may feel the same emotions as a man in this position—confused, rejected, wondering if there's something wrong with her—but also have the added worry that something is wrong with her partner's masculinity. It's not uncommon for women in this situation to ask their partner questions like *Why don't you want me?*, *Is there something wrong with you?*, or even *Are you gay?*

For men who are sexual withdrawers, this dynamic can feel uniquely isolating. The traditional trope of the male sexual pursuer is so ingrained in our culture that it can feel emasculating to acknowledge their lower desire. Male sexual withdrawers often feel inadequate or flawed, struggling to reconcile their experience with the dominant narrative of masculinity.

Those on both sides of the relationship can suffer from feeling unseen and shamed by society, their friends, and popular culture. They may feel like they "shouldn't" be in this role or even in the relationship. This ambivalence can add layers of hurt to an already deeply fractured bond.

Entitlement: The Kryptonite to Desire

As a starting point for George and Maria's struggle with a pursue/withdraw dynamic around sex, I suggest they take intercourse off the table for a while.

"How long?" George asks, already sounding uneasy.

"How about three or four months?" I reply. "This will give us time to work through things and take the pressure off."

Maria visibly relaxes, but George rolls his eyes and huffs, turning away in frustration.

"What just happened there, George?" I ask. "What did that huff mean?"

"What? I didn't do anything," George says defensively.

I turn to Maria. "Did you notice George's reaction?"

"Oh, yeah," Maria says. "I'm not surprised, though. It made me feel like he's not really on board, like I should be able to fix what's wrong with me faster so he doesn't have to go without sex."

George stiffens, clearly uncomfortable. "That's not what I meant," he says, his voice rising slightly. "It's just . . . I don't understand why we have to stop having sex to fix things. Can't we work on this without cutting it out completely?"

This defensive response revealed the tension George was grappling with internally—though he might not yet have the language to articulate it. On one hand, he wanted to be supportive of Maria and work through the issues they were facing. On the other, he couldn't shake the deep sense of unease that taking sex off the table triggered in him. To George, sex wasn't just about physical pleasure; it was about feeling loved, connected, and reassured in their relationship—something he had been desperately missing.

We've already discussed how a healthy sexual connection cannot thrive in an environment of entitlement. But while many people would never describe themselves as entitled when it comes to sex, the reality is that most of us have absorbed the cultural message that sex, especially in long-term monogamous relationships, is something we're "owed"—part of the unspoken contract of monogamy, if you will.

If anything, the shifts in modern gender expectations have made the situation more complicated, not less. In the past, a wife's role in the bedroom was often about duty, such as providing an heir to her husband; her enjoyment of sex was rarely considered necessary or even desirable. In today's more egalitarian relationships, however, partners are expected not only to provide access to sex but also to want and enjoy it, passionately and often. This shift, while seemingly positive, creates new pressures, particularly for partners whose desire might not align with these expectations.

For most people, the issue is not that they don't want to want to enjoy sex passionately and often; most of them do! The problem lies in the pressure and expectation that often accompany it. A well-intentioned partner asking, "What do you need to feel interested in sex more often?" might seem like a good starting point, but it still keeps the focus on sex as the ultimate goal. This can inadvertently bypass the real issue: underlying needs that may not seem directly connected to sex but are, in fact, intimately intertwined with the ability to feel desire and connection.

At the risk of understatement, this stuff is complicated. Some people need to feel emotionally connected to spark desire, while for others, too much emotional intimacy can dampen it. The truth is, it's deeply personal and often a paradox. Desire thrives in the tension between seemingly opposing needs: security and novelty, safety and risk, connection and autonomy. While these elements tend to remain consistent, the "recipe" for desire depends on the individual. Some people need deep emotional closeness to feel sexual, while others are turned on by the excitement of risk and novelty. This can be confusing, but it's also the fun part—discovering what ignites desire for you personally and exploring how that blends with your partner's unique needs.

Maria felt relief at the idea of taking the pressure off by abstaining from sex for three months, but George's huff instantly brought her back to feeling like she was letting him down—that she owed him sex and was failing to deliver. That moment of relief, followed by the crushing weight of expectation, revealed something crucial about what was inhibiting Maria's desire: the immense pressure she felt to meet George's needs despite feeling depleted herself.

Maria's nervous system was stuck in survival mode (the concept we discussed in chapter 4), with chronic stress, emotional exhaustion, and the unrelenting demands of daily life crowding out any space for desire to emerge. For her, sex had started to feel like one more item on an endless to-do list, further deepening her disconnection from her body and her desire.

Women's arousal systems, as described in chapter 5, also play a significant role in this dynamic. While spontaneous desire—the kind often stereotypically associated with men—can arise seemingly out of nowhere, Maria experienced more responsive desire, which requires the right context or conditions to emerge. For Maria, this meant her nervous system needed to feel calm and replenished, free from stress, self-judgment, and the invisible weight of emotional labor. Without these conditions, even thinking about being sexual felt overwhelming.

"I already feel inadequate," Maria says. "I worry about my ability to show up for you and the kids, like I am broken. I worry my brokenness will harm everyone around me and ruin everything. It's one of the things that keeps me up at night. So, when I see you roll your eyes, I feel like I'm disappointing you all over again. I just shut down when I know I've failed before I even start."

This realization genuinely shook George. He's always prided himself on being a good partner and father, especially given that he grew up in a traditional household with an emotionally unavailable father. He has worked hard to break these patterns, particularly with his two sons, yet here he was, unconsciously falling into a familiar trap: equating sex with his worth and using it as a measure of their relationship's health.

"George," I say gently, "it sounds like this idea is hitting you in a place that feels really vulnerable."

He exhales and nods reluctantly. "Yeah, maybe. I don't know . . . I guess it just feels like sex used to be a big part of our relationship, and without it, I don't know what we are. It makes me feel like I'm failing, like maybe she doesn't even want me."

This vulnerability wasn't easy for George to admit, but it reflected something deeper: his conditioning as a man. Like many men, George had been raised in a cultural framework that discouraged emotional expression and placed immense value on providing, protecting, and achieving. In his relationship, sex had become one of the few channels through which he felt comfortable expressing and receiving emotional connection. Without it, he felt adrift, unsure of how to maintain intimacy or validate his role as a partner.

Maria looks at him with a mix of compassion and frustration. "I don't think you're failing, George. I just feel like I need a break to figure out how to even want sex again. It's not that I don't love you. I just feel so exhausted all the time, and when I see you get upset about it, it makes me feel even worse."

This exchange laid bare the complex dynamics at play, shaped by deeply ingrained gender roles. For George, the cultural script of masculinity left him with few tools to articulate his emotional needs or find ways to meet them outside of sex. For Maria, the expectation to manage the needs of their children and household, carry the emotional labor of their relationship, and also fulfill George's sexual needs left her feeling overwhelmed and inadequate—leading her to worry that there was something deeply wrong with her. Both were stuck in roles they hadn't consciously chosen but felt powerless to escape.

"George," I say, "it sounds like sex has become a big part of how you feel connected and valued in your relationship with Maria. That's not a bad thing, but it might be helpful to explore other ways to feel close to her that don't rely on sex for now. This isn't about punishing you or denying your needs—it's about giving both of you space to reconnect in a way that feels sustainable."

George hesitates, his shoulders dropping slightly. "I guess I just don't know what that looks like."

"That's okay," I reply. "It's something we can work on together. And Maria, it sounds like for you, this break isn't about pulling away from George but about finding a way to feel more present and connected in your own body so that you can come back together in a way that feels good to both of you. Does that sound right?"

Maria nods. "Yeah, that's exactly it."

In that moment, both George and Maria began to see how the roles they had unconsciously inherited were impacting their dynamic. For George, the challenge would be to explore other channels for emotional connection and to untangle his sense of worth from sex. For Maria, it would be about reclaiming her sense of agency in her own sexuality and learning to ask for what she needed without guilt. By stepping out of their rigid expectations, they could begin to meet each other halfway, rebuilding a foundation for connection that felt authentic and balanced.

Meeting Each Other Halfway

The key to bridging this gender-based divide lies in mutual understanding and shared effort. For George, this meant diversifying how he met his emotional needs. Instead of relying solely on sex for validation, he began exploring other channels for connection, such as deepening friendships, pursuing hobbies, and creating moments of closeness with Maria that didn't revolve around sex. While unlearning societal messages about masculinity wasn't easy, George found that these new approaches reduced the pressure on sex and helped him feel more balanced and emotionally fulfilled.

For Maria, the challenge was equally nuanced. She needed to honor her boundaries and prioritize her emotional balance while also discovering how to access her own desire and sexuality in the context of family life. Part of this began with acknowledging how much sex meant to George—not just physically, but emotionally. Reframing sex as an opportunity for connection rather than an obligation helped Maria shift her mindset so sex was equally important to her, if for different reasons. By focusing on small, intentional moments that built her desire without the expectation of sex, Maria began to see her sexuality as something that could grow organically rather than under pressure.

The paradox is that stepping away from the need to "fix" their sex life allowed space for something new to emerge. George's willingness to find alternative ways to meet his emotional needs gave Maria the room she needed to reset her nervous system and access her own desire. In turn, Maria's openness to rebuilding sexual connection helped George feel valued and seen. Over time, this mutual effort laid a foundation where sex could return as a shared expression of love and connection rather than a source of conflict.

Examining Gender Myths Through Notice, Own, Connect

This chapter explored how deeply ingrained gender roles and societal expectations shape relationships, intimacy, and the way partners navigate the emotional and sexual dynamics that often operate beneath the surface, influencing behaviors and beliefs that impact connection and desire. By using the Notice, Own, Connect framework, couples can unpack these patterns, explore how they affect their relationship, and create a dynamic that feels balanced, authentic, and fulfilling. This isn't about conforming to new expectations. Rather, it's about having the freedom to choose what works best for both partners, building mutual understanding and stepping outside of limiting scripts that no longer serve the relationship.

NOTICE

The first step in challenging the impact of gender myths is noticing how societal expectations might shape your experiences, behaviors, and beliefs. These influences often operate beneath the surface, subtly guiding how you relate to yourself, your partner, and intimacy. Recognizing these patterns gives you the opportunity to assess whether they truly align with your values and the needs of your relationship.

Questions to ask yourself:

- What gendered messages did I grow up with about relationships, sex, and emotional expression?
- How might these beliefs influence my behavior or expectations of my partner?
- Are there moments where I am limited by expectations that don't feel authentic to me?

OWN

The next step is to own how these narratives have shaped your actions and your relationship dynamics. Owning this doesn't mean blaming yourself; instead, it's about taking responsibility for where these patterns may be showing up in your life. This awareness creates space for you and your partner to make intentional changes.

Questions to ask yourself:

- What role do I play in reinforcing gender roles or expectations in my relationship?
- Do I feel any resistance to shifting gender roles that may be limiting or harmful to me, my partner, or our relationship?
- Am I willing to challenge these patterns, even if it feels uncomfortable at first?

CONNECT

Finally, connect with your partner by exploring how these roles may have impacted each of you and discussing ways to create a dynamic relationship that feels authentic to *both* of you. This doesn't have to mean making huge changes—if you're playing more traditional roles and that works for you, that's great! The point is to assess what feels supportive and fulfilling, not to conform to new expectations about challenging gender roles. It's about having the freedom to choose, not the choices you make.

Questions to ask yourself:

- How have traditional gender roles shaped how we show up in our relationship—emotionally, sexually, or in daily tasks?
- Which parts of these roles feel good to us, and which ones feel unhelpful or restrictive?
- What can we do together to make our relationship feel more balanced and true to who we are?

By working through these steps together, couples can begin to see each other—and themselves—more clearly, creating space for deeper connection and a more authentic partnership. Moving beyond societal scripts and expectations isn't always easy, but it opens the door to a relationship where both partners can feel fully seen, valued, and loved. ♥

Chapter 7

The Work of the Pursuer

Relationships thrive when both partners feel seen, valued, and secure, but getting there requires understanding your own role in the dynamic. Whether you're the one leaning in as a pursuer or stepping back as a withdrawer, the key to deeper connection starts with recognizing and addressing your own individual patterns.

In the next two chapters, we'll explore what it means to do your personal work within the relationship. For pursuers, this means softening your approach by getting in touch with the deeper, more vulnerable feelings underneath the pursuit. The work of coming into connection isn't about assigning blame or fixing your partner—it's about understanding *yourself, your reactions, and how you can show up differently*. Together, we'll unpack the emotional needs driving these patterns and offer practical steps to move toward connection. Let's dive in.

A Love Letter (and Some Homework) for the Pursuer

First, let me say this: *Your longing for connection is beautiful.* It reflects the deep care and commitment you bring to your relationship. You're the one who notices when something feels off, who senses the distance and works to bridge it, who fights for the closeness that keeps love alive. That's an incredible strength, and it's something your partner likely values more than they show, even if it doesn't always feel that way.

But being a pursuer can also be lonely and exhausting. You've likely tried countless ways to create connection: staying quiet, speaking up, being patient, getting frustrated, and everything in between. I know you've felt unwanted, unappreciated, and unseen at times. Maybe you've questioned whether your partner truly desires you or if you're just coexisting in the daily grind of life. When your efforts to reach out are met with retreat or rejection, it's natural to feel upset, rejected, angry, or even helpless. These feelings are valid, and your longing for sexual connection is rooted in love and care. But here's the key: While your feelings and desire matter, they are yours to manage. Acting out of frustration or hurt—whether through criticism, withdrawal, or pressuring your partner—won't lead to the connection you crave.

Remember, pressure is the enemy of desire. When sex only happens out of obligation, it leaves both partners feeling disconnected and unfulfilled, which is the opposite of what you're longing for. Even when you're saying the right things or making thoughtful gestures, if your ultimate goal is to get to sex, your partner will sense it. This can reinforce their feelings of pressure and guilt, creating more distance instead of closeness. After all, your partner is likely primed to believe that you think they are the problem. Entitlement shuts down authentic connection because it positions sex as a transaction rather than a mutual act of love, desire, or connection. Focus instead on removing the emotional weight of obligation or expectation from your interactions. Be mindful of any sense of entitlement that might creep in: Expecting sex as a transaction or as something owed diminishes its authenticity. Intimacy thrives on mutual desire, trust, and connection, not coercion or guilt. By letting go of the idea that your partner is the problem, you create space for understanding and curiosity about what they might need to feel more open to being sexual.

Your work is to own your emotions—feel them, acknowledge them, and express them in a way that invites connection instead of blame. Instead of saying "You never want to have sex," try "I miss feeling close to you." This not only softens the approach but also shows your partner that you value them as a whole person, not just as someone who meets your sexual needs.

Owning Your Emotions

Feeling upset, rejected, angry, confused, or helpless is entirely understandable when faced with your partner's lower interest in sex or emotional withdrawal. These feelings are valid, and it's natural to experience them, but it's also crucial to understand that your feelings are your responsibility. Acting out of frustration or hurt won't bring you closer to getting your emotional needs met or to a satisfying sex life. To release the desire-killing pressure your partner feels, you must learn to own your emotions—that is, feel them, acknowledge them, and articulate how you feel without blaming your partner or implying that they are responsible for resolving those emotions. The following two examples of dialogue show the difference.

Example 1: Acting Out Feelings

Amara: "You never want to have sex anymore. You always reject me. I can't even remember the last time we did it."

Leo: "That's not fair, Amara. I'm just tired or stressed sometimes. You know that."

AMARA: "Tired and stressed? You're always tired and stressed. If you cared about me, you'd make time. I shouldn't have to beg for your attention like this."

In this example, Amara acts out her feelings through accusation and guilt-tripping. She's expressing hurt and frustration in a way that adds pressure to Leo, creating defensiveness. It turns the conversation into a blame game rather than sharing her vulnerable feelings and longing for connection.

Sometimes, the acting out can be more subtle:

AMARA: "You never seem to want to have sex with me anymore. I don't know what's wrong, but it's making me feel distant from you. Do you even want me?"

LEO: "Of course I do, but I've been stressed."

AMARA: "It doesn't feel like it. You're always too tired or busy, making me think something's wrong with us. I shouldn't have to be the only one wanting closeness."

LEO: "I know you feel that way, but I feel pressured whenever you bring it up, like you are saying something is wrong with me. It makes me want to have sex even less."

In this example, Amara is voicing her hurt but with a tone that indirectly blames Leo, creating defensiveness and adding pressure to the situation.

Example 2: Expressing Feelings

AMARA: "Hey, I know I've been pretty frustrated about our sex life lately. I realize I've been blaming you, and that's not fair. I've been thinking about it, and I don't want to make you feel like you're always in the wrong or that I'm pushing you."

LEO: "Yeah, I've felt that. It's hard because I'm not trying to make you feel bad."

AMARA: "I get that. I've been feeling disconnected, which makes me worry you're not attracted to me anymore. It makes me feel really insecure. I don't want to put pressure on you, but it's hard for me not to feel like something's off between us."

LEO: "It's not that I don't want you, it's just . . . I don't know; I've been exhausted and not in the right headspace. But hearing that you feel that way makes me feel bad, like I'm letting you down."

AMARA: "I'm not asking you just to have sex to make me feel better. That's not your job. But I do miss us being close."

In this version, Amara expresses her feelings without attacking Leo or pressuring him to meet her needs immediately. By sharing her vulnerability and making it about her own emotions, she opens up space for a more productive conversation. Leo responds from a place of empathy rather than defensiveness, allowing them to work toward understanding and connection.

How Entitlement Kills Enthusiasm

In order to have an enthusiastic yes to sex—which is what every high-desire partner I have worked with craves—there must also be the freedom to say no. It's an absolute necessity. A yes loses all meaning if no isn't allowed.

By "allowed," I'm not suggesting you would ever force your partner to have sex against their will. But let's be honest: Have you ever tried to convince them? Guilt them? Get cold or distant when they say no? Maybe you've gotten angry or threatened to leave if things didn't change. Have you ever questioned their sexuality or picked a fight out of frustration? Did you feel sorry for yourself or sulk when sex didn't happen when you wanted it? Maybe you've questioned whether they're still attracted to you, suggested they're withholding sex on purpose, or assumed they just don't care.

I know this is tough to admit, but if you're honest, the answer to some (or maybe all) of these is probably yes. You've been pretty desperate at times, which does not bring out the best in anyone. But here's the hard truth: All of these behaviors are taking away your partner's ability to freely say no. They are subtle (or not-so-subtle) forms of pressure and manipulation. You won't outright force them (because you're not a monster), but their no still comes with consequences. You're making them pay for it emotionally.

Before you get too down on yourself, I want you to know that I completely understand. You're feeling so much that it is hard to communicate. You've tried everything, yet here you are, still lonely, rejected, sad, and horny. The pain of feeling alone, especially while lying next to your partner in bed, is unbearable at times. No wonder you feel desperate enough to try anything to bridge that gap! You likely don't mean to pressure or manipulate your beloved—you just want them to understand and connect with you.

You're not a bad person for wanting more connection! But the hard truth is that a lot of your behavior is actually working against you. At best, your efforts result in pity or obligation sex. Neither of these will ever spark the true passion and desire you're longing for from your partner. In fact, obligation sex often suppresses any sparks of desire that might have been there.

I was recently talking to a friend, and she shared something that perfectly illustrates this dynamic. She told me that she frequently feels the desire to cuddle with her husband, who happens to be the sexual pursuer and emotional withdrawer in their relationship. Now, her desire is not to have sex, but it is desire, which is an amazing start! But she

Examining Your Entitlement

It's crucial to check your sense of entitlement when it comes to sex. Here are some questions to ask yourself:

- Do I feel like my partner owes me sex because we're in a committed relationship?
- Would my feelings about the situation change if my partner were physically unable to be sexual due to illness, injury, or other circumstances?
- Do I feel like my partner is not holding up their end of the relationship "bargain" when it comes to sex?
- Am I primarily focused on my needs, or am I also considering what my partner might be going through emotionally, physically, or mentally?
- Do I resent my partner for their lack of desire, and how is that resentment affecting our emotional connection?
- Have I communicated my needs in a healthy way, or do I expect my partner to automatically understand them?
- Am I able to enjoy intimacy in nonsexual ways, or do I feel frustrated when sexual activity doesn't happen?
- Do I equate my partner's love or commitment to me with their willingness to be sexual?
- Am I creating an environment where my partner feels safe and free to express their own needs and desires?
- Am I open to understanding the reasons behind my partner's lower desire, or do I focus more on fixing the problem to get what I want?

knows that after about five minutes of cuddling, he will start putting the moves on—rubbing, touching, poking her with his boner, and making it pretty clear that, in his mind, cuddling is just foreplay. Now, it's only natural to get aroused by close contact with your partner—there's nothing wrong with that. She wasn't upset by his arousal or the fact that he wanted to have sex with her. In fact, all of that made her feel desired and good.

And often, it worked! She described how her body would respond, and they would end up having sex, even though she hadn't wanted it to begin with. It wasn't that she wasn't consenting—she was—but it wasn't what *she* initially wanted. They ended up doing what *he* wanted because he convinced her rather than hearing and respecting what she desired and allowing that to be enough.

"My body always betrays me in those moments," she says. "He can turn me on, but that's not the point! It feels like he just wants whatever he can get, and in the end, it's like he didn't really care about what I wanted or what I was asking for. I know he'd love it if I initiated more, but if every time I show interest in being physical with him, it turns into him trying to convince me to go all the way, it makes me not want to start anything in the first place."

Her frustration is clear: While she enjoys feeling desired and can get physically aroused, it leaves her feeling unheard. Her body might respond, but emotionally, it feels like her original desire for closeness and nonsexual intimacy gets overridden. It's not that she's unwilling to be intimate, but when her needs for connection are consistently transformed into sexual encounters, she feels like *her* wants don't matter. What starts as a desire for affection ends up making her feel like her needs are secondary to his.

Many sexual pursuers feel so desperate for any kind of physical connection that they take every sign of touch, like a casual kiss or a caress, as a green light to go all the way. But this denies their partner the space to express their true desires. Over time, this pattern can overshadow the sexual withdrawer's need for connection, leaving them feeling like their wants are secondary. They may go along with sex, but it often comes at the cost of their own emotional or physical needs being ignored. This ultimately makes them less likely to offer a casual touch because they start associating it with pressure for more.

It's not that the pursuing partner has bad intentions; they're simply not fully tuning into the cues their partner is giving. Sometimes, their partner's need for closeness or physical affection without the pressure for sex is just as important. This space is critical, allowing the withdrawing partner to embrace and experience their own desires without feeling pushed. Without this, no one truly gets what they want. Sex starts to feel like a transactional cycle rather than a shared experience, and both partners can end up feeling unfulfilled and frustrated.

When casual physical touches—like a kiss, a passing touch, or a cuddle—are consistently seen as a green light for sex, the withdrawer may start to avoid those moments altogether. If they begin to feel that any affectionate gesture will be seen as an invitation for sex, it can create anxiety or reluctance around even nonsexual physical contact. Over time, they might pull away or avoid initiating physical affection, leading to a dynamic where the pursuer feels that their partner has become colder and less affectionate. This only builds on the negative cycle: One longs for more physical intimacy and feels rejected, while the other feels overwhelmed by the constant pressure for sex.

The first thing is to recognize that nonsexual touch and affection are just as important in building intimacy and connection, and sometimes, they need to exist without the expectation of sex (Campbell et al., 2024). When pursuers open the door to intimate touch without pushing for sex, the erotic charge has opportunity to build naturally.

I know that probably sounds difficult, especially if you've tried this in some form already or are apprehensive of how long it will take to achieve the sexual connection you want. But consider for a moment how much of your focus is on yourself—what *you* feel, what *you* need, what *you* think is normal or right. This viewpoint necessarily makes your partner wrong—not a great starting point for the enthusiastic, passionate sex you crave.

Just as you, as the pursuer, can't easily turn off your sexual wants, the withdrawer can't easily change how they feel. A difference in desire is a shared responsibility.

So, What's a Pursuer to Do?

You can start by asking yourself (and, more importantly, your partner), "What creates an environment where my partner feels open to being sexual?" And when I say "open," I don't mean enthusiastic right away. I'm talking about creating a space where your partner feels neutral and safe, able to explore sexual intimacy without pressure or expectations.

If neutrality and openness don't feel like enough for you, your next step is to reflect on what being desired by your partner does for you. In my work with couples, I've found that for sexual pursuers, having more sex is never just about being horny. If it were, masturbation could solve that need. But what pursuers often seek from sex with a partner is something deeper. So the important question becomes *What do you get from sex with a partner that you can't get from a solo orgasm?* Is it emotional closeness? The feeling of being seen and desired? Validation? Reassurance that the relationship is secure?

These are all great reasons to want sex. But when you start feeling like your partner's desire is a necessary validation of your self-worth, it turns intimacy into a transaction rather than a mutual and genuine connection.

Your work as a higher-desire partner is to figure out the deeper emotions and longings that fuel your own needs and desires and learn to fulfill those needs without placing the responsibility entirely on your partner. And while your partner can certainly be part of fulfilling those needs, you must learn how to express them in a way that fosters mutual connection rather than pressure.

It's important to be aware that because these entitlement patterns are often deeply ingrained and largely unconscious, breaking them can take time—sometimes months, even years. You may need support from

Emotional Pursuers, Take Note

It's important to note that nearly everything we've discussed in this chapter applies not only to sexual pursuers, but to emotional pursuers as well. On its face, it might seem more legitimate to get your emotional needs met through emotional closeness. But in practice, insisting that your partner "open up more" or "be more vulnerable," even when it comes from a place of love, rarely yields the soul-igniting connection you're hoping for, as you've probably learned all too well. Leaning in harder, seeking reassurance, or pressing for closeness tends to overwhelm your partner, leading them to withdraw even more. It's not because they don't care. More often, they pull back because they feel unequipped to meet the intensity of your need in that moment. This cycle isn't about fault—it's about learning a new way to connect that works for both of you.

One key change you can make is to soften—not to lose your voice or your needs, but to approach with vulnerability instead of urgency. Instead of saying "You never listen to me," try "I get worried that you don't care about me." This small shift creates space for your partner to step toward you rather than pulling away.

As you apply the principles throughout this chapter, it's also crucial to practice patience, with both yourself and your partner. Connection isn't something you can force. It's something you build together, moment by moment. Recognize that the effort you've put into improving the relationship is a testament to your strength. There's vulnerability in being the one to reach out, but it also shows your resilience and deep love. Keep going. There are ways forward that can bring more balance and connection—ways that ensure you feel seen, valued, and appreciated. You're not in this alone.

a coach or therapist. While this may feel overwhelming, I can tell you, from my experience working with couples, the effort pays off! The result is a healthier relationship and a deeper, more fulfilling connection for you and your partner . . . and yes, ultimately more satisfying sex.

Using Notice, Own, Connect to Build a Positive Cycle

Relationships thrive when both partners feel seen, valued, and secure—but achieving this requires understanding your role in the dynamic and taking responsibility for your part. For emotional and sexual pursuers, this means shifting from urgency to vulnerability and learning to soften your approach to foster deeper trust and connection with your partner without the pressure of entitlement or expectations. Tall order, right? Let's break it down.

NOTICE

Understanding your patterns starts with awareness.

Questions to ask yourself:

- What emotions, fears, or longings am I feeling, and how are they influencing my actions?
- What am I truly longing for in this moment—validation, closeness, reassurance, or something else?
- How do I typically react when I sense distance or disconnection in my relationship?
- When you pause to notice these patterns, you begin to understand the deeper emotional needs and fears that drive your pursuit. This awareness is the first step to shifting the dynamic toward creating a more authentic connection.

OWN

Taking responsibility for your emotions and actions helps create space for connection.

Questions to ask yourself:

- What part of this dynamic do I have control over, and how can I respond differently?
- Am I expressing my feelings as needs and desires, or as accusations and demands?
- How might my actions or words unintentionally add pressure or defensiveness to the situation?

By owning your feelings without blame, you show up in a way that fosters mutual understanding. Vulnerably expressing what's behind your actions invites your partner to lean in rather than pull away.

CONNECT

Fostering connection requires a shift from pressure to presence.

Questions to ask yourself:

- How can I approach my partner with curiosity about their experience instead of focusing on my own expectations?
- What's one small, vulnerable way I can share how I feel without blaming or pressuring my partner?
- How can I prioritize intimacy and mutual understanding in this moment, rather than focusing solely on the outcome I want?

Taking responsibility for your part in the cycle is a powerful step toward transforming your relationship. While you can't control your partner's reactions or behavior, you *can* control your own—your thoughts, your actions, and the way you communicate. True connection doesn't come from forcing change in your partner; it comes from showing up with openness, vulnerability, and a willingness to engage differently.

By focusing on small, intentional changes in how you express your emotions and needs, you create opportunities to shift the dynamic toward trust and intimacy. When you communicate with curiosity and compassion, you invite your partner into a space of mutual safety—one where both of you feel valued and understood. ♥

Chapter 8

The Work of the Withdrawer

Being the withdrawer isn't easy. Your partner's needs can feel overwhelming, the demands unending, leaving you unsure of how to meet their needs or your own. No matter what you do, it can feel like you're always getting it wrong. Maybe it feels easier to avoid intimacy altogether because it feels too hard to negotiate between what you want and your partner wants, or you've retreated to protect yourself from the vulnerability of feeling like there's something wrong with you and not knowing how to fix it. Any spark of desire you might feel instantly fizzles at the thought of the conflict or confusion that it could lead to.

Here's the tricky part: Your instinct to step back to prevent conflict actually does the opposite. Your partner interprets your withdrawal as disinterest or rejection, which only amplifies their pursuit . . . and, of course, your feeling that the disconnection is all your fault. But as a professional, I can promise you that it's not about fault; it's about a cycle that's hard to break.

As the withdrawer, your work is to reengage, get curious about your partner and yourself, and practice initiating connection even when your instinct is to retreat. This is risky, I know. You may not even be sure how to do it, and I'm sure you have some doubts about how it will go. The good news? When you begin to reengage while your pursuing partner is hard at work on their new moves (or even if they aren't quite there yet), you will actually both begin to get more of what you want.

A Love Letter (and Some Homework) for the Withdrawer

To start, let me make this clear: *There is nothing wrong with you.* You are not broken, and you didn't cause this issue in your relationship. If anything, your reluctance to jump into bed when your heart's not in it shows how important sex is to you. It's not just a way of satisfying physical urges—it's a manifestation of the trust, admiration, and affection you feel toward your partner.

So, don't let societal messaging (or things your partner has implied in moments of frustration) convince you that the desire discrepancy in your relationship is all your fault. This is a cocreated situation in which the conflict is created by the space between you, not by either of your individual positions. Comparing your level of desire to your partner's, or to what you think it should be, only adds pressure and diminishes your own ability to feel any desire at all.

You've probably tried a lot of different approaches to "fix" your desire discrepancy, including just doing it even when you didn't want to, for the sake of the relationship. Maybe sometimes you've enjoyed it, while at other times you've closed your eyes and thought about your to-do list. You might have had bad sex, transactional sex, or sex you didn't want far too often, to the point where you're not even sure what kind of sex you want anymore, or if you want sex *at all.*

You may realize that you no longer even have a sense of what turns you on. You've probably already tried reconnecting with your passion, and it's likely been frustratingly difficult. And I guarantee that feeling like you've let your partner down has made it harder for you to tap into your desire. Perhaps you've even questioned your attraction to your partner or your own sexuality—am I gay, bi, straight, or asexual? I'm certain that you've asked yourself, *Why is my partner's desire for sex my responsibility?*

I'm here to tell you that it's not. Just as your partner isn't responsible for your desire, you aren't responsible for theirs. At the same time, to break free from the negative sexual cycle, you need to decide *together* that creating a fulfilling sex life is worth working on. By committing to this shared goal, you've already begun to build a sexual dynamic that works for you both.

Owning Your Desire

We've talked already about how pressure and entitlement are surefire ways to kill desire. Sometimes, though, even when the pursuing partner eases up on their urgency around sex, the withdrawing partner continues to put pressure on themselves. This internal pressure often results into trying to guess what their partner wants from them. With this inauthentic foundation, the deed may get done, but neither partner feels truly satisfied.

As you've probably heard from your partner a hundred times, what they really want is for *you* to feel sexy. They don't just want you to be willing; they want you to be as aroused as they are, to come in with your own desires, ready to take as much as you give. You may read this and think, *That's just not me* . . . But what if it were? What if you got to call the shots for every sexual encounter, dictating the how, when, and where? Kind of a fun idea to play with, isn't it?

Owning your desire starts with stepping into a place of personal power. Instead of simply waiting for desire to show up, you're cultivating desire in the specific ways that do it for you. If you've ever wondered how sexual pursuers seem to be ready to get it on at a moment's notice, well, this is the answer. While the onset of their desire might seem sudden to you, it's likely been building over the course of several minutes or hours, maybe even all day. Sexual pursuers don't hesitate to follow their brain's arousal cues—on the contrary, they *pursue* them.

Take a cue from the pursuer in your life and ask yourself, *What helps me move into a space where I feel open to being sexual?* Often this warm-up process starts outside the bedroom, so get curious. Does moving your body make you feel more sexy, like after a workout? Maybe you feel more "lit up" following a fun date night, on a relaxing vacation, when your partner has been especially helpful at home, or when you see them in a different light, like interacting with others at a party. Or maybe what gets you turned on is some kind of artistic or visual input—an erotic short story, a steamy love scene in a favorite movie, or even a suggestive social media reel. (It's incredible how some of those food influencers can turn baking or sautéing into softcore porn!) Nothing is too silly to count as a turn-on.

Building Bridges

Once you've identified what helps you feel more sexually open, take some time to explore what helps build that openness into excitement. Is it more foreplay or a different kind of foreplay? Deeper emotional intimacy? Nonsexual touch throughout the day? Or perhaps it's about giving yourself permission to fantasize or engage in self-stimulation before being intimate with your partner. Getting clear on what sustains that spark can help you build a bridge between the idea of sexual fulfillment and the reality as manifested in your relationship. It empowers you to tell your partner, "This is what I need to get in the mood."

Owning your desire means prioritizing time to explore your own body—whether alone or with your partner—so you can better understand what feels good and what you need to experience pleasure and connection more fully. For some, especially women, this may mean starting or rediscovering a masturbation routine, particularly if it's been weeks, months, or even years since they last engaged in solo pleasure. This gap in practice can stem from various factors, including feelings of shame or guilt surrounding self-pleasure or simply never having learned how. Prioritizing solo sexual exploration enhances your self-awareness and builds confidence in communicating your desires with a partner.

Sometimes, what turns someone on is just the opportunity to get turned on. For example, a friend recently shared that on nights when she and her husband decide to have sex, he cleans up the kitchen while she goes into their room alone for 20 to 30 minutes. She takes a shower, puts on a "good" bra and underwear, then settles into bed with a steamy novel. Reading a few chapters of something erotic helps her shift into the right mood. Sometimes, she fantasizes about what they might do together and masturbates (but not to orgasm) with lube because she's found that the feeling of wetness turns her on, jumpstarting the foreplay before her husband joins her. This alone time is her opportunity to connect with her own desire, rather than relying on her partner to get her in the mood. This sets the stage for a more connected and pleasurable experience with her partner.

Your turn-on techniques may be completely different. The specifics don't really matter. What does matter is creating conditions where you feel more in control of your own arousal and pleasure. When you take ownership of that process, it invites more connection and intimacy with your partner because you're coming to the experience from a place of self-awareness and intention rather than pressure or obligation.

Masturbation and Sexual Satisfaction: How Does It Fit Into Your Sex Life?

Masturbation affects people differently when it comes to desire and satisfaction. For some—especially men—it's more often linked to lower sexual satisfaction, possibly because it becomes a stand-in for partnered sex rather than enhancing it. This can happen when desire feels out of sync or when masturbation is more about habit or stress relief than pleasure.

For others—particularly women—masturbation can boost sexual well-being by increasing body awareness, fostering a positive relationship with pleasure, and even sparking more desire for partnered sex. Rather than replacing intimacy, it can complement it by building confidence and reducing pressure (Cervilla et al., 2024).

These patterns aren't set in stone—everyone's experience is different. Does masturbation fuel your desire and connection with your partner, or does it sometimes pull you away? Exploring its role in your sex life can help you find what works best for you.

Removing Obstacles

Along with figuring out how to warm yourself up to sex, it's vital to figure out what thoughts, feelings, or experiences make you go cold.

First, it's worth exploring whether any biological or medical obstacles might be getting in your way. Hormonal factors can play a significant role in suppressing sexual desire and function. For many women, this might be related to the natural hormonal shifts throughout their menstrual cycle, as well as pregnancy, postpartum changes, and of course perimenopause. These shifts can make desire unpredictable or absent altogether.

Maybe you're on a medication that makes it difficult to feel desire, experience pleasure, or reach orgasm. One of the most common classes of medications that can have these side effects is antidepressants, particularly SSRIs. If that's the case for you, you may find yourself facing a difficult choice: Do you stop taking medication that helps you feel less depressed or anxious (both of which can also kill desire), or do you stay on and manage the sexual side effects? There's no easy answer here, and it's a deeply personal decision. While some SSRIs may have lower sexual side effects, most do to some degree, and some people are more sensitive to them than others.

And then there's our old friend, body image. What we see in the mirror can have a significant impact on desire, especially as we age or after having kids. Changes in your body, such as weight fluctuations, stretch marks, or scars, can make it harder to feel confident, let alone sexy. When you're caught up in thoughts about how you look, it's easy to disconnect from your body and its capacity for pleasure. Rebuilding this connection starts with focusing on how your body feels, rather than how it looks, appreciating all it's done rather than focusing on what it can't do (or isn't ready for just yet). Mindful practices such as touch, movement, or even simply acknowledging your body's strength can help. Another practical solution is to keep some clothes on or dim the lights during sexy moments. If this feels awkward to you or your partner, remember that none of this is set in stone—it's just what works for you right now. Sexual connection is remarkably dynamic, constantly evolving with both partners' changes in biology, psychology, emotions, and circumstances.

Outside of biology, there are many factors that can influence your desire. Some of them might be environmental, like hearing the laundry running in the background, worrying that the kids might walk in, or having the room feel too hot or the lights too bright. Some of them might be mental distractions, like intrusive thoughts about work, politics, or family concerns. Maybe it's something your partner brings to the table—it could be as superficial as bad breath or body odor, or perhaps it's something deeper, like a festering fear or resentment that you haven't been able to resolve with them.

Maybe the obstacle is that the sex you're having isn't pleasurable for you anymore. It's even possible you've been going through the motions without ever experiencing the kind of connection and pleasure that make you look forward to intimacy. Or maybe you feel so emotionally connected that your partner is in the nonsexual "family" category in your mind. Whatever it is, taking the time to understand your no can eventually help guide you toward a yes. It's not about forcing desire, but rather about creating a space where it can naturally emerge once the roadblocks are cleared.

Do I Need Professional Help?

Some of these issues you can address on your own; others you might need professional guidance to navigate. Working with a coach or therapist can be incredibly beneficial, especially when it comes to overcoming sexual obstacles such as shame, poor body image, or past trauma.

Seeking therapy is not an indication that you are the problem with your sex life—it's all part of owning your desire and understanding what works for you. Except in cases where trauma or attachment issues make sex feel unsafe or triggering, low desire isn't an individual therapy issue. (Even in those cases, it's not your fault, and helping your partner understand and support you is a crucial part of the healing process.) When we treat low desire as if it's solely the responsibility of the person experiencing it, we reinforce a harmful narrative: that the higher-desire partner is "healthy" and the lower-desire partner is "broken." This simply isn't true. Yes, part of your work may involve addressing emotional and physical blocks, but it's not entirely your burden to bear. Desire exists within the context of the relationship, and the dynamic between partners plays a significant role.

That's why I strongly recommend couples therapy for desire differences. Seeking individual therapy to "fix" the withdrawer's low desire can actually exacerbate the relationship issues. No one feels sexy when they're told the lack of intimacy is their fault. While both partners are responsible for managing their own needs and emotions, one of the best things a pursuer can do to restore sexual connection is to stop making the withdrawer feel like they're the problem.

Emotional Withdrawers, Take Note

As with the last chapter, just about everything we've said in this chapter about sexual withdrawal applies to emotional withdrawal, as well. If you find yourself pulling away when things get heated, retreating to avoid conflict, or feeling stuck in a pattern where you're unsure how to make your partner happy, you're not alone. Being the withdrawer often means carrying the weight of keeping the peace while feeling like you're always one step behind your partner's needs. It's a tough spot to be in, especially when your efforts to create calm are misunderstood as indifference.

Let me start by saying this: Your desire for calm in your relationship is a gift. You bring a sense of steadiness and thoughtfulness that often keeps things from spiraling out of control. You withdraw not because you don't care about the relationship, but because you *do*.

Your desire for harmony and protection is just as valuable as your partner's longing for connection. This chapter isn't about changing who you are. It's about learning new tools to engage in ways that feel authentic and doable for you. The work of reengaging may feel challenging, but it's essential.

So, What's a Withdrawer to Do?

In any relationship, desire exists on a spectrum, with each partner bringing their unique rhythm to the shared experience of intimacy. Instead of seeing themselves as the problem in the relationship or overidentifying as "low desire," it's more helpful for withdrawers to see themselves as collaborators with their partner, working together to create a sexual connection that both find fulfilling.

The withdrawer arguably has the more fun role in this collaboration: exploring their turn-ons and cultivating a sense of personal power. Of course, this might not initially feel like fun for a withdrawer. But the more permission you give yourself to indulge what feels good to you, the more freedom you'll find from the pressure you put on yourself to meet someone else's expectations. You might be surprised how sexy that freedom makes you feel.

Both partners need to recognize that restoring sexual connection is a long game, not a quick fix. It's challenging work to open up when you'd rather shut down, to approach when you'd rather retreat. The pursuing partner can support a withdrawer by learning to manage their expectations and cultivate patience, which gives the withdrawer confidence to explore and access their authentic sense of desire. This shared approach transforms intimacy from a source of conflict into an opportunity for growth, trust, and deeper understanding.

Stepping In with Notice, Own, Connect

Relationships are a delicate dance, and as a withdrawer, your steps are just as important as your partner's. Whether you pull back emotionally, sexually, or both, you likely retreat to protect yourself and the relationship. Conflict may feel overwhelming, and the weight of your partner's needs can make it hard to believe that your own wants, needs, and feelings matter.

But here's the truth: They *do* matter. And your role in the relationship isn't just about keeping the peace or stepping back when things feel like too much—it's about learning to step in. This doesn't mean you have to change who you are or abandon your need for calm and safety. Instead, it's about taking responsibility for your part in the dynamic and trying new moves that invite connection rather than distance.

NOTICE

Awareness is the first step to understanding your patterns.

Questions to ask yourself:

- What emotions am I feeling when I step back—overwhelm, fear, inadequacy, or something else?
- What triggers my withdrawal? Is it a fear of conflict, a sense of not being enough, or feeling overshadowed by my partner's needs?
- How does my withdrawal affect my partner, and how might they interpret it differently than I intend?
- Noticing your emotions and patterns helps you see where you're stuck and how you might begin to step forward.

OWN

Taking responsibility for your feelings and actions empowers you to change the dynamic.

Questions to ask yourself:

- What am I afraid of when I avoid conflict or connection—getting it wrong, being misunderstood, or feeling overwhelmed?
- How does staying silent or stepping back keep me from expressing my own wants and needs?
- What small step can I take to share my feelings without fear of "messing things up"?
- Owning your role doesn't mean taking all the blame. It means recognizing that your wants, needs, and feelings are valid—and that expressing them is a way to build connection, not harm it.

CONNECT

Connection begins with small, intentional steps.

Questions to ask yourself:

- What's one simple way I can communicate my needs or emotions, even if I'm unsure how they'll be received?
- How can I let my partner know I'm invested in the relationship without feeling pressured to "fix" everything? For example, "I want to talk, but I need time to gather my thoughts."
- How can I create a space where both my needs and my partner's are valued, so neither of us feels overlooked or overwhelmed?

True connection doesn't require perfection. It comes from showing up as you are, taking small risks, and believing that your voice matters just as much as your partner's.

By applying the Notice, Own, Connect framework, withdrawers can begin to break free from cycles of disconnection and rediscover their own desires and needs. The process isn't about becoming someone you're not—it's about recognizing that your wants, needs, and feelings are just as important as your partner's. Small, intentional steps can pave the way for deeper emotional and physical intimacy, creating a relationship where both partners feel seen, heard, and valued. ♥

Part Three

MOVING INTO CONNECTION

Chapter 9

Pleasure

Pleasure can take many forms. It might mean enjoying your partner's pleasure, taking turns giving and receiving, savoring sensual touch, or even just making out on the couch like teenagers. What if you focused on what feels good instead of stressing about doing it "right"? What if that definition of pleasure evolved from day to day, week to week, or year to year as you follow what feels good in your body and relationship? Imagine allowing your sexual relationship to be guided by your pleasure and that of your partner, rather than both of you adhering to a script that you may not have had much say in writing.

This all may sound wonderful, but one key element is essential to making it work: communication.

Masturbation often leads to quicker orgasms because there's an effortless and nearly instantaneous communication between action and sensation. You know what feels good and can adjust immediately without explaining or negotiating. In contrast, partnered sex requires dialogue that's more explicit and multilayered. It involves expressing desires, giving and receiving feedback, and being attuned to verbal and nonverbal cues, as well as psychological factors such as emotional connection and differing arousal patterns, and it's no surprise that orgasm during partnered sex often takes longer, not only because of the need to synchronize with a partner's movements but also because of the focus on mutual pleasure.

♥

"Sometimes it's hard for me to cum when we have sex," Mateo admits. "I start overthinking, like wondering if this is taking too long or maybe Carrie isn't really into it because she usually doesn't orgasm from intercourse. Even though she says she enjoys it, sometimes it doesn't always seem like she's fully engaged. It becomes a bit of a vicious cycle."

"I struggle to orgasm from penetration," Carrie shares. "I love having intercourse with Mateo—the friction and the fullness feel amazing—but it just doesn't make me cum."

"When we don't have sex as often, I end up masturbating more, and that seems to make it harder to cum when we do have sex. It's easier when I know she's enjoying what we're doing, but it's tricky because what gets her off isn't always what works for me," Mateo continues.

"I can have really pleasurable sex without reaching orgasm," Carrie explains. "But sometimes, I feel pressure to finish because I know you want me to. And when there's pressure, it becomes even harder."

"Oh, I get that," Mateo replies. "It's the same for me. If I feel like I'm taking too long and you might be getting sore or wishing it was over, it takes even longer for me to finish. That pressure is tough."

Mateo and Carrie's situation illustrates the complex interplay between goal-driven and pleasure-driven approaches to sexual intimacy. When the primary focus of sex shifts toward achieving orgasm, especially under the pressure of time or performance expectations, it can create an environment of anxiety that ultimately reduces the overall pleasure for both partners. This pressure can lead to a negative feedback loop, where the more one worries about reaching orgasm, the more elusive it becomes.

For many, if not most, orgasm is essential for sexual satisfaction—after all, it's the culmination of building arousal. When sex consistently lacks the potential for orgasm, it may start to feel incomplete or less rewarding, potentially leading to a decrease in sexual desire over time.

But orgasm isn't the only payoff in sex. Carrie's experience in the story above highlights the fact that pleasurable sex involves a rich tapestry of experiences, including the emotional connection between partners, the satisfaction of fulfilling relational needs, and the reward of knowing that your partner is enjoying the experience as much as you are. Knowing this helps us create a more holistic and satisfying sexual experience where orgasm is a possibility but not the sole focus, allowing both partners to fully engage in the moment and derive pleasure from the entire spectrum of what sex can offer.

The Orgasm Gap

When couples approach me with concerns about low desire, one of the first steps is to evaluate the pleasure they experience during sex. If the sex isn't mutually pleasurable, it's understandable that desire might be lacking.

One common culprit behind less-than-pleasurable sex is unrealistic expectations. The portrayal of sex in TV, movies, porn, or literature often centers heavily on intercourse—intense penetration, simultaneous orgasms, quick resolution (Séguin et al., 2018) . However, these make-believe depictions fly in the face of research showing that 95 percent of women cannot achieve orgasm from intercourse alone (Mintz, 2017). In fact, for the majority of women, intercourse actually isn't their greatest source of pleasure. Sex therapist Dr. Laurie Mintz notes in *Becoming Cliterate* that 88 to 99 percent of women don't include penetration during masturbation, and those who do almost always combine it with clitoral stimulation. This statistic is especially staggering given our cultural tendency to equate intercourse with sex. Most of the time, when a couple encounters barriers to intercourse or is told by a doctor that it's off the table, they end up abstaining from all sexual activity, assuming that nothing else can deliver comparable pleasure.

Both men and women tend to believe that penetrative sex is the ultimate source of sexual satisfaction. This belief affects sexual satisfaction for both, as well, making it a major contributor to the orgasm gap: the statistic that while 91 percent of men report usually or always reaching orgasm during partnered sex, only 64 percent of women do (Frederick et al., 2018).

This statistic is not fueled by physiological differences in men and women; rather, it is shaped by cultural expectations and misunderstandings about sexual responsibility (Salisbury & Fisher, 2014). When women feel they are failing to achieve orgasm through penetration alone, they often internalize these feelings. This mental burden can create a vicious cycle where anxiety and self-doubt further suppress arousal and make it even more difficult for women to reach orgasm (Hevesi et al., 2022). Meanwhile, this belief leads men to feel that it's their job to physically stimulate their partner to orgasm. When a woman doesn't climax, both partners often worry about its effect on the man's ego. It's not uncommon for women to fake orgasms due to feelings of insecurity or with the goal of protecting their partner's self-esteem (Hevesi et al., 2022; Salisbury & Fisher, 2014). This dynamic reflects broader cultural scripts that place pressure on men to perform and leave women prioritizing their partner's feelings over their own satisfaction (Salisbury & Fisher, 2014).

Let me be clear: I am not anti-penetration, nor am I suggesting that couples give up anything they enjoy together. Intercourse fosters deep intimacy and brings immense pleasure for many couples. However, viewing penetration as the ultimate form of sexual connection can limit the capacity for pleasure and, over time, dampen desire. It's essential to recognize that the clitoris, often misunderstood and overlooked, is the true epicenter of female pleasure; in fact, it's unique in having no purpose beyond pleasure.

Many people think of the clitoris as just a small external nub. But it actually extends beyond the visible glans and hood into the pelvic floor with structures that surround the vaginal canal, and its "legs" are positioned on either side of the vaginal walls. These internal parts contribute significantly to the sensitivity and functionality of the clitoris as the center of sexual pleasure. This deep internal structure makes clitoral stimulation, including the elusive "G-spot" stimulation, an integral part of many women's sexual experiences.

Embracing a more accurate view of female anatomy can reduce pressure and thereby enhance sexual satisfaction. By acknowledging and incorporating diverse forms of stimulation and intimacy beyond penetration, couples can experience more fulfilling sexual encounters.

Research-Backed Sexual Positions Most Likely to Enhance Female Orgasm*

- Face-to-face, man lying down, woman on top
- Face-to-face, woman lying down with hips elevated, man on top
- Face-to-face, man sitting, woman sitting on top

* Krejčová et al. (2020); Lovie & Marashi (2022)

The Biggest Erogenous Zone: Your Brain

Can we be honest? Between the jerky movements and the profusion of body fluids, the undignified facial expressions and the animalistic sounds, partnered sex is downright weird. Its mechanics boil down to friction and lubrication; what makes it magical is the element of fantasy. It's fantasy that supplies the erotic charge between two people and stokes the sense of fulfillment beyond a mere physical release. Fantasy is what elevates sex from a purely animal act to a means of exploring desire, indulging emotion, and escaping everyday stress. It's the "spice" we crave in a relationship that keeps us coming back for more.

You may have heard it said that the brain is the biggest erogenous zone. For many, if not most, the erotic experience is largely driven by imagination. The brain is where desire takes shape, stories unfold, and fantasies come to life. It's where anticipation, curiosity, and longing build toward climax. Most importantly for parents, it's what allows us to see our partner (and ourselves) in new, unexpected ways, keeping desire fresh and alive.

By the same token, many sexual difficulties arise when the brain's erotic powers are blocked by mental anti-aphrodisiacs such as anxiety, shame, or self-doubt. Often caused by poor self-image, constrictive cultural or religious beliefs, or past traumas or abuse, negative thoughts and feelings pull our attention away from the present moment or, at worst, cause us to subconsciously suppress our libido. Men may experience erectile dysfunction, delayed ejaculation, or premature ejaculation, while women may struggle with arousal or reaching orgasm.

Perhaps it's more accurate to say that the brain *can be* the most erogenous zone. If its powers of imagination shift focus from erotic fantasy to our fears, hurts, or perceived shortcomings, it creates a negative feedback loop that closely mirrors the negative emotional cycle. One partner's sexual anxiety, shame, or self-doubt feeds into the other's, until both of them feel frustrated, inadequate, and isolated.

A Pleasure-Focused Path

When I help couples stuck in a negative sexual cycle, I typically suggest a period where intercourse and their usual sexual routine are taken off the table. In its place, I guide them through a technique known as *sensate focus*.

Initially developed by therapists William Masters and Virginia Johnson in the 1960s, this technique has proven effective in treating a number of sexual issues by shifting partners' focus away from performance and toward sensation and connection (Weiner, 2022). The practice begins with nonsexual touching, encouraging partners to tune in to sensory experiences such as the texture, temperature, and feel of each other's skin. Over time, this progresses to more intimate touch, including genital areas, but always with the goal of intensifying sensation rather than achieving outcomes like arousal or orgasm. With practice, sensate focus helps couples experience intimacy more easily and more deeply by allowing the mind and body to be fully immersed in sensation.

Communication is a crucial component of sensate focus. Partners are encouraged to share their experiences and sensations with each other. This exchange builds emotional intimacy and trust, making it easier to discuss sexual preferences and boundaries. As partners become more comfortable with each other's touch and communication, they can gradually move to more intimate forms of contact, keeping the priority on pleasure over performance.

The process typically begins with nonsexual touching exercises, where one partner is the "toucher" and the other the "receiver." During this stage, the couple focuses on exploring various parts of the body, noticing how different types of touch feel—whether it's soft, firm, slow, or quick. The receiver's role is to pay attention to how their partner's touch feels without evaluating or analyzing the sensations, allowing them to fully engage with their body in the present moment. The toucher, in turn, is encouraged to focus on the act of touching itself rather than trying to provoke a reaction or sexual response. As the exercises progress, partners move toward more intimate areas of the body, including the genitals and breasts. Even at this stage, the focus remains on the sensation rather than on reaching arousal or engaging in full intercourse. If either occurs, it's accepted, but the central goal remains sensory awareness. Instead of slipping into automatic responses (like rushing toward orgasm) or evaluating the experience (Is this good? Am I turning my partner on? Can I cum?), the goal is to simply be in the moment, enjoying sensation for its own sake. Needless to say, this practice can be a game-changer for those struggling with sexual performance anxiety or feelings of disconnection in the relationship.

Take Grace and Matthew, a couple in their early 50s who have been together for 20 years. Despite describing their relationship as close, they haven't had sex in three years. Grace is in perimenopause, and as a result, intercourse has become more painful. Matthew is on heart medication that causes unreliable erections. Sex "just always worked" for them, so they never really talked about it.

Now, they are caught in a sexual cycle where Matthew, having struggled with erectile dysfunction, has become a sexual withdrawer driven by shame, anxiety, and fear of disappointing Grace. Meanwhile, Grace feels increasingly insecure and questions whether Matthew is still attracted to her. She craves the validation and connection that sex once provided but often feels disappointed and alone.

Grace looks at Matthew, her voice hesitant. "I feel like we haven't really connected in years, and . . . I don't know. It makes me wonder if you're still attracted to me. Especially now, with everything changing. My body feels different. I feel different."

Matthew shifts uncomfortably, avoiding her gaze. "It's not that. I'm still attracted to you. It's just . . . every time we try, I get stressed. I know what's going to happen—I won't be able to keep an erection or stay hard, and I don't want to disappoint you again."

Grace sighs, her frustration mingling with sadness. "I get that it's hard for you, but when you pull away, it feels like I'm the problem. I start to worry, maybe you don't want me anymore. And, with everything going on with my body, I guess I just want to know you still see me that way."

Matthew's shoulders slump, his voice softening. "It's not you. I just feel like I've already failed before we even started. And the more it doesn't work, the more anxious I get."

Grace frowns. "I just feel so . . . disconnected. It's not just the sex; it's everything. It's feeling like we're drifting apart."

Matthew looks down, taking a deep breath. "I get that, but I'm so worried about failing that it's hard for me even to try anymore."

This kind of dialogue highlights the dynamic that keeps Grace and Matthew trapped in their sexual cycle. Grace seeks validation and connection through physical intimacy, while Matthew, consumed by anxiety and fear of failure, withdraws. Grace's insecurities around her body change during perimenopause, adding another layer to the disconnection, making her feel older and less desirable, which intensifies her need for reassurance. Neither one feels understood, and the lack of communication further reinforces their disconnection.

This couple can't simply be asked to map their sexual cycle and "give it another try." They need a more structured approach to rebuild confidence and reduce anxiety as they learn to view their physical interactions differently. Through sensate focus, couples can start to reconnect. A key aspect of sensate focus is communication. It's a series of communication exercises where touch serves as the vehicle. Couples focus on touching and noticing pleasure, then communicating about it slowly and deliberately. This practice is often unfamiliar to many couples, especially outside the early days of their relationship, but it can significantly improve their connection and intimacy.

Ease Your Way In

Like any sex therapy technique, sensate focus can feel strange or awkward initially. This awkwardness is eased by consistent practice and by making space for whatever emotions come up. Often, feelings of anxiety, disconnection, and worry will surface at the outset of practice. This is actually a positive sign, indicating that underlying anxieties present in sexual encounters are being brought to light. For this reason, having a trained therapist guide couples through the process can be very helpful.

There are a number of quality apps available to guide couples through the steps of sensate focus. The one I recommend is called Blueheart; it has been studied by independent researchers and found effective, particularly with couples who saw the work as a joint endeavor and not one person's sole responsibility to fix (Vowels, 2023). You can also use the instructions provided on the following pages.

Sensate Focus: A Step-by-Step Guide*

First, choose one or two times a week for these "dates." Be specific and put them on the calendar. The length of time that the date will last should be agreed upon beforehand and divided evenly so each person is the toucher and receiver for equal amounts of time. Many couples work though these stages over the course of 6 to 12 weeks. The key is to approach with curiosity and openness and not rush the process.

Set the Stage for Sensuality, Not Sexuality

- **Remove Pressure:** On these nights, agree in advance that there will be no assumption of genital or breast touching, oral sex, or intercourse. This removes the pressure to perform and shifts the focus to pure sensation.
- **Create the Environment:** Ensure the space is private, comfortable, and distraction-free. Both partners should feel relaxed and at ease. Aim for 30 to 40 minutes for each session.
- **Clothing:** Nudity is ideal to allow full skin-to-skin contact. Avoid constrictive clothing.

Step 1: Non-Genital Touching

- **Designate Roles:** One partner is the toucher, and the other is the receiver. The receiver focuses solely on feeling and experiencing touch without reciprocating or analyzing.
- **Explore Different Areas:** The toucher can experiment with various parts of the body—arms, back, legs, neck—avoiding genitals and breasts.
  - ***Texture game:*** Notice how different parts of the skin feel. Compare the softness of the inner arms to the roughness of the heels or the smoothness of the thighs.

  - ***Vary pressure and speed:*** Switch between light, slow touches and firmer, quicker strokes. Notice how the tempo affects the sensations.
  - ***Use hands and fingers:*** Explore how touching with the whole hand feels compared to just fingertips. Try using two hands to enhance the tactile experience.
- **Communication:** The receiver can speak up if something feels uncomfortable, but otherwise, they should focus on simply experiencing the sensation without thinking or judging.

Step 2: Include Genital and Breast Touching

- **Expand Exploration:** After several sessions without genital touch, include breasts and genitals in the touching, but with the same non-goal-oriented mindset.
- **Keep It Slow:** The toucher should gently explore the genital and breast areas, not as a means to arousal but as a way to notice different sensations. Alternate between genital touch and other parts of the body to keep the exploration broad.
- **Hand-Riding Technique:** The receiver can place their hand on top of the toucher's hand to gently guide pressure or tempo, offering subtle feedback without taking control.

Step 3: Introduce Lotion or Oil

- **Enhance Sensation:** Incorporate lotion or oil to add a new texture to the experience. Warm the lotion in your hands before applying it to the skin.
- **Contrast Sensations:** Start without lotion, then add it midway through to compare sensations. Try using lotion on just one hand and notice the differences as you explore your partner's body.

Step 4: Mutual Touching

- **Touch Together:** Now, both partners touch each other simultaneously. Focus on the dual sensations of being touched while also touching your partner.
- **Explore Oral Touch:** This isn't oral sex, but rather using lips and tongue to sensually explore the body. Take time to notice how the sensations differ from those of the hands.

- **Stay Present and Mindful of the Sensations:** Avoid thoughts or fantasies that shift the focus toward sexual performance.

Step 5: Sensual Intercourse

- **Introduce Genital Contact:** After practicing the previous steps, explore the sensations of genital contact, including intercourse. The goal here is still to focus on the physical sensations rather than achieving orgasm.
- **Slow Penetration:** If intercourse is a goal, begin with partial penetration, taking time to notice the warmth and sensations of contact. Hold still for a moment to feel the subtle differences that even the smallest movements make.
- **Vary Movements:** After slow penetration, experiment with different types of thrusts—quick and shallow or slow and deep—while maintaining focus on the sensations rather than any goal.
- **Communicate Needs:** If you feel like transitioning to full intercourse or pulling back, communicate clearly with your partner, ensuring both are comfortable and focused on the experience.

Key Tips

- **Start Slow:** Don't rush the process or feel pressure to move to the next step until you're both comfortable.
- **Stay Mindful:** Keep the focus on the sensations you're feeling in the moment, not what should or could happen next.
- **No Judgment:** Sensate focus is about the experience, not whether something is "good" or "bad." Let yourself feel without evaluating.
- **Switch Roles:** After one partner explores as the toucher, switch roles to ensure both experience giving and receiving.

* Adapted from *Sensate Focus in Sex Therapy: The Illustrated Manual*, by L. Weiner and C. Avery-Clark. Copyright 2017 by Routledge.

Fiddling with the Formula

One of the main generators of erotic energy is novelty, something hard to come by in domestic life. Routines become the lifeblood of many families, and for good reason. Children need predictability and structure for optimal growth and development. By sticking to an established schedule and framework, parents save themselves a lot of pain and suffering from sleep-deprived, overstimulated, hungry, or anxious behavior. It also can help grease the wheels of the domestic partnership—rather than having to guess or arbitrate who is taking care of what from one day to the next, a predictable routine ensures that both partners are accountable for their share of the load and, over time, lessens the difficulty associated with various tasks. As the saying goes, practice makes perfect.

However, this maxim does not apply in all aspects of the relationship. In creating this framework of predictability and structure for their children, parents often adopt it for themselves, limiting their access to spontaneity, mental stimulation, and excitement. This orientation toward routine can gravitate into the bedroom, with many couples developing a set routine of sexual moves that become their go-to favorites. While this is a natural part of exploring each other's bodies and preferences and very often leads to consistent and pleasurable sex, it can also reduce excitement, exploration, and playfulness. Familiar routines, while enjoyable, can limit the erotic energy fueled by novelty and discovery. As a result, couples may start to feel that their sex life becomes formulaic, potentially leading to less desire and excitement if they don't actively seek ways to refresh their connection and introduce variety (de Oliveira et al., 2023).

The good news? A little novelty can go a long way!

"We have a formula," says Maria matter-of-factly. "When we have sex, we do the same few things in the same order. It works, but . . . I wouldn't say it's always very exciting."

"Recently, I felt like we got outside our norm a little," says George. "Remember when we made out against the car in the driveway? That was so hot. It was like the best sex we've had in ages, and we didn't get past second base. I've been thinking about it ever since."

"Oh yeah, I remember," says Maria, flushing a little. "You asked me if I remembered the time we had sex in the back seat of your old car on the way home. We were laughing about how hot and uncomfortable it was. Then, when we got out of the car, you grabbed me and shoved me up against the car; I felt how much you wanted me. But then you walked away and didn't take it past the driveway. You left me wanting, which I haven't felt lately."

As George and Maria came to realize, the richest experiences of eroticism go beyond traditional definitions of sex. The delicate dance of creative energy intertwined with intimacy indeed nourishes fulfilling connections. Yet, as couples become accustomed to their sexual routines and mired in the minutiae of domestic life with children, they might unknowingly channel this vital energy elsewhere, leading to a decline in desire.

This isn't to suggest that this erotic energy necessarily gets diverted into other sexual encounters, such as affairs, although that can certainly happen. More often, the creative, vital excitement that erotic energy contains gets redirected into nonsexual pursuits such as parenting or work. The demands of raising children and managing a household can be all-consuming, leaving little room for the spontaneous, imaginative elements that once fueled a couple's passion.

Maria shares that she tends to find herself prioritizing George's pleasure in their sexual encounters. This is not because she feels like her pleasure doesn't matter—far from it, in fact. It's because a reciprocal relationship exists between her pleasure and her perception of his pleasure. When Maria senses that George isn't thoroughly enjoying himself, it diminishes her enjoyment, making them both more inclined to narrow their sexual menu to activities that are mutually agreed upon and pleasurable to both.

"I used to really enjoy doggy style. It hit the right spot and gave great access to my clit, a perfect recipe for great sex for me," says Maria. "But George said once that he likes to see my face when we have sex, and ever since then, I haven't asked him to do me from behind. I care what he wants, too, and knowing he's not really into it makes it less sexy for me."

When time is short and sex is hard to come by, there is a tendency for couples to prioritize practicality and expediency over sensuality. In other words, couples tend to stick to what they know works for their partner, and this can limit their sexual options and creativity. In addition, couples who share a deep emotional connection and a genuine concern for their partner's pleasure may inadvertently limit their exploration of individual desires and preferences (Muise et al., 2023).

This is not inherently negative. It means that many couples are maximizing both practicality and pleasure. However, over time, this tendency can make sexual encounters less exciting and, therefore, less desirable. The erotic energy is constricted by the regular and routine, and excitement becomes the casualty.

To understand why this happens, it's important to remember what we said earlier about the brain being the most powerful erogenous zone. When the brain is stimulated and the imagination is engaged, even the lightest of touches or a look from across the room can become incredibly erotic. Encounters that involve no physical touch at all can be intensely sensual. Just imagine the palpable heat that can be generated between two people by a meaningful gaze or a few words.

However, this mental heat often lessens in long-term relationships as the familiarity with domestic life slowly replaces the mystery and eroticism of early dating. Recognizing the importance of mental stimulation and novelty can help couples keep their relationships vibrant and exciting, even amid the demands of domestic life. This involves an ongoing effort to keep the brain engaged and the imagination alive. Prioritizing the mental aspect of intimacy and actively seeking out new experiences in and out of the bedroom can help maintain a sense of excitement and connection. It's about balancing the necessary routines that support family life and the spontaneous, imaginative elements that keep the romantic relationship alive.

Hot vs. Warm Sex

When people think of great sex, they often picture passion-fueled, can't-keep-your-hands-off-each-other encounters—what we might call *hot sex*. It thrives on spontaneity, novelty, and intensity, making it most common in the early stages of a relationship (or on vacation). While exhilarating, hot sex can be harder to sustain as life responsibilities, stress, and routine set in. And honestly—who has the time or energy for high-intensity, erotic sex *all* the time?

Warm sex, on the other hand, is about connection, comfort, and deep emotional safety. It's the kind of sex that happens when trust and tenderness create a space for intimacy to unfold more slowly. While it may lack urgency, it brings a different kind of satisfaction—one rooted in closeness and security. For many long-term couples, warm sex becomes the foundation of their intimate life, even as passion ebbs and flows.

The key is to value *both* kinds of sex rather than seeing warm sex as a consolation prize for when hot sex isn't happening. Hot sex brings excitement and novelty, while warm sex fosters deep connection and intimacy. A fulfilling sex life isn't about choosing one over the other—it's about appreciating what each brings to the relationship. By embracing both and letting go of the pressure to make every encounter mind-blowing, couples can create a rich, sustainable, and satisfying sex life that evolves over time.

Redirecting Erotic Energy

When my husband and I go out to eat, we often opt for a seat at the bar, enjoying observing the goings-on around us. One of our little games involves gauging the length of couples' relationships based on their interactions. On a recent occasion, a couple caught our eye. They were seated facing each other, engrossed in conversation, with one of the man's legs positioned between the woman's. There was a certain glow about them, accompanied by an undeniable tension, evident in their lidded eyes, lingering gazes, and hushed voices.

Their absorption in each other was so complete that when their food arrived, they seemed startled, as if snapping out of a trance. It dawned on me that what we were witnessing was more than just a mealtime chat—it was an intimate connection, bordering on something more. It was sex, even though they were just sitting at the bar like the rest of us, barely touching each other. As my husband and I observed them in what was hopefully a discreet way, I couldn't shake the charged atmosphere they created. It was almost as if their energy permeated the entire bar, making it impossible for anyone not to notice. We found ourselves stealing glances at them throughout our meal, and we weren't the only ones—their chemistry drew the attention of everyone in the room.

In a telling moment, both my husband and I surmised that they were in the early stages of dating. Looking back, I'm annoyed that we made that assumption. Who says that longtime couples and co-parents can't maintain that kind of vibrant connection? When did we decide that being in a committed relationship meant giving up the brain's capacity for erotic excitement?

In my work with clients, I frequently encounter individuals whose lack of desire has nothing to do with biological issues or even mental blocks; often, it's the result of their erotic energy being channeled into other areas of their lives. In her book *Mating in Captivity*, Esther Perel explains that erotic energy is the creative force that drives us in our passionate endeavors. Once people have achieved the "goal" of sexual eroticism—that is, finding a committed partner—many of them redirect that energy into their professional endeavors, immersing themselves in high-powered careers or striving for financial success. Others pour this energy into their roles as parents, becoming deeply involved in the joys and challenges of their children's education or sports activities, or the day-to-day demands of parenting.

While these areas of life undoubtedly require considerable energy, it's crucial to reserve a portion for nurturing the sexual connection within our relationships. After all, unless one is in a nonmonogamous arrangement or engaging in extramarital affairs, the intimate bond with a romantic partner remains unique to any other relationship. Unfortunately, our trust in each other's commitment means that this relationship tends to receive only the scraps of time and energy left over from a day of work, domestic responsibilities, and of course, parenting.

Parenthood: The Great Sex Killer

A friend recently told me a story that perfectly embodies the tragicomedy of trying to maintain sexiness with kids around. She was in the driveway with her boys, who are seven and nine, when her husband arrived home from work. Feeling a bit playful, she flashed him the peace-fingers-to-the-mouth sign—you know the one—behind the boys' backs. Her husband smirked, and she flushed with the little thrill of surprising and delighting him and herself. And then . . .

"Mom, what does that mean?"

Seeing her seven-year-old mimicking the gesture, my friend panicked. "Uh . . . it means 'victory'!"

For a moment, she thought she'd dodged a bullet. Alas, no—her boys *loved* this new secret signal. They started doing this "victory" sign all the time—not just at home, but at friends' houses, at the park, in front of everyone! Watching this unfold, my friend remembers thinking, *Oh no, what have I done? And more importantly, how can I undo it without explaining the real meaning?!* After about a week of this, tortured by visions of getting called into the principal's office, she finally pulled them aside.

"Hey guys, just so you know, it only means 'victory' if you hold it *away* from your mouth."

"Okay, Mom," they agreed dutifully, then carried on as if nothing happened.

My friend remembers standing there for a moment, caught between relief and barely contained laughter. Crisis averted, but not without a good story and a reminder of how messy it can be to navigate life as both lovers and parents.

The truth is, even when you do everything right—plan dates, communicate, stay emotionally connected, prioritize your sex life, keep the spark alive with spontaneous surprises—kids will still find a way to interfere. In our house, my husband and I can't even sneak a hug without one (or both) of the kids quite literally squeezing themselves in between us. It's sweet, in a way, and we often smile at each other over the top of their tousled heads, thinking, *What can you do?*

The reality, though, is that there are things we can and must do if we want to keep the erotic charge alive in our long-term relationships. Along with examining our relational patterns and improving our communication, we can reignite our erotic charge by redefining what sex means to us.

It's Time to Redefine Sex

When I mention the word *sex*, what comes to mind for you? For many heterosexual individuals, it's often limited to good old "P-in-V." Within the LGBTQ+ community, there tends to be a broader and more diverse understanding of what constitutes sexual activity, paired with a willingness to communicate openly. This alternate view could serve everyone struggling with sexual disconnection: What if all couples broadened their understanding of sex beyond the traditional heteronormative sex-for-reproduction scenario? What if we considered that numerous everyday interactions hold elements of sensuality? By expanding our definition of sex, we can encompass much more than just intercourse. This broader perspective can include a variety of intimate and pleasurable experiences that deepen connections and enhance relationships.

Early in your relationship, there were likely moments of playful flirting, stolen glances, and sexy interactions, both in person and over the phone (or email or social media). Parenthood leaves little room for those effortless moments of erotic connection. If you're lucky, you might squeeze in a few minutes of foreplay before moving straight into penetrative sex, but that's often the extent of it. Is it any wonder that desire can start to fade?

I'm going to suggest something radical: that sex can be whatever you and your partner define it as. Instead of only counting intercourse and orgasm in your weekly "sex quota," factor in all the ways you experience erotic thrill together. Lingering kisses, playful touches, flirty texts throughout the day, sensual touch—for busy parents, it *all* counts as sex.

For this to work, both partners should have a mutual intention to redefine what being sexual together looks like. Desire thrives on imagination, so it's unrealistic to expect that sex can be boiled down to just the "bare bones" (foreplay and penetration) in perpetuity while still maintaining a high level of desire. By broadening your definition of sex, you can create space for connection and satisfaction without the pressure for it to always look a certain way. When you start to view these small acts of intimacy as part of your sexual life and not just as stepping stones to "the real thing," it changes the game.

Reclaiming Pleasure with Notice, Own, Connect

In many parents' busy lives, pleasure is something that happens along the way to a bigger goal like a quick orgasm or, perhaps even better, going to sleep afterward. But what if pleasure itself became the focus? What if we stopped measuring success in the bedroom in terms of performance and instead embraced what felt good, moment to moment?

Pleasure isn't static. It evolves with time, experiences, and circumstances. It can look like sensual touch, a spontaneous dance to a special song, or making out on the kitchen counter. It's not about following a script, but rather about letting curiosity guide you toward what feels good in your body and your connection with your partner. When you focus on pleasure, you can redefine your sexual relationship, shifting away from performance-driven intimacy to something more fulfilling, playful, and present.

This chapter is about making pleasure central to your sexual experience. It's about noticing what brings you pleasure, owning your role in creating that, and connecting with your partner in ways that are deeply satisfying. Let's explore how you can cultivate more pleasure and make it the foundation of a more connected and fulfilling sexual relationship with Notice, Own, Connect.

NOTICE

The first step in cultivating pleasure is to notice what feels good in your body. Too often, we get caught up in what we think sex "should" look like or worry about meeting expectations. Instead, try tuning into your body and noticing the sensations you enjoy.

Questions to ask yourself:

- What types of touch or sensation do I find most pleasurable?
- When do I feel most at ease and able to enjoy being sexual?
- What are my brakes? What hits my gas pedal?

OWN

Owning your pleasure means taking responsibility for communicating about what feels good for you. This might involve exploring solo pleasure to better understand your own body or learning to advocate for what you need during partnered sex. Remember, your pleasure is yours to cultivate, and you deserve to prioritize it.

Questions to ask yourself:

- Do I feel comfortable exploring my own pleasure, either alone or with my partner?
- Are there any cultural or personal beliefs that make me feel shame or hesitation about pursuing pleasure?
- How can I communicate with my partner about my brakes and gas pedals?

CONNECT

Pleasure thrives in connection—not just with your partner, but also with yourself. Tuning in to what you enjoy, communicating openly, and staying curious about your partner create a positive feedback loop that deepens intimacy and enhances satisfaction.

Questions to ask yourself:

- How can I communicate my needs and desires to my partner in a way that fosters connection?
- When I feel distracted or anxious during sex, do I share it openly or try to hide it?
- What small changes could we make together to prioritize mutual enjoyment over performance?

When both partners prioritize pleasure—individually and together—it creates a more balanced and fulfilling dynamic. By noticing what brings you joy, owning your role in cultivating pleasure, and connecting through open communication and shared exploration, you can redefine intimacy as something rich, playful, and deeply rewarding.

Pleasure isn't about perfection. It's about presence. By stepping away from rigid scripts and embracing curiosity, you can create space for pleasure to flourish in ways you may not have imagined. Whether through sensual touch, playful experimentation, or simply savoring each other's presence, the possibilities are endless when you allow pleasure to lead the way. ♥

Part Four

AGES AND STAGES

I had mixed feelings about including this section in the book. While writing it, I struggled to thread the needle between speaking to the challenges parents face in each stage specifically enough to feel helpful, yet keeping it broad enough to apply to a wide range of people and families. In every stage, there are countless reasons why couples may get stuck, and I wanted to avoid oversimplifying these complex dynamics or offering advice that feels trite or patronizing.

At its core, the advice for reconnecting often circles back to the same themes: Notice the negative cycle and blame it for the problems, rather than each other. Pay attention and tend to your nervous system. Prioritize the relationship, even when it's hard. All while maintaining the delicate balance between individual needs, relationship needs, and family needs—the *me*, the *we*, and the *three* (or more). Differentiating and balancing these needs is essential for sustaining a strong emotional and sexual connection throughout each stage of parenthood.

While these themes might feel repetitive, the reminders are necessary. It's simple to say these things but incredibly hard to do them, especially when messy feelings take over and the relentless demands of schedules, children, and life seem specifically designed to pull your attention away from each other.

This balance isn't a one-time achievement; it's an ongoing practice. It's about continually returning to the lessons of support, connection, and maintaining the individuality that keeps each partner both attractive to the other and grounded in their own erotic energy. While these suggestions might seem obvious, they aren't "set it and forget it" solutions. Every stage of parenting offers a new opportunity to practice these skills, and depending on how disconnected you feel or how escalated your negative cycle has become, some seasons will inevitably feel more challenging than others.

In this section, I've highlighted common challenges based on the age of your children. The goal is to normalize the struggles that arise at each stage while also encouraging you to see these moments as opportunities—opportunities to refocus on each other, strengthen your connection, and navigate challenges in ways that ultimately bring you closer together. ♥

Chapter 10

The Early Years

When a couple starts planning for a baby, they're not only imagining cute onesies and Pinterest-worthy nursery decor. Beneath the surface, they're beginning to navigate weightier conversations about finances, work-life balance, shared parenting philosophies, and how they'll handle the inevitable exhaustion and overwhelm. At their core, these discussions boil down to the ultimate question: How do we become good parents while holding on to "we" and still making space for "me"?

The considerations that go into this question aren't just logistic; they're also deeply emotional. They reflect a shared fear of losing the intimacy, playfulness, and connection that brought you together in the first place. While becoming parents is a profound and meaningful experience, it's also one of the most intense transitions a relationship can face.

Even before pregnancy becomes a reality, these conversations set the stage for a significant lifestyle shift.

It's common during this period for couples to vow, "The baby won't change us! They'll fit into our life, not the other way around!" It sounds reasonable—certainly, it looks possible in books and on Instagram. And for some couples, maybe it is. But more often, this mindset serves as a convenient denial, a way to soothe fears and muster the courage to take the plunge into parenthood.

For many new families, the changes start well before the baby arrives. The decision to start trying can shift the dynamic almost immediately. Spontaneous sex might take a back seat to ovulation tracking and the perfectly orchestrated meeting of egg and sperm, turning moments of connection into goal-oriented tasks.

During the journey from conception to pregnancy and into the newborn phase, the accompanying changes and heightened emotions can make it hard for either partner to consistently be at their best. The emotional highs and lows are intense—while you may feel a deeper love and connection than ever before, miscommunications and existing cracks in the relationship can become more noticeable and troubling.

It raises important questions: Why aren't we advocating more for open discussions about these challenges? Why aren't couples encouraged to seek counseling or attend parenting classes before the baby arrives? During this pivotal period, much of the focus is misplaced. We often obsess about achieving the perfect pregnancy or childbirth experience—factors largely beyond our control. What we can control, however, is how we prepare for the transition into parenthood together as partners.

You can start by engaging in meaningful conversations with each other about your expectations for parenting, discussing potential changes to your relationship dynamic, and addressing fears or concerns. Seeking out counseling or relationship workshops specifically designed for new parents can help you build communication skills, learn conflict resolution strategies, and create a shared vision for parenting. Parenting classes can also offer practical tools for caregiving and managing the inevitable stress of raising a newborn.

This proactive approach is effective because it strengthens the foundation of the relationship before the baby arrives, equipping you to handle challenges as a team rather than in opposition. It fosters a sense of partnership and reduces the likelihood of unresolved conflicts turning into long-term resentment. By investing in your relationship even before the baby arrives, you set yourselves up not just to survive the early parenting years but to thrive as you grow into your new roles together.

Exercise: A Parenting Vision Map

This activity will help you align your values, expectations, and goals for parenthood.

Step 1: Reflect Separately

First, each partner should take 10 to 15 minutes to journal their responses to the following prompts. Writing things down helps bring clarity and allows space to process your thoughts individually. Write about:

- Three qualities you want to bring to parenting (for example, patience, playfulness, structure).
- One challenge you think you'll face and how your partner can help you through it.
- Something from your own childhood you'd like to replicate, and something you'd like to do differently.

Step 2: Share and Discuss

Come together and talk through your answers. Take turns listening without judgment and ask clarifying questions to deepen your understanding of each other's perspectives. These conversations can reveal important insights. If any parts feel particularly sensitive or bring up strong emotions, it may be helpful to revisit them with a therapist or another trusted third party.

Some key themes and follow-up questions to explore with each other include:

Parenting Roles

- How do you see our roles as parents?
- Are there specific tasks or responsibilities you'd like to take on or share?

Fears and Hopes

- What excites you most about becoming a parent?
- What scares you the most?

Support and Connection

- When things get stressful, what's the best way I can support you?
- Tell me about one time you felt really supported in the past—what was it that worked for you?

Boundaries with Others

- What boundaries do you want to set with friends and family after the baby is born?
- What outside help do we want to ask for?

Maintaining Our Relationship

- What do you think we can do to keep our connection strong while adapting to life as parents?
- What makes you feel most connected?

Step 3: Create Your Vision

Using a piece of paper or whiteboard, map out your shared values and goals for parenting. Start by identifying which values you both feel strongly about prioritizing, and then explore ideas for how, specifically, you can work together to uphold those values. For example:

- **Shared Values:** Love, consistency, communication
- **Practical Goals:** Divide responsibilities, set weekly check-ins, prioritize one-on-one time

Step 4: Action Plan

Identify one small step you can take together this week to work toward your vision, such as reading a parenting book, scheduling a date night, or practicing a new communication skill.

From Pleasurable to Purposeful

When sex shifts from being about pleasure and connection to just making a baby, it can take the magic out of the experience. Tracking ovulation and timing intercourse can turn sex into a clinical process, stripping away the spontaneity and fun that once defined it. It can start to feel like a chore rather than an act of love, leading to stress, frustration, and a sense of loss for both partners. It's crucial to recognize when sex becomes more about conception and less about connecting with your partner. While recognition won't necessarily change it back—for most couples, it is just a fact of this phase of their parenting journey—naming it together can be the linchpin that helps partners stay connected.

One helpful strategy when trying to conceive is to separate reproductive sex from pleasure sex. While the physical actions might look the same, the emotional and mental experiences are often worlds apart. In fact, many couples find it helpful to give them entirely different names to emphasize their distinct purposes. These differences tend to become more pronounced the longer conception takes. For some couples, the process can eventually culminate in a purely clinical experience—one that involves no physical intimacy at all and is often far from pleasurable, sometimes even painful.

To counter this, it can help to intentionally nurture pleasure-based intimacy. During nonfertile weeks, focus on sexual activities purely for enjoyment, like oral sex, mutual masturbation, sensual massages, cuddling, or even just making out without an agenda. Many couples I've worked with decide to reserve the expectation of intercourse specifically for ovulation week. This approach builds anticipation, keeps intercourse tied to the shared goal of starting a family, and reduces the sense of obligation around sex for the rest of the month. At the same time, prioritizing connection and pleasure throughout the rest of the month helps maintain the erotic charge and emotional intimacy that can so easily get lost in the stress and pressure of trying to conceive.

Communication is critical here. Often, one of the most stressful parts of trying to conceive is the perception that one partner wants it more than the other (Carver & Peterson, 2022). This can lead to disconnection, resentment, and feelings of loneliness. Share frustrations and fears about the conception process as well as its impact on your sexual connection. Talk about your needs and desires with your partner and be honest about what feels good and what doesn't. This kind of transparency helps both partners understand each other's experiences and find ways to provide support.

If a couple is experiencing significant fertility challenges, the stress it places on their sex life can be overwhelming. A therapist, especially one specializing in couples or sex therapy, can provide strategies to navigate this period without losing sight of your relationship's emotional and physical intimacy. They can offer techniques to manage stress and keep the connection strong, ensuring your relationship remains healthy and supportive.

The Pregnancy Roller-Coaster

When that positive pregnancy test finally comes, it's like everything shifts into hyperdrive. There's this mix of excitement, nerves, and "Oh my gosh, what do we do now?" Suddenly, the focus shifts to preparing for the baby—baby showers, nursery prep, birthing classes, you name it. Amid all the chaos, it's easy for the relationship to get lost in the shuffle.

Within the first few weeks of pregnancy, hormones kick into overdrive. If you're the birthing partner, your emotions start to zigzag like a pinball machine, you suddenly need to pee every 10 minutes, you find yourself in a constant state of ravenous hunger or, conversely, sickened by even the thought of food. Another area significantly affected by pregnancy hormonal changes is the sex drive. It's common for many women to experience a lower or even nonexistent sex drive during the first trimester. Often, this dip in libido recovers during the second trimester, only to decrease again in the third trimester. Understanding these hormonal fluctuations can help expectant mothers and their partners navigate changes in sexual desire throughout the pregnancy.

While it's common for pregnancy to bring shifts in sexual desire, not every expecting couple experiences a dip. Some individuals find their sex drive remains steady or increases during pregnancy, often due to hormonal changes and increased blood flow to the pelvic region. For those with heightened desire, this can be a surprising and even empowering experience, as their body feels more sensitive and attuned to pleasure.

Low- or No-Sex Pregnancy

Hormonal factors aren't the only things that can throw a wrench into an expecting couple's sex life. Concerns about the baby's health during penetrative sex are also common, with many worrying that intercourse might harm the baby, even though it is generally safe up until the water breaks. These fears, combined with the physical and emotional changes of pregnancy, can create significant mental barriers to maintaining a healthy sex life. For some couples, the idea of a baby "in the room" can make sex feel less appealing, as nonbirthing partners may feel an intense sense of protectiveness rather than sexual desire. Others may struggle with stress or anxiety about impending parenthood, which can lower sexual satisfaction for both partners (Zhao et al., 2022). It's also common for pregnant individuals to feel desexualized or self-conscious due to body changes such as weight gain, leading to insecurities that can affect intimacy. Without open communication, these shifts can result in misunderstandings or feelings of rejection for either partner.

In some cases, abstaining from sex during pregnancy is medically necessary. Conditions like placenta previa, a shortened cervix, or a history of preterm labor may require couples to avoid intercourse to reduce the risk of complications. However, it's important to distinguish between sex and being sexual. When couples hear "no sex," they often assume this means avoiding all forms of intimacy, but in most cases, pelvic rest or medical restrictions don't mean all physical connection needs to stop. Being sexual can include a wide range of activities, such as kissing, cuddling, sensual massage, and other nonpenetrative touch, which can help maintain closeness without compromising safety. Exploring these alternatives can help couples stay connected while navigating medical limitations or personal preferences.

Every pregnancy is unique, so couples should always seek guidance from a health care provider to understand what is and isn't recommended during pelvic rest. This clarity allows them to confidently find ways to maintain intimacy without fear of doing harm. Shifting focus from intercourse to creative, intentional acts of connection can keep the emotional and physical bonds strong, ensuring that both partners feel loved, valued, and supported.

Supporting Postpartum Partners: Moving Beyond "What Do You Need?"

Babies don't need much: a way to feed them (a breast or a bottle), a way to change them (a pack of diapers), and a few outfits. It's the parents' needs that skyrocket during the first several months of postpartum life. The sleep deprivation, the nerve-jangling effect of a newborn's intermittent crying, and the bewilderment of trying to interpret those cries (Is baby hungry? Gassy? Overtired? Not tired enough?) deepen both partners' longing for the comfort of each other's arms and attention. Maybe it shouldn't be a surprise that by the time baby

Hormonal Changes During Pregnancy

Estrogen and Progesterone

- Levels of estrogen and progesterone increase dramatically during pregnancy.
- These hormones can enhance blood flow to the pelvic area, potentially increasing sexual desire and sensitivity for some women.
- However, they can also cause mood swings, fatigue, and nausea, which might reduce sexual interest.

Oxytocin

- Levels of oxytocin—known as the love hormone—rise during pregnancy and childbirth.
- It plays a crucial role in bonding and can increase feelings of affection and closeness.
- Oxytocin also facilitates uterine contractions during labor and helps with milk ejection during breastfeeding.

Prolactin

- This hormone increases significantly, especially in the late stages of pregnancy and postpartum, to prepare for breastfeeding.
- High prolactin levels can suppress ovulation and reduce sexual desire.

is asleep for the night (or at least for a few hours), neither partner has anything left to give. But that rarely makes it any less of a letdown.

The postpartum phase is one of the most intensely demanding periods in a couple's life, often leaving both partners feeling overwhelmed and unsure how to best support each other. New parents, especially mothers, are often so stretched thin that identifying what they need most can feel impossible. Even when they do pinpoint something, there may be barriers to truly feeling supported, such as standards they have a hard time letting go of or needs that can't easily be met. As a result, even well-intended questions like "What do you need?" or "What can I do to help?" aren't always as helpful as they sound.

Instead of relying on open-ended questions, here are some specific ways partners can step up for each other:

- **Offer Concrete Options:** Rather than asking "What do you need?," try offering choices: "Would you rather I take the baby for an hour so you can rest, or would it help if I folded the laundry while you nurse?" This narrows the field and makes it easier for a sleep-deprived parent to say yes to something that feels doable.
- **Anticipate Needs by Observing:** Instead of waiting to be told, take initiative by paying attention to daily rhythms. Notice when the house feels cluttered, the diaper pail is full, or meals are getting skipped. Doing things like vacuuming, meal prepping, or stocking up on snacks for late-night nursing sessions without being asked can make a huge difference.
- **Normalize Emotional Check-Ins:** Partners can create space for postpartum feelings by asking thoughtful questions: "How are you feeling today?" or "What's been the hardest part of today for you?" These are less about problem-solving and more about listening and validating. A mother who feels heard is more likely to feel supported overall.
- **Offer Nonjudgmental Help:** Sometimes the most supportive thing a partner can do is lower their own expectations and meet their partner where they are. Maybe having the laundry folded perfectly isn't what's needed; maybe just getting it clean and put away is enough. Releasing the need for things to be done "the right way" can alleviate tension.
- **Be Proactive with Self-Care Time:** Often, postpartum parents won't ask for a break even if they desperately need one. Say

something like "I've got the baby—why don't you take a nap, go for a walk, or take a long shower?" Offering a specific activity and reassurance that things are covered can make it easier for them to step away.

- **Get Educated About Postpartum Needs:** Learn about the physical and emotional changes that happen during this phase, including such common challenges as breastfeeding, healing from birth, and postpartum mood disorders. The more informed a partner is, the less likely they are to ask for guidance during moments when a new mom might already feel tapped out.

Ultimately, postpartum support isn't about getting it perfect. It's about showing up, trying, and adjusting as you learn. When communication feels strained, naming it together can help: "I know you're carrying so much, and I want to support you. Can we figure out a way that feels easier for both of us?" This acknowledgment not only builds teamwork but also keeps the connection strong during a phase that often feels anything but.

What Your Doctor Doesn't Tell You About Having Sex Again

"Congratulations on reaching the six-week mark!"

This is health care code for "medically cleared for intercourse." For many new parents, these words can evoke complicated emotions: excitement, anticipation, anxiety, and perhaps even dread. As much as you may have looked forward to this day, the reality may feel far from appealing. After giving birth, hormonal shifts persist and can have significant effects on libido and sexual desire. Many women continue to experience discomfort or pain long after this time frame, while others may find certain erogenous zones particularly sensitive or unresponsive to touch. In short, even beyond the somewhat arbitrary milestone of six weeks, the journey to reclaiming one's sexuality after childbirth is often far from straightforward.

While most women resume sexual activity between six weeks and one year postpartum, it often takes 6 to 12 months to feel more in sync with prepregnancy sexual patterns and desire levels (Delgado-Pérez et al., 2022). Physical healing—such as recovery from tears or scarring—hormonal changes, and pain during sex can make postpartum intimacy challenging. Emotional factors, including postpartum depression, adjusting to new roles, body image concerns, and the mental load of motherhood, also play a significant role in how women feel about post-childbirth sex.

On top of this, exhaustion, limited personal time, and less opportunity for connection with a partner can add further strain. These factors often contribute to lower sexual desire, vaginal dryness, and reduced sensitivity, making pleasure or orgasm more difficult to achieve. As a result, both individual satisfaction and mutual enjoyment as a couple can be affected.

While all of this can feel frustrating in the moment, it's important to remember that it's perfectly normal—and, for most couples, temporary! You've just had a baby together, and the pressure to bounce back is an unfair expectation that sets women up to feel like they're doing it wrong. But you aren't. There's no one-size-fits-all approach to navigating sexuality after childbirth, and there's certainly no right or wrong way to feel about it.

Changes Postpartum

Hormones

Estrogen and Progesterone

- After childbirth, levels of estrogen and progesterone drop sharply.
- This sudden decrease can lead to vaginal dryness, making intercourse uncomfortable and reducing sexual desire.

Oxytocin

- Oxytocin remains high, especially during breastfeeding, promoting bonding between mother and baby.
- This hormone can also enhance emotional connections with a partner, but the physical exhaustion of caring for a newborn might offset its effects.

Prolactin

- Continued high levels of prolactin during breastfeeding can suppress ovulation, leading to low estrogen levels.
- This suppression can result in reduced libido and vaginal dryness.

Physical and Emotional Factors

Physical Recovery

- The body needs time to heal after childbirth, especially after a vaginal delivery or C-section.
- Birth trauma is very common (especially for first-time moms) and can impact both physical and psychological healing. Working with a pelvic floor physical therapist, psychotherapist, or support group can really help.
- Pain, fatigue, and changes in body image can impact sexual desire and comfort.

Sleep Deprivation

- The demands of a newborn often lead to significant sleep disruption.
- Lack of sleep can decrease energy levels and reduce interest in sex.

Emotional and Psychological Factors

- The emotional adjustment to parenthood, including stress, anxiety, and changes in identity, can influence sexual desire.
- Some women experience postpartum depression, which can significantly affect libido and sexual satisfaction.

Physical Preparation

Many women feel emotionally and mentally ready to rekindle their sexual spark before they feel ready for penetrative sex. If this is where you find yourself, exploring solo sex can be a gentle way to reconnect with your body and identify newfound sensitivities (both pleasurable and not) that result from the significant body changes of pregnancy, childbirth, breastfeeding, and postpartum recovery. Women who take this time for individual pleasure commonly describe feeling relieved that they are still able to orgasm or that everything still "works."

Even when your doctor clears you, it's entirely normal to feel apprehensive about resuming penetrative sex after childbirth. Concerns often range from worries about their partner's enjoyment to fears of experiencing pain or discomfort. A common concern is that vaginal childbirth may leave the vagina stretched out and potentially reduce pleasure during penetrative sex. While every woman's experience is unique, it's actually not uncommon for the vagina to feel tighter after childbirth rather than stretched out. Some women even liken the sensation to losing their virginity again.

Guided Masturbation Practice

A guided masturbation practice for rediscovering sexuality after childbirth can be a gentle and empowering way to reconnect with your body and explore your sexual desires at your own pace. Here's a suggested step-by-step approach:

1. **Set the Mood:** Create a comfortable and relaxing environment in your chosen space. The most challenging part of the exercise is choosing a moment when you are not disturbed!
2. **Mindful Breathing:** Begin with a few deep breaths to center yourself and bring awareness to your body. Focus on each inhale and exhale, allowing tension or stress to melt away.
3. **Self-Exploration:** Start by gently touching and exploring your body, paying attention to sensations and areas of pleasure. Use different strokes, pressures, and techniques to discover what feels good.
4. **Focus on Sensations:** As you continue to touch yourself, focus on the physical sensations you're experiencing. Notice any areas of tension, pleasure, or discomfort, and adjust your touch accordingly.
5. **Incorporate Fantasy:** Allow your mind to wander and explore erotic thoughts or fantasies that arouse you. Visualize scenarios or experiences that excite you, and let your imagination guide your arousal.
6. **Utilize Toys:** If you feel comfortable, add a vibrator or other toy into your practice to enhance stimulation and pleasure.
7. **Practice Self-Compassion:** Be kind and compassionate toward yourself and your body throughout your practice. Let go of any expectations or judgments and embrace whatever feelings or experiences arise without self-criticism.
8. **Communication with Partner:** If you feel comfortable, consider sharing your experiences and desires with your partner. Open and honest communication can strengthen your connection and intimacy as you navigate this journey together.

The "Husband Stitch"

A troubling historical practice known as the husband stitch underscores how societal expectations about women's bodies have sometimes influenced medical practices. This procedure involved the physician adding an extra stitch to a perineal repair after childbirth to make the vagina tighter for the husband's sexual pleasure. While now considered unethical and harmful, it is a painful reminder of the ways women's autonomy over their bodies has been compromised. Fortunately, awareness and advocacy around consent and evidence-based care have led to broader discussions and challenges to such practices.

For this and other reasons, it's not unusual for sex to be uncomfortable the first few times after childbirth. (If it's painful rather than just uncomfortable, talk to your doctor.) Working with a pelvic floor physical therapist is often very beneficial. While the human body is designed to carry and birth babies, the process takes a toll. For pain with sex, pelvic floor PTs often use dilators or manual massage combined with breathing exercises to gradually stretch the vaginal opening to alleviate pain during intercourse.

It's important to remember that once a health care provider has given the green light, the risk of severe injury or lasting damage during intercourse is low. However, persistent pain should never be ignored and should prompt a discussion with a health care provider. Remember, there's no right or wrong way to explore your sexuality after childbirth, as long as it is pleasurable. Trust yourself, listen to your body, and honor your needs and desires as you embark on this journey of rediscovery.

Emotional Preparation

The six-week milestone refers solely to physical recovery, such as healing birth injuries or giving scar tissue time to heal. It doesn't necessarily mean you're emotionally ready for sex. Amid the whirlwind of parenthood at this early stage—sleepless nights, around-the-clock feedings, and the overall adjustment to life with a newborn—sex may be the furthest thing from either partner's mind. That's perfectly normal. The energy and emotional reserves that used to go into maintaining a romantic connection are often expended in caring for children. Thanks to the ongoing drip of oxytocin, dopamine, and other bonding hormones, new parents can easily find themselves simultaneously drained and fulfilled by the time baby is asleep. This can inadvertently lead to a reduced desire for intimacy with their partner.

Eventually, even the rosiest postpartum glow transitions into a demanding and somewhat monotonous cycle of physical and emotional labor. A baby's constant demand for attention, affection, and care can leave the primary caregiver, usually the mother, feeling both deeply fulfilled and profoundly depleted. Nursing, snuggling, and gazing into her baby's eyes often already meets her emotional needs for connection, leaving her longing not for more closeness, but for solitude or nurturing.

Even as she craves personal space—to exercise, take a shower, or (gasp) simply enjoy a quiet moment alone—she may also feel guilty for prioritizing these needs. In many cases, her need for caregiving or solitude to recharge naturally takes precedence over her desire for sexual intimacy with her partner.

This makes sense, but it can still leave the other partner feeling neglected, frustrated, and even resentful. After all, they've been working hard during this phase as well. They understandably miss the intimacy and affection that used to meet their needs, but they may feel like they have no right to ask for it or fear being rejected if they do.

When One Partner Isn't Ready for Sex After Six Weeks

While the six-week postpartum mark is often seen as a safe time to resume sexual activity, readiness doesn't always align with the timeline for either partner. Unsurprisingly, research shows that parental stress has a greater impact on mothers' sexual satisfaction than on fathers'. Higher levels of parenting stress in mothers are strongly linked to lower sexual satisfaction, both individually and within the couple dynamic (Leavitt et al., 2017).

Cultural narratives further complicate this dynamic, often idealizing the "selfless mother" who prioritizes her children's needs above all else. This framing can push sexual satisfaction—a fundamentally self-focused drive—to the bottom of the priority list. Additionally, societal messaging frequently portrays motherhood and sexual identity as incompatible, suggesting that a "good mother" cannot simultaneously embrace her sexuality. Research indicates that these negative cultural perceptions, such as judgments about mothers being "too sexual" or assumptions that prioritize nurturing over sensuality, are linked to poorer sexual functioning (Sims & Meana, 2010).

It's worth noting that while fathers' parenting stress doesn't seem to have the same predictive effect on sexual satisfaction, it's not unusual for the nonbirthing partner to feel hesitant about sex for a variety of reasons. Physical exhaustion, the weight of added responsibilities, and a general feeling of uselessness or being unwanted can take a toll on desire.

Finally, some couples, whether due to medical reasons, personal preference, or comfort, may have avoided sexual activity for much of the pregnancy. After such a pause, it's natural for feelings of awkwardness or trepidation to arise when trying to rekindle that connection. For some, feelings of emotional distance or fear of causing pain during intimacy can add to the reluctance.

These feelings are normal, temporary, and not a reflection of their love for or attraction to each other. Desire often rebuilds with time and through nurturing the connection in other ways. This starts with showing patience and understanding for each other and practicing open dialogue: "I'm feeling nervous about reconnecting sexually" or "I know you're going through so much, emotionally and physically, but I really miss feeling your touch." Sharing fears, worries, or hesitations can help prevent either partner from feeling rejected or alone.

Redefining sexual connection to include smaller, pressure-free forms of touch also helps intimacy to reemerge naturally. It's essential to recognize that sexual intimacy encompasses a broad spectrum of activities, and prioritizing pleasure and comfort for both partners is paramount. Expanding the scope of sexual activity beyond penetrative intercourse can be immensely beneficial, particularly during the postpartum period. Physical closeness through cuddling, massages, or simply holding hands can maintain a sense of connection while readiness develops. In fact, research shows that affectionate touch fosters love, acceptance, and body confidence, enhancing both relationship and sexual satisfaction (Campbell et al., 2024).

By shifting the focus away from intercourse as the main event, couples can alleviate pressure and discomfort, especially if there's pain or nervousness surrounding penetrative sex after childbirth. (In cases where the gap feels challenging, seeking support from a couples or sex therapist can provide tools to navigate this transitional period.) Ultimately, the postpartum phase is an opportunity for couples to build deeper emotional and physical intimacy by prioritizing communication, compassion, and flexibility.

The Payoff: Sexual Afterglow

It is crucial for couples to recognize that their feelings of exhaustion, disconnection, and mismatched desires are a normal part of new parenthood. Understanding this as a temporary reality can help reduce guilt, shame, and concern about the health of the relationship, all of which are powerful blockers of connection. Couples who can normalize this disruption in their romantic partnership are already taking an important step toward reigniting it. Even if the desire for sex isn't present, engaging in other forms of physical intimacy can help maintain the connection between you and your partner.

While there are many nonphysical ways to foster intimacy, the physical connection is essential to maintain, even when it feels challenging. Physical touch, after all, is a shortcut to our bonding hormones. Often, even if parents aren't initially enthusiastic about a sexual encounter, they describe feeling lighter, more connected, and happier afterward if they can approach it with willingness.

There is a good reason for this. Research tells us that sex helps strengthen bonds between partners, even between sexual encounters! It's called *sexual afterglow*. It's that lingering sense of satisfaction and connection that you feel after a satisfying sexual encounter, and it turns out, it doesn't fade immediately. Researchers have found that the effects of sexual afterglow lasted about 48 hours, keeping partners feeling more connected and satisfied during that time. Perhaps unsurprisingly, it's also been shown that couples who reported a stronger sexual afterglow also reported higher overall relationship satisfaction, both in the short term and several months later (Meltzer et al., 2017).

The sexual afterglow acts like a bridge, keeping partners bonded and emotionally close in the time between sexual encounters. It's not just about the act itself—it's about how it lingers and reinforces emotional intimacy long after the moment has passed. During the strain of the early years, these moments are invaluable.

Finding Your Way Back Together with Notice, Own, Connect

Falling in love with a new baby both strengthens and challenges even the strongest bonds. But the intensity of this phase can ultimately bring couples closer together, not just as parents but also as partners and lovers.

Given the intense emotions and significant life changes involved, couples must be patient with themselves and each other, and prioritize reconnection in whatever form it takes. Above all, partners must keep in mind that there is no "normal" standard for this time in a family's life. Expecting either partner to behave in a certain way or be ready for sex by a certain time is a setup for disappointment and disconnection. Instead, it's crucial to approach this period on a case-by-case basis, recognizing that every individual's readiness for sexual activity varies.

NOTICE

The first step in navigating the early years is to notice how your relationship is evolving. These shifts likely come with both positive and negative aspects—like a deeper sense of partnership and shared purpose alongside less time for spontaneity or increased tension around parenting and household tasks. Paying attention to these changes helps you celebrate the strengths you're building together while also identifying areas that need care before they escalate into larger issues.

Questions to ask yourself:

- Are there patterns of disconnection or tension that feel new or more frequent?
- How do I want my partner show up for me during this time, and what makes me feel most supported?
- How have my feelings about myself as a sexual being changed since the baby arrived?

OWN

Owning your feelings and role in the relationship means taking responsibility for how you show up and expressing your needs with honesty. It's about recognizing what's within your control and being intentional about addressing it. This might mean sharing fears about parenthood, acknowledging changes in your sex life, or actively working to prioritize your relationship.

Questions to ask yourself:

- Are there unspoken expectations or assumptions I'm holding that might be creating tension?
- How am I contributing to cycles of disconnection in our relationship?
- Am I able to connect with my sexual self? What gets in my way?

CONNECT

Connection is the glue that holds relationships together during times of stress and transition. It doesn't always require grand gestures—often, it's the small, consistent acts of care and kindness that matter most. A lingering hug, a thoughtful text, or a few uninterrupted minutes can go a long way. Prioritizing time for each other, both individually and as a couple, even amid sleepless nights and chaotic schedules, helps nurture intimacy and keeps the bond strong.

Questions to ask yourself:

- What are small ways we can carve out time to reconnect, even during busy days?
- How can I show my partner appreciation for their role in this new chapter?
- Are there ways we can carve out time to prioritize being sexual?

The early years of parenthood can feel overwhelming, but they also present an opportunity to grow closer as a couple. By noticing the changes in your relationship, owning your emotions and actions, and intentionally nurturing your connection, you can transform this period into a time of profound growth and bonding.

Every couple's journey is unique, and there's no one-size-fits-all solution. The key is to approach this time with patience, empathy, and a commitment to supporting each other and your relationship. By doing so, you're not just surviving early parenthood—you're laying the foundation for a partnership that thrives through every stage of life. ♥

Chapter 11

Preschool to Preteen Years

From the sleepless fog of the postpartum period to the cute yet hair-tearing toddler years, many parents fantasize about reaching the next level: the time when their child is potty-trained, sleeping through the night, and can entertain themselves for longer periods. It's true that this stage of development can give parents some much-needed breathing room. And if you ask parents on either side of this stage—those still awash in diapers and bottles and those dealing with the heightened intensity and conflict of the teen years—they'll likely tell you to enjoy this period of calm.

Of course, for the parents actually in this phase, it might not feel quite as calm as they expected. While you're spending less time cleaning spit-up off your clothes and playing endless games of peekaboo, your schedule quickly fills up with school obligations, extracurricular activities, sports practices, and playdates. Nevertheless, the replacement of early childhood chaos with a sense of order and structure usually means parents have more available energy than they did for the previous five years. This extra energy often gets channeled into work or personal interests, leading to neglect of the relationship. Many couples may have gotten out of the habit of paying attention to or caring for their relationship by this time. It's easy to do! In the full-contact-parenting stage of the early years, we get used to putting the relationship aside and asking it to wait.

If dating means treating a relationship like a delicate orchid, being a parent can train us to treat it like a cactus, assuming that it can survive on little time, energy, or water. Couples often get so used to channeling their resources—time, energy, and money—into the needs of their children and family that they don't stop to ask themselves, *What would it be like to make the relationship a priority again?*

♥

Back in chapter 1, we met Avery and Sam, a lesbian couple in their mid-30s who came to see me due to increased conflict, lack of connection, and a desire difference. They have been married for eight years and have two children, aged three and five.

Avery says softly, "I love our kids so much, but I gotta admit, things between us have changed since we became parents."

Sam nods, leaning back on the couch. "Yeah, I feel that too. I mean, we're always in parent mode now. Sometimes, there's just no room left for *us*."

Avery runs a hand through her hair, her voice tinged with frustration. "I think that's been the hardest part for me. I still have this need for intimacy, but it's like we're never in sync anymore. I get that you're exhausted after a long day, but sometimes I miss the physical connection we used to have."

Sam shifts, looking down for a moment before meeting Avery's eyes. "It's not that I don't want you, but I'm just wiped out when the kids are finally asleep and the day is over. My mind goes straight to wanting to sleep rather than anything else."

Maybe *Calm* Isn't the Right Word?

During this stage of parenting, the focus moves from primary caregiving to supporting children's growing independence and ensuring they have opportunities for social and academic development. Culturally, there's a strong push and expectation to prioritize our children's needs and activities above almost everything except work. It's easy to fill up this time with gymnastics and soccer, music lessons and math tutoring, weekend playdates and the endless parade of classmate birthday parties. For parents, this often means juggling a multitude of responsibilities. Coordinating schedules, managing homework, attending school events, and shuttling children to various activities create a whirlwind of daily demands. Despite the kids being more independent than they were during the toddler years, the complexity and volume of their activities lead to a different kind of hectic pace.

This continuous demand for parents' time and energy can lead to conflict over seemingly routine issues, like whose turn it is to pack lunches, coordinate soccer practice, or manage homework battles. These everyday disagreements often go beyond the task itself, surfacing deeper frustrations about the division of labor and feelings of inequity. If couples haven't established a system that feels balanced and sustainable for both partners, these conflicts can build over time, creating resentment and pulling them further apart. Left unresolved, these seemingly small disputes can erode connection and make it harder to approach each other with patience and care.

In addition, many families consider adding a second or third child during this time, meaning parents might find themselves in more than one parenting stage simultaneously. For instance, they may be handling the challenges of toddlerhood while also navigating the sleep-deprived fog of the postpartum period. Juggling these different stages requires immense patience, resilience, and a robust support system, all of which may feel like they are in short supply at times!

As a result of these factors, you might be reading this and wondering, *Where's the calm in this calm phase?* Both of you are working just as hard as before to support the family's growing number of commitments, only now it's without the help of parental leave. In the whirlwind of family life, finding time to reconnect emotionally and sexually as parents can feel like an impossible task. Many parents say, "We just don't have the time."

They probably aren't wrong. Studies have found that modern working mothers spend as much time with their children as stay-at-home mothers did in the 1960s and 1970s (Bianchi et al., 2006). I don't know about you, but I find this shocking, especially since most parents I know carry immense guilt about not spending enough time with their kids!

The researchers found that mothers achieve this by—no surprise—sacrificing sleep, personal time, housework, and time with their spouses (Bianchi et al., 2006). They also found that fathers have significantly increased their involvement in childcare and household responsibilities compared to previous generations. This shift reflects a move toward more shared parenting, with fathers actively participating in tasks traditionally seen as maternal roles. However, both mothers and fathers often face intense pressure from work and societal expectations, leaving them juggling their time and energy in ways that can strain their relationship and personal well-being (Bianchi et al., 2006). As a result, this phase can feel almost indistinguishable from the postpartum phase, with both partners kicking the well-being can down the road ("Maybe once they're in high school, we'll have time for ___ again") and sustaining their connection with the sexual and relational habits they established during babyhood. That is, until one of them starts making time for themselves again.

Self-Care Is Relationship Care

Typically, one parent catches on more quickly than the other to the pockets of free time that show up during this phase of parenting. Whether it's taking advantage of weekend mornings while the kids are watching cartoons or realizing that bedtime now only requires one parent instead of both, the prospect of a few hours to do something—*anything they want*—by themselves is irresistible. After spending the last few years effectively fused with this new little person, it feels amazing to reconnect with your individual identity by reengaging with the hobbies you used to enjoy, resuming the personal habits that used to fuel you, or just having time to be with your own thoughts.

Of course, for the parent who hasn't caught on, hearing their partner announce, "I'm heading out for a nature walk!" or learning that their time running errands included a stop at the sports bar to catch the end of a game can feel like a slap in the face. *When did we agree that we got to start taking personal time? And when do I get mine?*

Self-care is often framed as an individual pursuit—something we do alone to recharge, reset, or nurture our well-being. But the truth is that self-care is also relationship care. When you prioritize your own mental, emotional, and physical health, you bring a more present, grounded, and resilient version of yourself into your partnership. You're better equipped to listen, communicate, and show up with empathy and patience.

Some parents will read this paragraph and think, *Yes! Permission to take time for myself!* Others will read it and think, *That sounds great—but what about all the stuff I'd be neglecting?* After all, spending an hour or two on yourself means an hour or two of grocery shopping, housecleaning, or homework helping that will be left undone. And what about quality time with kids? What will they feel, knowing that their parent neglected them in favor of spending time alone?

If you're the second kind of parent, you deserve to be acknowledged. Your willingness to sacrifice your own preferences and needs to care for your family shows how much you love them. That said, I have a blunt truth for you: It's not working. Parenting naturally requires self-sacrifice from time to time, but as a lifestyle, it's a breeding ground for resentment and frustration. These two feelings effectively cancel out any love or care that your sacrifice might convey. Your kids won't feel the love you put into making them a healthy dinner if you're seething with repressed rage about the book club you're missing out on. And I probably don't need to tell you that self-sacrifice is not high on the list of qualities that partners find sexy. (Try whispering "I skipped yoga to scrub the bathroom floor" in your partner's ear and see how hot it makes them.)

Think of self-care as tending to the roots of a tree. While the leaves and branches represent your partnership and family, the roots—your individual well-being—must be nourished to keep everything else thriving. When both partners invest in their own self-care, they create a ripple effect that strengthens the whole family. This might look like carving out time for exercise, rest, pursuing personal passions, or seeking support through therapy or meaningful friendships. Admittedly, these pursuits often look different from how you used to practice them. For instance, my husband and I alternate getting up at 5:00 a.m. to sneak in daily workouts. Before having kids, neither of us would have chosen to work out that early, but between all our obligations, it's what works best for us. It's not ideal, but it's better than not doing it.

Ultimately, self-care and relationship care aren't separate—they're deeply intertwined. Taking care of yourself isn't selfish. It's an essential act of love and respect for both yourself and your relationships. By showing up for yourself, you're better able to show up for each other, creating a dynamic where you can each bring more of your best self to the family.

What Are You Saying Yes To?

Parenthood is a juggling act, no doubt, but sometimes the way we fill our schedules reflects not just our kids' needs but also societal pressures that push us toward high-intensity parenting. It's that constant drive to do *more*—more activities, more enrichment, more opportunities—that can leave little room for anything else, including our relationships.

Ask yourself: *Do my kids really need to participate in three different extracurricular activities at once, or could they thrive just as well with one? Am I overcommitting to things like volunteering, playdates, or work obligations, when loosening the reins a bit might actually benefit everyone?* Cutting back on the relentless schedule doesn't mean you're failing as a parent. In fact, it can mean the opposite—it shows your kids that balance is important and that it's okay to prioritize what truly matters, including your partnership.

What many parents don't realize is how much their relationship sets the tone for the entire household. When you feel connected as partners, it creates a sense of security and warmth that positively impacts your children. By scaling back the endless busyness, you create space—not just to be less stressed, but also to nurture the relationship that serves as the foundation of your family. This doesn't have to mean elaborate date nights or hours of alone time. It could look like taking a walk together while the kids are at soccer practice or having an uninterrupted conversation after bedtime. Small moments can be deeply impactful when they're *intentional.*

Reconnecting sexually can feel like an even bigger challenge, especially when exhaustion and resentment from the daily grind have piled up. But the payoff isn't just about sex—it's about carving out time to remind each other that you're not just co-parents, but partners, friends, and lovers as well. By letting go of the pressure to do it all as parents, you may find the energy and space to lean into these moments of connection, both emotional and physical. And while it might feel indulgent or even selfish, it's important to remember that prioritizing your relationship is one of the greatest gifts you can give your children.

Parenting doesn't come with a perfect formula, and the pressure to give your kids everything can feel overwhelming. But sometimes, scaling back can be the most loving thing you can do—for them, for yourself, and for your partnership.

When Parenting Styles Clash

As behavior manifests more prominently during toddler years and beyond, differences in parenting styles can become a significant source of tension. While the newborn phase often centers around basic caregiving tasks, the toddler years introduce more complex challenges related to discipline, boundaries, and developmental milestones. These emerging differences in parenting approaches can lead to significant disagreements on managing behavior, which in turn may cause emotional distance and distress in a couple's relationship.

During the newborn phase, parents might not have had the opportunity or need to explore their parenting philosophies. However, as toddlers assert their independence, test limits, and develop their personalities, parents often face situations that require thoughtful responses on the fly—a tall order even when you aren't trying to co-parent with someone who may have a different approach. One parent might prefer a more lenient and nurturing approach, while the other might advocate for stricter rules and consequences. These differences can lead to arguments and a sense of being undermined or unsupported.

Significant disagreements on parenting can erode the emotional connection between partners. When one parent feels that their approach is constantly being challenged or dismissed, it can lead to frustration, resentment, and isolation. The stress of these disagreements can create emotional distance, making it difficult for couples to maintain a united front and a supportive partnership, let alone a satisfying sex life.

Parenting can become especially challenging when one partner's parenting style mirrors the painful experiences the other partner remembers from their own childhood. In his Relational Parenting course, Terry Real (n.d.) refers to this dynamic as "parenting hell." In these moments, unresolved hurts can surface, making parental conflict feel disproportionately intense. You'll know you're in parenting hell when you see your partner interacting with your child in a way that echoes the very thing that caused you distress as a child.

To be clear, we're not talking about abusive behavior here. Every parent carries childhood wounds, no matter how loving or well-intentioned their caregivers were. For example, if you grew up with a parent who yelled when angry, and you found it terrifying, chaotic, or unnecessary, you might have promised yourself, "When I grow up, I won't yell at my kids." Now imagine you've partnered with someone who yells when they're frustrated. They might not see it as a problem—they might even say, "I always repair afterward, and I think it gets the message across." But for you, it feels like watching history repeat itself, and it stirs up deep emotional distress, which often comes out as conflict in the relationship.

This dynamic helps explain why parenting differences can trigger seemingly disproportionate reactions in both partners. The pain of unresolved childhood wounds, combined with the high stakes of raising children, can amplify even minor disagreements.

Parenting is a deeply emotional task that brings out both our best and our worst. While we may like to think of our parenting decisions as purely rational, they are often shaped by our beliefs and emotions, our hopes, our fears, and our deep desire to help our children turn out *okay*. Each parent carries their own emotional blueprint, shaped by their family of origin and their unique experiences of being parented. These emotional undercurrents influence not only how we parent, but also how we react to our partner's parenting choices.

In a parenting partnership, both individuals are often guided—and sometimes burdened—by different emotional considerations and fears. These dynamics can lead to misunderstandings, tension, and conflict, even when both partners have the same ultimate goal: raising happy, healthy children. Recognizing and naming these emotional drivers is a crucial first step. Developing realistic expectations for co-parenting and understanding how your upbringing influences your parenting style allows couples to approach differences with more compassion and clarity. From there, partners can begin to build new strategies for managing their children's behavior and, perhaps more importantly, communicating effectively about parenting disagreements without falling into cycles of blame or defensiveness.

Reinvesting in the Relationship: A Gift for the Whole Family

As children gain independence, it's natural to reinvest newfound time into ourselves, our work, or personal pursuits. This reinvestment in self is often necessary before we feel ready to focus on the relationship—a process that can be difficult for a partner to understand. But what if, alongside these personal efforts, we also chose to reinvest in our relationship? This relatively calm period offers a unique opportunity to address any challenges in communication or feelings of disconnection. What might it look like to intentionally refocus on your partnership?

Prioritizing your relationship doesn't have to mean grand gestures or elaborate plans—it's about *small things, often*. This concept, highlighted by relationship experts Dr. John Gottman and Dr. Julie Gottman (2015), emphasizes that consistent, intentional acts of care and attention are what truly sustain emotional connection over time.

Think of it like dating your spouse again: approaching them with curiosity, paying attention to the little things, and intentionally seeking moments to connect. Parenting changes us, often in profound ways, and it's easy to assume we already know everything about our partner. But what if you approached them with fresh curiosity? What if you asked about their dreams, their fears, or what's bringing them joy *right now*?

These small, intentional moments—a genuine compliment, an affectionate touch, or an uninterrupted conversation—can rebuild emotional intimacy and remind you both of the bond that existed before parenting took center stage. Small things, done often, are powerful building blocks for lasting connection.

And of course, there's therapy.

Readers might take this with a grain of salt considering the source—a therapist—but I firmly believe, based on my years of experience, that couples seek therapy way too late. A recent study showed that couples are, on average, unhappy for two and a half years before seeking professional help (Doherty et al., 2021). This is an improvement from a previous study that cited six years, but still, it's way too long (Gottman, 1994)! When couples come to see me, they are often in great distress, looking for an emergency relationship fix. This is like starting to watch your diet and exercise after a heart attack rather than making healthy lifestyle choices as a preventive measure before a health crisis hits.

It's natural to have periods of disconnection, misunderstandings, and resentments that lead to hurt and anger. Two humans sharing a life will never be free of conflict. The longer couples wait, the more they have to wade through to reconnect. However, many people believe that couples therapy is a precursor to separation or divorce. This belief prevents couples from seeking support to improve their relationship, not just to repair it when it's broken.

This parenting period is a great time to seek professional help to improve communication and better understand each other.

Strengthening your relationship now can prevent more significant issues and help you navigate the inevitable ups and downs with greater resilience. Investing time and effort into your relationship during these calmer years benefits you and your partner. Not only does it create a healthy and loving environment for your children to thrive in, it also sets a positive example for your children about love and connection.

Scheduling Is Sexy

Scheduling sex as busy parents might feel unromantic at first, but let's be honest—so are guilt, shame, conflict, and the sting of repeated rejection! Making time for sex sends a clear message: Your relationship matters, even in the chaos of parenting. Whether it's penciled into the calendar or decided with a playful text earlier in the day, planning builds anticipation, gives you something to look forward to, and creates space to emotionally reconnect or flirt, so connecting sexually feels intentional rather than like just another task.

Planning also takes the pressure off finding "the perfect moment" and keeps sexuality from getting lost in the shuffle of busy schedules or sheer exhaustion. Over time, this habit can grow into a meaningful ritual: a consistent way to check in and nurture both physical and emotional connection. It's not about rigid scheduling. Sometimes it's as simple as saying, "Let's make tonight about us." Knowing that being sexual—whatever that looks like for you both on any given day—is on the menu can give both partners, especially the lower-desire partner, the space to mentally and emotionally prepare. This preparation makes it easier to transition into a headspace where connection feels natural, enjoyable, and aligned with what works for both of you.

Ultimately, this small, intentional effort helps sex feel prioritized, sustainable, and even exciting, even in life's busiest seasons. It's a healthy, loving, and dare I say, grown-up way to realistically approach being both lovers and parents. Sexual desire doesn't always show up on demand, and that's okay. Giving yourselves the time, space, and compassion to lean into learning how it *does* show up can lead to a deeper emotional and physical connection that works for both of you.

Prioritizing Intimacy with Notice, Own, Connect

Parenting often feels like an endless marathon, with every moment consumed by schedules, responsibilities, and emotional demands. Intimacy—both emotional and physical—can easily fall to the bottom of the priority list. But if connection, especially sexual connection, feels important to you and your partner, it's worth making space for it.

The so-called calm years of parenting often feel anything but calm. Endless to-do lists, packed schedules, and the pressure to excel at high-intensity parenting can leave little room for quality time—with yourself or your partner. But what if this stage could be more than a juggling act? What if it's an opportunity to pause, reassess, and refocus on what truly matters: fostering a meaningful, balanced partnership where both of you feel seen, valued, and cared for?

Using Notice, Own, Connect, you can take steps to redefine these years, prioritizing connection and balance over perfection and pressure.

NOTICE

Start by noticing the pressures and beliefs shaping how you spend your time and energy, not just in your daily life, but also in your emotional and physical connection with your partner. Are you saying yes to every extracurricular activity, work commitment, or social event out of fear of falling behind or feeling not good enough as a parent? Notice how these choices impact not just your time, but also your well-being, your emotional availability, and your desire for intimacy. Are stress, exhaustion, or resentment getting in the way of closeness with your partner? Pay attention to how these pressures influence your ability to show up in your relationship with presence and openness.

Questions to ask yourself:

- How does my current pace of life impact my ability to connect with my partner?
- When do I feel most open to sexual connection, and when do I feel most closed off?
- What beliefs or values might be holding me back from prioritizing myself and my relationship over the kids at times?

OWN

Owning your role means taking an honest look at how your actions, habits, and mindset contribute to cycles of disconnection. Have you unintentionally deprioritized your relationship in favor of caregiving or productivity? Are there unspoken expectations or unaddressed resentments creating distance?

The truth is, if you're being honest, the answer to these questions will almost certainly be yes. How could it not be? Owning isn't about blame—it's about recognizing where you have agency to make meaningful changes, even if they're small ones.

Questions to ask yourself:

- Have I prioritized my children's activities and needs at the expense of myself or my partnership?
- How big a role does my stress play in the challenges we face as a couple?
- What small, meaningful changes could I take ownership of today to create more balance?

CONNECT

Connection is about aligning your actions with what matters most: your partner, your family, and your values. This might mean scaling back on commitments, redefining "good enough" parenting, and prioritizing small, meaningful moments of connection over endless busyness. Letting go of the race to meet every societal expectation can free you to nurture a rich and fulfilling relationship—not just with your partner but with yourself and your kids, too.

Questions to ask yourself:

- What small moments of connection—sexual or nonsexual—make me feel closest to my partner?
- What small changes can I make to prioritize connection over busyness?
- How can I create space where sexuality feels like an opportunity rather than an obligation?

By intentionally stepping away from the hamster wheel of high-intensity parenting, you model balance and care for your children. They'll learn that relationships require attention, time, and effort—and that loving your partner and yourself is just as important as loving them.

Remember, intimacy isn't just about sex; it's about feeling seen, valued, and desired by your partner both in and out of the bedroom. The goal isn't to recreate your relationship as it was before parenting, but rather to build something new, something that aligns with the reality of your current life while still honoring the closeness you both crave.

The so-called calm years may never feel entirely serene, but they can be a season of recalibration. By noticing what isn't working, owning your role in the dynamic, and intentionally choosing to reconnect, you create a foundation where your relationship doesn't just survive the demands of parenting—it thrives because of the care you've invested in it. ♥

Chapter 12

Teen Years to Empty Nest

The teen years can be an exhilarating yet challenging time for parents. As kids grow more independent and navigate their transitions into adulthood, parents often experience a mix of pride, nostalgia, worry, and stress. While teenagers face the roller-coaster of puberty, parents are frequently juggling the demands of raising teens alongside their own life changes.

Teenagers are not the only ones weathering the storm of biological changes. For many women, perimenopause begins around this time, bringing hormonal fluctuations, fatigue, changes in libido, and mood swings. Men may face their own midlife challenges, including less predictable erections, shifts in energy levels, and existential questions about a life half spent. The familiar tropes of this life phase—the balding man in a red sports car or the aging woman melting down during a hot flash—make for relatable memes, but the reality often feels far less amusing for couples living through it.

These biological shifts impact more than just physical health. They also influence emotional well-being and mental clarity. Sleep disruptions, mood swings, and feelings of overwhelm can make it harder for parents to stay connected and present with each other. When combined with the emotional turbulence of raising teens, these changes can create a perfect storm.

♥

Remember Grace and Matthew? Both in their early 50s, they have been together for 20 years and haven't had sex in three years. While they both want to be sexual, they both struggle to initiate for different reasons. Grace is in perimenopause and struggles with unpredictable libido and vaginal dryness, and Matthew's erections have become unreliable. They also have conflicts regarding their three teenage daughters. Grace feels unsupported in setting limits, while Matthew feels he has no say in parenting decisions.

"I don't want to be in a sexless marriage—that thought is horrible," Grace says. "But I don't feel emotionally connected or supported by him, so even though I want to be sexual, it's hard to think about it."

Matthew looks down, his voice filled with uncertainty. "I don't even know how to talk about it. How can I ask her to have sex if I don't know if I can . . . perform?"

Grace sighs. "We need to find a way to reconnect emotionally before we can even think about sex again. It's not just about the physical aspect. I need to feel close to you in other ways as well."

Matthew and Grace have a pursue/withdraw dynamic outside the bedroom, with Grace pursuing and Matthew withdrawing. While historically they have had a crossover-cycle dynamic where Matthew was the sexual pursuer, his loss of confidence in his ability to perform sexually has led to a withdrawal-withdrawal sexual cycle. This change in relationship dynamics has proved difficult to adapt to for both.

Aging Bodies and the Impact of Erectile Dysfunction

Erectile dysfunction (ED) is a common issue for men, growing more common as they age, often arising from a complex combination of physical and psychological factors. Medical conditions such as heart disease, diabetes, and obesity can impair blood flow to the penis, making it challenging to achieve or maintain an erection. Additionally, treatments for prostate cancer—such as surgery, radiation, or hormone therapy—are a well-known cause of ED, as they can damage nerves, blood vessels, or hormonal balance. Testosterone levels, which naturally decline with age, may further complicate the issue by reducing sexual desire. Medications prescribed for managing chronic conditions can also contribute to ED by interfering with vascular or hormonal processes. Lifestyle factors including smoking, excessive alcohol consumption, and a lack of exercise often exacerbate these physical challenges, creating further barriers to a satisfying sex life.

The emotional toll of ED can be equally impactful, often amplifying its physical causes. Stress, anxiety, and depression frequently contribute to performance difficulties, trapping men in a frustrating cycle: Worry about sexual performance increases the likelihood of issues, which in turn deepens anxiety. For men like Matthew, who faces ED related to both health conditions and medication side effects, this cycle can feel insurmountable. His self-esteem has taken a hit, and the fear of failure has made him hesitant to initiate sexual activity. This reluctance creates emotional distance, leaving both partners feeling undesirable and disconnected.

Holistic Approaches to Addressing ED

While ED is a challenging issue, it's important to recognize that effective treatments are available. Medical interventions, such as prescription medications like Viagra, Cialis, and Levitra, can improve blood flow to the penis, offering a good solution for many men. Lifestyle changes, such as weight loss, regular exercise, stopping smoking, and moderation of alcohol intake, can also significantly enhance erectile function, improving overall health in the process. If medication and lifestyle changes do not work, penis pumps, injections, and implants are all options to discuss with a doctor.

For those with low testosterone, hormone therapy may help restore libido, which can have an impact on sexual functioning. However, because ED often results from a combination of physical and psychological factors, a multifaceted approach is typically the most effective.

Addressing the psychological components of ED is essential, as they often fuel a cycle of shame and anxiety that worsens performance issues and creates distress for both partners. Therapy offers tools to reduce shame, improve communication, and ease the pressure to perform, helping couples create a more relaxed and supportive dynamic. It also fosters understanding and connection, ensuring both partners feel valued and united in addressing the issue.

Therapy can further help couples redefine intimacy by exploring ways to be sexual even when erections are unpredictable. It opens the door to discovering that pleasure and even orgasm are possible without an erection. By addressing shame and redefining expectations, couples can embrace creative, fulfilling expressions of sexuality that strengthen their bond and reduce performance-related anxiety.

Beyond medical and lifestyle interventions, reframing sex can be a powerful way for couples to navigate the challenges of ED. Intercourse doesn't always have to be the focal point of sexual connection. Exploring other forms of intimacy—such as sensual touch, oral sex, incorporating sex toys, or simply enjoying skin-to-skin closeness—can reduce performance pressure and create space for connection and enjoyment. Ironically, for many men, shifting the focus away from achieving or maintaining an erection often eases anxiety, making successful intercourse more likely.

"The Change"

Perimenopause and menopause bring significant hormonal changes that can lead to various sexual issues for women. As estrogen levels decline, many women experience vaginal dryness and thinning of the vaginal walls, which can cause discomfort or pain during intercourse. This condition, known as *vaginal atrophy*, can make sexual activity less pleasurable and sometimes painful, leading to a decrease in sexual desire. Hormonal fluctuations can also contribute to reduced libido, making it challenging for women to feel sexually aroused. Additionally, the various symptoms of menopause, such as hot flashes, night sweats, and difficulty sleeping, can impact overall well-being and energy levels, further diminishing interest in sexual activity. Emotional factors, including mood swings, anxiety, and depression, often associated with hormonal changes, can also affect sexual desire and satisfaction. These combined physical and emotional changes can lead to a decreased frequency of sexual activity and challenges in maintaining sexual intimacy within relationships.

Before we start painting menopause as the end of your sexual life, let me reassure you that there are highly effective treatments available to manage symptoms. And, just as importantly, once symptoms are under control, it's common for women to experience a newfound sense of freedom in their sexuality during this time. With the worry of unwanted pregnancy off the table, many women find this phase to be liberating—a chance to embrace their desires without hesitation. For some, it feels like a sexual revolution, offering the opportunity to redefine intimacy and pleasure on their own terms.

Common (and Not-So-Common) Symptoms of Perimenopause

- Hot flashes
- Night sweats
- Vaginal dryness
- Thinning of vaginal walls (vaginal atrophy)
- Reduced libido
- Mood swings
- Anxiety and depression
- Difficulty sleeping
- Fatigue
- Weight changes
- Loss of muscle tone
- Cognitive changes (brain fog, memory lapses)
- Dizziness
- Joint pain or stiffness
- Heart palpitations
- Dry skin or thinning hair
- Changes in body odor
- Headaches or migraines
- Urinary incontinence or urgency
- Breast tenderness or changes
- Changes in menstrual patterns (before cessation)

Treatment Options

Treatment options for sexual issues caused by perimenopause and menopause are widely available and highly effective, addressing both physical and emotional aspects to bring much-needed relief and renewed intimacy for many women.

For vaginal dryness and discomfort, local estrogen therapy—like creams, tablets, or vaginal rings—can work wonders by restoring moisture and elasticity to the vaginal tissues. Nonhormonal lubricants and moisturizers are also great options for easing discomfort during sex. Hormone replacement therapy (HRT), which suffered some bad press in the early 2000s, is now widely regarded as safe and effective for most women, especially when started near the onset of perimenopause. HRT can alleviate symptoms including hot flashes, night sweats, and mood swings while supporting sexual function and overall well-being. If you've been hesitant about HRT due to concerns about health risks, it's worth consulting a health care provider who's well-versed in the current formulations and guidelines to see if it could be a good option for you.

Low-dose SSRIs (selective serotonin reuptake inhibitors) are another option that can alleviate mood swings, irritability, or anxiety related to menopause. These treatments, while traditionally used for depression, are now recognized as valuable tools for addressing hormonal and emotional shifts.

Lifestyle changes can also be transformative, particularly in combination with other treatments. Regular exercise, a balanced diet, and good sleep hygiene are the foundation of better sexual health and overall well-being. Stress-reduction techniques, mindfulness practices, and relaxation exercises, such as yoga or meditation, can further enhance arousal and satisfaction by reducing stress and fostering a stronger mind-body connection.

The key is finding a combination of treatments and practices tailored to your specific needs, whether physical, emotional, or sexual.

With the help of a trusted health care provider, it's possible to navigate these changes and reclaim a sense of vitality that aligns with your evolving self.

Correcting the Cultural Imbalance

In health care, there's an established understanding of the psychological and emotional ramifications of ED for men. This condition is widely recognized for its physical implications and how it impacts a man's self-esteem and overall psychological well-being. The medical community and society at large are generally empathetic and proactive about providing treatments, widely covered by insurance, which are prescribed not just for reproductive purposes but also for maintaining overall mental health, self-identity, and the quality of intimate relationships.

However, this level of awareness and response does not uniformly extend to women's health issues, especially those associated with menopause. Vaginal dryness, hormonal fluctuations, and other physiological changes during perimenopause and menopause can severely impact a woman's ability to engage in and enjoy sexual activity and affect her overall quality of life. These changes can be as debilitating as ED in terms of their impact on intimate relationships and personal identity. Yet, acknowledgment of and urgency in addressing these issues lag, lacking the same comprehensive support system readily available for men.

It's essential to recognize that menopause and its effects are not mere inconveniences but significant health concerns that warrant the same serious attention as any other condition affecting bodily autonomy and quality of life. The conversation about menopause needs to shift toward a more empathetic and medically thorough approach, mirroring the care provided for ED. This includes a broader societal recognition of the challenges women face during menopause and a more robust medical approach to managing these symptoms effectively.

The progress seen in the domain of birth control is a prime example of how women's health issues can be handled with sensitivity and respect. Women have access to various contraceptive methods, and discussions about these options are typically handled in a supportive, patient-centered manner. This kind of care demonstrates what is possible when health care providers focus on empowering patients with choices and information.

Expanding this model to include all aspects of women's health, particularly menopausal care, is essential. Equipping women with comprehensive information about hormonal therapies, alternative treatments, and supportive therapies can enable them to make informed decisions that align with their health needs and lifestyle preferences. By fostering a health care environment that is as responsive to the needs of women during menopause as it is to men with ED, we can achieve a more equitable and effective health care system.

Grace and Matthew's challenges extend beyond the physical and emotional changes that come with aging. Their differing approaches to discipline and boundary-setting have become a significant source of tension. When Matthew manages feelings of inadequacy by retreating, Grace feels the weight of managing day-to-day conflicts with their daughters. This dynamic has left Grace feeling unsupported and isolated, intensifying the disconnection between them.

Grace often feels like the disciplinarian who sets limits and enforces rules with their teenage daughters. "I'm always the bad guy," she says. "I set curfews, enforce homework time, and deal with the pushback. I feel like Matthew isn't backing me up, which makes me feel alone."

Matthew responds, "It's not that I don't care about discipline. I just think we have to pick our battles. Sometimes I feel like my opinion doesn't matter. It's like I'm stepping on your toes when I try to help."

Grace shakes her head. "I need us to present a united front. The girls need to see that we're in this together. When you undermine me, even unintentionally, it just adds to the stress I'm already feeling. It feels like such high stakes—I worry we're going to lose them if we don't get this just right."

Matthew nods. "I want to support you, but I also need to feel like we're a team again. It feels like I don't have a seat at the table. You tell me I'm not supporting you, but I don't feel supported either."

Parenting teens can be emotionally exhausting, not just because of their behavior but also due to the intense pressure parents often place on themselves. This stage brings heightened anxiety about preparing children for adulthood, with uncertainty fueling cycles of worry and overcompensation. Finding the right balance between freedom and limits can feel overwhelming, often leading parents to lean toward too-controlling or too-permissive tendencies as a way to manage their anxiety. While these approaches stem from the desire to set their child up for success, they can unintentionally create tension within the family and strain the relationship between partners.

For some parents, the anxiety focuses on specific concerns, such as substance use, declining academic performance, or eating disorders. Similarly, when teens deviate from family traditions or shared values—such as choosing not to attend religious services, exploring different lifestyles, or pushing back on long-held expectations—parental anxiety and family conflict can increase, especially if one partner sees the behavior as a phase to be weathered while the other views it as a problem to be fixed.

Parenting differences quickly create a rift between partners, especially when they disagree on how to approach discipline or foster independence. One parent might advocate for stricter rules to maintain control, while the other prefers a more lenient approach in an effort to preserve the relationship with the teen. These disagreements can leave both parents feeling unsupported and misunderstood, compounding the stress of managing their teen's unpredictability.

This dynamic can be challenging for both partners: One may feel excluded and unheard, while the other feels unsupported and alone. Adding to the complexity is the reality that teens often naturally connect more strongly with one parent than the other, sometimes creating a good cop/bad cop dynamic. This bond might form for practical reasons, such as one parent handling most of the daily routines or driving to activities, or for emotional reasons, like a teen feeling more comfortable confiding in one parent over the other. While this is normal teen behavior, it can still leave partners feeling hurt or misunderstood, especially if they interpret their child's preference as a lack of care.

The emotional challenges of parenting teens also intersect with parents' own mental health. Anxiety over the teen's future, combined with the stress of daily life and increased conflict at home, can leave parents feeling exhausted and overwhelmed. This can also bring underlying insecurities or unresolved personal issues to the surface, such as fears of being irrelevant as their children grow more independent or worries about their own worth and identity outside of parenting.

Midlife and Meaning

The teen years often coincide with a pivotal stage in parents' personal development as well. For many, midlife is a period of deep reflection and, at times, an existential crisis. With children becoming more independent, parents are confronted with questions about their own identity and purpose beyond raising kids. This transitional phase can bring a mix of emotions: relief at no longer being needed as intensely, sadness at the inevitability of children growing up, and even a sense of emptiness or confusion about what comes next.

For some, the realization that they are entering a new life stage can trigger behaviors commonly associated with a midlife crisis. These might include impulsive career changes, a desire to pursue long-neglected dreams, or even a yearning to relive youth through new hobbies, social circles, or lifestyle shifts. While these changes can be healthy and revitalizing, they can also create friction in a relationship if partners aren't on the same page. For instance, one partner may embrace a newfound sense of freedom, while the other feels left behind, stuck in the familiar routines of parenting and family life.

This period of self-reflection often brings up questions about the longevity and health of the relationship itself. Partners may begin to examine their roles within the marriage, their shared goals, and whether the relationship still fulfills their emotional and sexual needs. These questions aren't inherently negative—in fact, they can provide an opportunity for growth and deeper connection. However, when these feelings remain unspoken or unmet, they can create resentment, withdrawal, or conflict.

Parenting teens can amplify these midlife questions. As children test boundaries and assert their independence, parents may find themselves questioning their own parenting decisions or struggling with the shifting dynamics of the parent-child relationship. Watching teens grapple with their own identities can act as a mirror, forcing parents to confront unresolved feelings about their own adolescence or paths not taken in their adult lives. The combination of these internal struggles and external parenting pressures can feel overwhelming, especially if partners don't feel equipped to navigate them together.

To move through this phase constructively, couples can approach midlife as a shared journey rather than an individual crisis. Open conversations about each partner's fears, desires, and evolving goals can foster understanding and reduce the sense of isolation that often accompanies this stage. Finding ways to support each other's growth—whether through pursuing individual interests or rekindling shared dreams—can help couples redefine their relationship beyond the roles of parenthood and find meaning and revitalization in their shared life.

Tackling the Cycle of Disconnection

As I listened to Grace and Matthew, it was clear how intertwined their challenges had become. Their sexual struggles, emotional distance, and parenting conflicts were feeding into each other, creating a cycle of disconnection that felt overwhelming. But beneath the frustration and silence, I sensed a shared desire to find their way back to each other.

"Let's take a moment to look at where you both are right now and where you'd like to go," I say, my eyes meeting theirs. "You're feeling stuck, but I hear from both of you that you want things to get better. That's a hopeful starting point."

Grace nods, her tone softening. "Honestly, I don't care that much about Matthew's erectile issues. I just don't want him to feel bad or embarrassed. I hate seeing him pull away."

Matthew glances at her, his expression a mix of relief and sadness. "I don't initiate anymore because I don't want to face that failure. But I don't want to keep avoiding it either. I hate how distant we've become."

"You both really care for each other," I point out. "Even though things feel frustrating and difficult right now, that love is still there. That's a strong foundation to build on."

Grace offers a small smile. "I don't want to go the rest of my life without sex. I used to love having sex with Matthew—it was fun and amazing. But we didn't know what to do when it stopped being easy."

Matthew takes a deep breath. "We're stuck in this cycle. I feel useless because I can't perform, and Grace is dealing with pain and a lack of desire. It feels like every time we try, we just make it harder. But I don't want to give up. I want us to figure this out together."

"That willingness to work on this is huge," I reassure them. "You don't need to have all the answers right now."

Grace adds, "It's not just about sex. I want us to be a team again. I feel so alone when I'm the only one setting limits with the girls. They hate me, and I feel like Matthew doesn't have my back."

Matthew nods, his tone more determined. "You're right. I haven't been showing up the way I should, but I want to do better. We need to start talking about this stuff instead of avoiding it."

I smile. "Exactly. When you're willing to have these conversations and take even small steps toward connection, it's amazing how quickly things can shift. Rebuilding intimacy—emotionally, physically, and as parents—takes effort, but you're both already showing that you care enough to begin. That's a powerful place to start."

Grace and Matthew's story reflects how layered these challenges can be, but their willingness to engage with each other is the first step toward untangling the disconnection. The struggles they face encapsulate the complex challenges of this parenting phase, where personal, relational, and parenting difficulties intersect. Their avoidance of uncomfortable topics—whether it's Matthew's erectile issues, Grace's physical discomfort and waning desire, or their misaligned parenting approaches—has created a cycle of disconnection that affects every part of their lives. Each issue feeds into the next, deepening their frustration and making it harder to find common ground.

Their story highlights how personal challenges, from physical changes to emotional insecurities, can spill over into the relationship, creating barriers to intimacy. The pain and complexity of midlife physical changes have left Grace feeling unsexy and isolated, while Matthew's struggles with ED have led to feelings of failure and withdrawal. Both feel stuck in a loop of avoidance, reluctant to address these vulnerabilities head-on but yearning for the connection they once shared.

The impact extends beyond their relationship. Their disconnection as a couple has made it harder for them to present a united front as parents. Grace feels isolated as the disciplinarian, while Matthew feels disconnected from both his partner and his role in the family dynamic. Their teenage daughters sense this tension, interpreting it in ways that only escalate family conflict. This further underscores the importance of addressing their relationship issues—not just for their own well-being, but to create a stable and supportive environment for their children.

Grace and Matthew's realization that they're avoiding instead of tackling their issues marks an important turning point. While the challenges they face feel overwhelming, their willingness to acknowledge them is the first step toward change. By confronting these uncomfortable topics and working together, they can begin to rebuild trust, communication, and intimacy. This isn't just about fixing their sex life or parenting struggles; it's about reclaiming the partnership that forms the foundation of their family.

An Opportunity to Reconnect

While the teen years come with their fair share of challenges, they also offer unique and often overlooked opportunities for couples to strengthen their relationship. As teens require less hands-on parenting, many parents find themselves with more free time than they've had in years. This shift can feel disorienting at first, as the constant demands of earlier parenting stages fade, but it also opens the door for couples to rediscover each other outside of the roles of Mom and Dad. Instead of automatically filling this time with more work, individual hobbies, or endless commitments, couples can choose to intentionally turn toward each other, setting the stage for a deeper and more fulfilling partnership.

This period provides a chance to explore shared interests that may have been sidelined during the busier years of raising younger children. Whether it's reigniting a love for travel, taking up a hobby together, or simply planning regular date nights, couples can use this time to prioritize activities that foster closeness and joy. Even something as simple as enjoying a quiet evening at home or going for a walk together can help rebuild the closeness that often gets overshadowed by the demands of parenting. These moments don't have to be extravagant to be meaningful—they're about carving out space to reconnect and enjoy each other's company.

Beyond strengthening the relationship, this intentional reconnection also benefits the entire family. When teens see their parents prioritizing their partnership, it provides them with a model of healthy, loving relationship dynamics. Teens learn that even as life grows busy, it's important to make time for the people you care about most. This modeling can have a profound impact on how they approach their own future relationships, instilling values of respect, communication, and intentional connection.

"The Talk"

As kids navigate the physical, emotional, and social changes of puberty, parents often find themselves caught off guard by the intensity and complexity of these shifts. Adolescents may become moody, withdrawn, or rebellious, which can leave parents feeling unprepared, disconnected, or unsure of how to offer support. The mix of hormones, identity exploration, and social pressures creates a perfect storm of challenges and opportunities for meaningful conversations. One of the most important (and most avoided) topics during this time is sex and puberty. These conversations, while sometimes awkward, are essential in building trust, reducing shame, and helping teens develop a healthy relationship with their bodies and sexuality.

Talking to kids about sex and puberty isn't a one-time "big talk" but instead an ongoing conversation that evolves with your child. It's about creating a safe space where questions are welcomed, curiosity is met without judgment, and accurate information is provided. Parents often worry about saying the wrong thing or fear that discussing sex will encourage risky behavior. In reality, studies consistently show that open, honest conversations about sex and relationships lead to healthier choices, better boundaries, and more responsible behavior (Widman et al., 2015). Instead of approaching the topic with dread, think of these conversations as opportunities to share your values, offer guidance, and demonstrate that no question is off-limits.

It's also important to recognize that teens are getting information about sex and puberty from many sources—friends, social media, and the internet—and not all of it is accurate or appropriate. By being proactive in these discussions, parents can provide a reliable foundation of information and help teens critically evaluate what they see and hear elsewhere. Conversations about sex shouldn't be limited to the mechanics; they should also include topics like consent, respect, emotional readiness, and the importance of healthy communication in relationships. These discussions not only prevent risks but also equip teens with the confidence and knowledge they need to navigate relationships safely and meaningfully.

Last, don't underestimate the power of modeling openness and vulnerability. It's okay to acknowledge that these conversations might feel uncomfortable or that you don't have all the answers. What matters most is showing up, being available, and demonstrating that you are a safe and trusted resource. Puberty and sexuality are natural parts of life, and treating them as such reduces shame and stigma. In the end, even if your delivery isn't perfect, your willingness to engage in these conversations sends a powerful message: Your child's questions, feelings, and experiences are valid, and they can always turn to you for support and guidance.

Beyond the Outburst: Curiosity for Connection

When faced with a teenager's outburst, eye roll, or slammed door, it's easy for parents to focus solely on the behavior itself. After all, these moments can feel disrespectful, frustrating, or even hurtful. But beneath every behavior lies a feeling—a deeper emotion driving the reaction. Teens, like everyone else, act out when they feel something intensely, whether it's fear, embarrassment, sadness, or frustration. Instead of reacting immediately to the surface-level behavior, parents can pause and ask themselves, *What might my child be feeling right now?* This small mental shift creates space for curiosity instead of defensiveness and can lead to more meaningful interactions.

Approaching teen behavior with an eye toward the emotion underneath doesn't mean ignoring unacceptable actions or letting them off the hook. It means addressing the root cause rather than just the symptom. For example, a teen snapping at a parent when asked about homework might not be about defiance—it could stem from feeling overwhelmed, anxious about failure, or even embarrassed about not understanding the material. When parents focus on uncovering the underlying emotion and respond with empathy, teens are more likely to feel seen and heard, reducing the need for repeated outbursts.

This approach also models emotional intelligence and regulation. By naming and validating emotions ("It seems like you're really struggling right now—do you want to talk about it?"), parents show teens how to process their feelings in healthier ways. Over time, this builds trust and emotional safety, creating an environment where teens are more willing to share openly instead of lashing out. While it's not always easy to pause and look beneath the surface in the heat of the moment, doing so can shift patterns of conflict into opportunities for connection and understanding.

When Teens Go Quiet

Silent teens can be just as challenging for parents as loud, emotional teens. While silence might look like indifference, defiance, or avoidance, it often signals something deeper—fear of judgment, uncertainty about how to express emotions, or simply feeling overwhelmed. Teens may also withdraw because they believe their feelings won't be understood or because they're struggling to process something internally.

Instead of pushing for immediate conversation, parents can focus on creating a safe, low-pressure environment for connection. This might mean sitting together quietly, sharing an activity without an agenda, or offering gentle invitations to talk: "I'm here if you want to chat about anything." It's also helpful to notice when teens are more naturally open—maybe during a car ride, before bed, or while doing a shared task.

Sometimes, a teen's silence isn't about shutting parents out—it's about figuring things out on their own. Patience, consistency, and a calm presence can reassure kids that when they're ready to talk, their parents will be there, ready to listen without judgment.

Fostering Privacy (Not Secrecy)

The difference between privacy and secrecy lies in intent and impact. Privacy fosters trust and respect by maintaining healthy boundaries and allowing personal autonomy, while secrecy often involves withholding information in ways that can harm trust and relationships. While privacy protects individuality and promotes openness, secrecy tends to create isolation, mistrust, or potential harm.

Modeling privacy also means teaching children to respect their parents' boundaries by setting clear family expectations around respect. For example, establishing a household rule of knocking before entering a private space—like a bedroom or bathroom—sends a powerful message. When parents follow these rules themselves, they demonstrate that privacy and autonomy are mutual values. This not only models healthy boundary-setting but also sets the expectation that teens should respect their parents' boundaries in return.

Parents who set aside time to nurture their relationship—such as implementing a "no interruptions" policy during date nights or quiet evenings—show children that prioritizing connection as a couple is healthy and necessary. This teaches children that maintaining boundaries doesn't detract from family unity; instead, it fosters balance and well-being for everyone.

At the same time, parents can emphasize that privacy is not secrecy. Open conversations about when sharing is necessary, such as addressing safety concerns or emotional struggles, help kids understand the distinction. Framing these discussions around trust and mutual care reinforces that privacy is about respecting boundaries, while secrecy often leads to harm or disconnection.

Empty Nest: A Second Honeymoon

The empty nest is a unique milestone in the journey of parenthood, marked by endings and beginnings. It can feel both liberating and destabilizing. As children leave home to pursue their own lives, parents often find themselves at a crossroads, experiencing a mix of emotions that can feel as overwhelming as they are contradictory. Sadness may arise from the absence of day-to-day parenting responsibilities that once filled family life, while excitement brews at the thought of newfound freedom and the possibilities it brings. It's a bittersweet time, and both feelings are valid.

For many parents, this stage prompts reflection. The years spent raising children can feel like a blur of schedules, milestones, and countless sacrifices. Now, with fewer demands pulling your focus outward, you have the chance to turn your attention toward yourself, your partner, and the relationship that has often taken a back seat to the needs of the family. The empty nest may feel unfamiliar at first, but it's also an opportunity to rediscover who you are as individuals and as a couple.

This period also invites you to reimagine your partnership. After years of prioritizing parenting, it can feel both liberating and daunting to return to a relationship that isn't centered around co-parenting. The empty nest is more than a transition; it's an opportunity to rekindle the connection and joy that first brought you together. However, for couples who have been disconnected for a long time, it can be difficult to know where to begin. Feelings of hesitation, conflict, or awkwardness may arise, leading some to question their path forward now that the necessity of "doing it for the kids" is no longer front and center.

The empty nest is also a time when couples are at greatest risk of separation. Sometimes it's the right choice for individual happiness, but it doesn't have to be. With mutual intention and effort, this phase can become a time of rediscovery and renewal, allowing you to build a relationship that thrives beyond the shared role of parenting.

When the Nest Just Won't Empty

For many parents, the empty nest symbolizes a long-awaited chapter of freedom and reconnection. But what happens when the nest doesn't empty—when adult children remain at home well into their 20s or even 30s? Whether due to financial challenges, the rising cost of housing, job instability, or cultural norms, more young adults are living with their parents for longer. While this arrangement can offer practical benefits, it also brings unique emotional and relational challenges for couples.

One of the most common struggles is the blurred boundary between parenting and partnership. With an adult child still in the home, couples may find it difficult to fully shift out of the parenting mindset and reclaim space, both physical and emotional, for themselves. Conversations and decisions that should center on the couple's goals and desires often get sidetracked by the ongoing needs of their child. This dynamic can create feelings of resentment, frustration, or guilt, especially if one partner feels more burdened by the situation than the other.

Sexual connection can also suffer when adult children remain at home. Couples may feel a lack of privacy or self-conscious about expressing affection. Over time, this can lead to disconnection or even avoidance of being sexual altogether. Addressing these challenges requires clear boundaries, open communication, and shared expectations about how space, responsibilities, and independence will be managed.

It's also important for parents to ask themselves, *Is this for working for us?* If the answer is no, then it's helpful to reflect on their own roles in the arrangement. Are they unintentionally enabling their child to stay dependent, either financially or emotionally? Are they avoiding conversations about independence because they fear their child's failure or discomfort? While every family has different values, fostering independence can be a key part of supporting adult children. Encouraging them to take on responsibilities, contribute to household expenses, or set a timeline for moving out can help everyone feel more empowered.

Embracing the Transition

After years of structuring life around the needs of children, their absence creates a void that is both practical and emotional. For many parents, the departure of children from the home brings up unexpected feelings of grief. The daily routines—preparing meals, attending events, or simply sharing conversations—are no longer part of the rhythm of life, leaving parents to grapple with the loss of those moments. Alongside this grief often comes a sense of anxiety about identity: *Who am I now, beyond being a parent?*

The practical changes of the empty nest can be equally disorienting. Without the demands of managing children's schedules, parents suddenly find themselves with more unstructured time than they've had in decades. While this newfound freedom can be exciting, it can also feel unfamiliar and overwhelming. Long-held routines and habits centered around children must now be reimagined, which can leave couples wondering how to prioritize their time and energy. These shifts often highlight the need to create new structures that reflect the goals and desires of this stage of life.

For many couples, this transition exposes differences in how each partner approaches the empty nest. One partner may eagerly embrace retirement and the freedom to travel, explore hobbies, or focus on personal growth, while the other might feel more grounded in nostalgia or unsure of what's next. These differing responses are natural, but they can lead to tension. Giving each other space to process the transition in your own ways, while finding common ground for shared goals, is key to navigating this period as a team.

One of the simplest ways to reconnect is to revisit shared hobbies or discover new ones together. Think back to the activities you enjoyed as a couple before parenting took center stage. Did you love hiking, cooking, or dancing? Or is there something you've always wanted to try but never had the time for? Exploring these interests can bring a sense of playfulness and excitement back into your relationship. Shared activities create opportunities for teamwork, laughter, and conversation, strengthening the bond between you.

Reigniting your sexual connection can be another important aspect of rediscovery. Without the interruptions and stress that often accompany parenting, couples can create intentional moments of closeness. Depending on what your level of sexual activity is already, this doesn't have to mean rushing to rekindle a spark overnight. It's about small, meaningful gestures that rebuild connection. Working with a therapist on a sensate focus protocol or trying an app can be helpful for couples, especially those who may be in low- or no-sex partnerships. For most couples, conversations about how their needs and desires have evolved over time are a very helpful first step.

This stage also offers an opportunity to recenter the relationship. With the demands of parenting no longer front and center, couples have the chance to reconnect and rediscover each other as partners rather than just co-parents. The energy once spent managing children's needs can now be redirected toward shared hobbies, greater intimacy, and new adventures. This period can become a time to reflect on what brought you together, what you've built, and what you want to create in the years ahead.

The emotional complexity of the empty nest is entirely normal, and it's important for couples to give themselves grace during this adjustment. Grief, excitement, anxiety, and relief often coexist in this transition. By approaching this stage with openness and curiosity, couples can transform what might feel like an ending into a beginning—a time to honor the family they've nurtured while embracing the possibilities that lie ahead.

And, if all else fails, chances are you'll be able to count on the little birds returning to the nest periodically to recharge and regroup. The intensive parenting of earlier years may be over, but the job of providing a safe place to land never ends.

♥

When Matthew and Grace dropped their youngest child off at college, they stood in the dorm parking lot, looking at each other with a mix of pride and disbelief. After raising three children, their house was finally empty.

"What now?" Matthew asked, half joking but also a little uncertain.

Without missing a beat, Grace smiled and said, "Let's go to Ireland!"

They'd always dreamed of visiting Ireland, but life had a way of putting that dream on hold. First, it was diapers and daycare, then school events, and finally, college tuition. But now, with their nest empty and their schedules wide open, they decided it was time to make it happen. They booked their trip as a celebration of beginning a new chapter in their lives.

In Ireland, they rediscovered something they hadn't realized they'd been missing. With no soccer games to rush to or homework to supervise, they had time to simply *be* together. They wandered through cobblestone streets, drank pints of Guinness in cozy pubs, and hiked along the Cliffs of Moher, holding hands like newlyweds. Grace told me later, "It was like we were back to dating—getting to know each other all over again, but with all the history and love we've built over the years."

That trip didn't just reignite their sense of adventure. It also brought them closer in ways they hadn't anticipated. They talked about their dreams for the future: what they wanted for themselves and for their relationship. They laughed about parenting mishaps and shared quiet moments reflecting on the family they'd built. Most importantly, they celebrated *them*—not as co-parents or caretakers, but as partners.

Their story reminds us that the empty nest isn't an ending; it's a beginning. It's a chance to step back from the demands of parenting and rediscover the joy of being together. Whether it's a trip to Ireland or a simple date night at home, the important thing is to prioritize your connection and celebrate the life you've created as a couple.

The journey of parenting evolves, but the relationship you've nurtured remains the anchor. This is your moment to embrace a second honeymoon—an opportunity to write a new chapter in your love story, filled with curiosity, adventure, and a renewed sense of togetherness. Like Grace and Matthew, you might just find that the best part of your relationship is still ahead.

Embracing Good-Enough Sex in the Empty Nest Years

Barry McCarthy and Emily McCarthy's concept of "good enough sex" offers a refreshing perspective (Metz & McCarthy, 2011). This approach encourages couples to redefine their expectations for sex, shifting the focus from performance and perfection to connection and mutual satisfaction. For many couples, especially those facing the physical and emotional shifts of aging, this framework provides a practical and compassionate way to maintain sexual connection without pressure.

McCarthy and McCarthy emphasize that sexual encounters don't have to be spontaneous or mind-blowing every time. Instead, they celebrate sex that is intentional, emotionally connected, and fulfilling within the context of a couple's current reality. This approach acknowledges the challenges that often come with midlife—such as hormonal changes, health issues, and shifting energy levels—and encourages couples to adapt their expectations and activities rather than avoid being sexual altogether.

The framework also highlights the importance of communication in maintaining a healthy sexual relationship. Couples are encouraged to talk openly about their needs and desires, and any barriers they may be experiencing. This honesty can help demystify challenges such as decreased libido or physical discomfort, reducing the shame or frustration that can sometimes arise. By creating a space for vulnerability, partners can work together to foster intimacy that feels satisfying and meaningful for both.

In the context of the empty nest, good-enough sex offers couples the chance to view this phase as an opportunity to explore intimacy with renewed curiosity and care. It's a reminder that the goal isn't to recapture what intimacy looked like in the past, but rather to create a new, realistic vision for the future. By embracing this approach, couples can prioritize connection and find joy in closeness, no matter how it looks.

From Good Enough to Magnificent

Dr. Peggy Kleinplatz and Dr. A. Dana Ménard (2020), in their book *Magnificent Sex: Lessons from Extraordinary Lovers,* offer a refreshing and hopeful perspective on sexual fulfillment, particularly as people age. Their research identifies elements that make up truly extraordinary sexual experiences, including authenticity, vulnerability, engagement, communication, exploration, and connection—qualities that often flourish with age. Older adults, with their years of experience and deeper understanding of themselves and their partners, tend to prioritize emotional intimacy and meaningful connection over performance or physical perfection. This shift allows for a richer, more satisfying approach to sexuality—one grounded in pleasure, trust, comfort, and mutual understanding.

Kleinplatz and Ménard (2020) challenge the common belief that declining physical abilities inevitably lead to diminished sexual vitality. Instead, they emphasize that while physical changes may require adaptability, these shifts can inspire couples to explore new ways of connecting and experiencing pleasure. Far from being a limitation, aging becomes an opportunity to focus on emotional depth, shared joy, and the qualities that make intimacy truly meaningful. Their work reframes aging as a time for growth and enhanced sexual satisfaction, where connection takes precedence over mechanics.

This perspective is especially powerful for couples navigating the empty nest stage. With more time and fewer distractions, partners have the chance to rediscover each other and cultivate a deeper connection. Without the daily stresses of parenting, they can slow down and tune in. Magnificent sex, as Kleinplatz and Ménard describe, isn't about spontaneity or flawless technique—it's about creating an environment of trust, openness, and shared joy. By embracing these principles, couples can build deeply fulfilling intimate experiences that enrich their relationship.

The Legacy of Love

As couples move into the empty nest stage, it's easy to think that the impact of their relationship on their children diminishes. After all, the kids are grown, more independent, and living their own lives. However, the truth is that a strong, thriving partnership continues to play a vital role in shaping the emotional and relational health of adult children. The love and connection you cultivate as a couple creates a legacy that benefits not only your relationship but also the broader family dynamic.

When adult children see their parents prioritizing their relationship, it sets a powerful example of what healthy love and connection look like. Watching you navigate the empty nest years with intentionality teaches them that relationships require effort and care. This modeling gives them a blueprint for fostering their own healthy partnerships, showing that love isn't static but evolves and deepens with time and commitment.

A strong relationship between parents also provides a stable foundation that supports family bonds, even as dynamics shift. In the empty nest stage, the family unit undergoes a reconfiguration: Children establish their independence, and parents transition into a new phase of life. Amid these changes, a thriving partnership anchors the family, offering a sense of continuity and security. When children see their parents connected and content, it reassures them that their family remains a safe and supportive space, even as they grow into adulthood.

Investing in your partnership during this stage can also prevent your children from feeling burdened by concerns about your happiness. Adult children often carry a sense of responsibility for their parents' emotional well-being, especially if they sense disconnection or dissatisfaction in the relationship. A thriving partnership allows your children to focus on their own lives without the weight of worrying about your fulfillment. They can engage with you as adults and equals, rather than feeling the need to mediate or "fix" your relationship.

Ultimately, the love and effort you pour into your relationship creates a ripple effect that strengthens the entire family. By prioritizing your connection as a couple, you're not just building a fulfilling life for yourselves—you're also creating a legacy of love, stability, and resilience that will shape the emotional landscape of your family for generations to come. This is the gift of a thriving partnership: It nurtures not only the bond between partners but also the bonds that tie the family together, even as you all grow and change.

Navigating Change with Notice, Own, Connect

Parenting isn't just about raising children. It's also about navigating the changes that ripple through your relationship at every stage. Whether you're managing the emotional turbulence of raising teens or adjusting to the quiet of an empty nest, these transitions can disrupt sexual connection, emotional closeness, and the sense of partnership you once relied on. Hormonal changes, shifting identities, and evolving family dynamics create challenges that are both logistic and deeply emotional.

For many couples, these seasons highlight where patterns of disconnection have quietly taken hold—conversations that remain surface-level, intimacy that feels forced or absent, or unspoken resentments simmering just below the surface. It's easy to become reactive, responding to each stressor as it arises without taking time to notice the bigger patterns at play. But these transitions also offer something powerful: an opportunity to pause, reflect, and choose how you want to show up for your partner, your family, and yourself.

The Notice, Own, Connect framework isn't about fixing everything overnight. Instead, it's about shifting your focus back to what matters most. It's about recognizing the real emotional and physical barriers to intimacy, being honest about your role in those dynamics, and taking small but intentional steps to rebuild connection. Whether you're navigating the chaos of parenting teens or settling into a quieter home, this framework offers a practical guide to understanding yourself, your partner, and the relationship you share.

NOTICE

Start by noticing the emotional, physical, and relational changes happening within yourself, your partner, and your relationship. Parenting teens often brings heightened stress, fluctuating moods, and ongoing identity shifts for both parents and kids. Similarly, transitioning to an empty nest can stir grief, relief, or uncertainty as parents adjust to a new rhythm of life. Notice how these emotions—whether exhaustion, anxiety, excitement, or longing—show up in your interactions, your intimacy, and your willingness to connect.

Questions to ask yourself:

- How are my physical or emotional shifts affecting how I engage with my partner?
- What patterns of avoidance, disconnection, or resentment am I noticing in myself or our relationship?
- Have my wants and needs—both emotional and physical—shifted over time? If so, have I shared these changes with my partner?

OWN

Midlife and parenting teens—or adjusting to an empty nest—come with their own unique set of challenges. These stages often highlight patterns and habits that have quietly taken root in your relationship over the years. Maybe parenting responsibilities have made it easier to avoid difficult conversations about intimacy or emotional needs. Perhaps exhaustion, stress, or resentment have become unspoken barriers to closeness. Owning your role in these dynamics isn't about assigning blame; it's about recognizing how your actions, expectations, and emotional responses contribute to the current state of your relationship.

Questions to ask yourself:

- What are my unspoken expectations around sexuality, connection, or parenting roles?
- Am I holding on to old assumptions about what sex "should" look like?
- Have unspoken fears or insecurities prevented me from expressing my desires?

CONNECT

Connection is about aligning your actions with your values and what truly matters to you and your partner. Whether you're in the thick of parenting teens or adjusting to life without kids at home, intimacy—emotional and physical—requires intention. For some couples, connection might mean scaling back on external commitments or getting more involved in shared activities. For others, it's about redefining intimacy beyond intercourse and prioritizing touch, presence, and emotional openness.

Questions to ask yourself:

- What small, meaningful gestures can I make this week to connect with my partner?
- Are we having open conversations about how our emotional and sexual needs are evolving?
- How can we create space for both emotional closeness and physical connection in ways that feel sustainable?

These transitional periods, whether filled with the chaos of teenagers or the stillness of an empty nest, often bring unspoken fears to the surface. Will we still have anything in common once the kids are gone? Why do I feel more like a roommate than a romantic partner? Why does intimacy feel like one more chore on an endless to-do list? These questions are normal, and they're not a sign of failure—they're signposts pointing toward areas that need your attention.

Grace and Matthew, like many couples, found themselves caught in patterns of avoidance and resentment during midlife and parenting shifts. Instead of leaning into these questions, they turned away from each other, letting silence fill the gaps. But when they began to notice their patterns, own their roles in those dynamics, and make intentional efforts to reconnect, their relationship began to shift—slowly, imperfectly, but meaningfully.

These years don't have to be about simply surviving the chaos or enduring the quiet. They can be about curiosity—rediscovering who you are as individuals and as a couple. They can be about rebuilding—letting go of outdated expectations and creating intimacy that feels real and sustainable for the current season of the life you're building together. ♥

Conclusion

This book explores parents' challenges in maintaining a vibrant emotional and sexual connection while raising children. Parenting is a yearslong commitment that demands enormous financial and emotional energy. It's often a thankless job, filled with conflict, worry, and sleepless nights. However, it's also an enriching journey filled with love, joy, and moments of pure connection with your child. The challenge for many couples is maintaining a strong attachment to each other while navigating the intense focus required to raise children together.

Falling in love with your child can sometimes feel similar to the experience of falling in love outside of the relationship, like an affair. The bond with your child is deep, powerful, and all-consuming and can leave little room for your partner. To maintain a healthy relationship, it becomes crucial to reconnect intentionally and, sometimes, to repair the attachment with your partner. This requires effort, as the focus often shifts away from each other and toward the child, making it easy for couples to drift apart if they don't actively work to nurture their connection.

Understanding the attachment science behind bonding with a child and how that bond interacts with the one between partners can help identify areas where you might get stuck, both in and out of the bedroom. Sexual intimacy is often impacted as desire naturally fluctuates over time, especially during parenthood. The pressures, exhaustion, and emotional shifts that come with raising children can create negative sexual cycles fueled by differences in desire and all the feelings that go along with the mismatch. These fluctuations are not only expected but nearly inevitable. However, recognizing these patterns can help couples navigate these cycles without feeling disconnected or resentful.

Another crucial element in maintaining emotional and sexual connection is understanding how your nervous system responds to attachment disconnections. When partners are emotionally or sexually disconnected, it's typical for the nervous system to respond to this disconnect as it would to a physical threat, by activating in sympathetic fight, flight, or freeze mode, even if we're not consciously aware of it. In this state, it becomes more challenging to connect with a partner. Learning to befriend your nervous system—understanding its responses and what triggers them—can make you more receptive to connection and intimacy. By calming these responses, couples can create an environment that allows for both emotional closeness and sexual intimacy.

The challenges of maintaining a vibrant sexual relationship over the long term, especially when children are involved, are significant. Both as a therapist and as a human being, I don't know anyone who hasn't struggled with this at one time or another. Open communication and mutual understanding are crucial to navigating these challenges successfully. Throughout this book, we explored practical ways to maintain intimacy and connection despite and because of these challenges. It's in navigating these struggles together that relationships grow more robust.

My hope is that this book speaks to the experience of being parents in love. As both a practitioner and a consumer of therapy, I strongly encourage everyone to seek out a therapist they connect with—not because their relationship is on the verge of collapse, broken, or even in immediate need of repair, but because it is entirely natural for two people sharing their lives to experience conflict. Misunderstandings, communication issues, and disconnection are inevitable in any relationship. When these misattunements are left unaddressed, they can fester and have a lasting impact on the overall health and happiness of the relationship.

I've seen firsthand how therapy can create meaningful, positive change. It provides a space where partners can communicate more effectively, understand each other on a deeper level, and learn to navigate the inevitable challenges that arise. A fresh perspective and guidance can truly elevate the quality of your connection. Therapy isn't just about fixing problems—it's about strengthening the bond you already have and finding ways to grow together.

Investing in your relationship can help you to be proactive rather than reactive. Instead of waiting for conflicts to reach a breaking point, having regular check-ins, with or without a professional, can help keep your relationship thriving. It's not a sign that something is wrong; it's a commitment to making your relationship the best it can be. By doing so, you can avoid the pitfalls that come with neglecting issues and instead focus on enhancing the love and connection that brought you together in the first place.

Additionally, therapy can provide valuable tools that help couples communicate better and deepen their emotional and physical intimacy. It allows each partner to reflect on their own needs, learn to understand their partner's needs, and develop strategies for nurturing their relationship. This kind of attention can be significant during life transitions, such as becoming parents, when relationship dynamics often shift unexpectedly.

In the end, investing in your happiness and the health of your relationship is one of the most worthwhile commitments you can make. Taking the time to work on your connection, with the support of a therapist or coach, can lead to a more fulfilling, joyful partnership. Your relationship deserves that care, and so do you.

By reading this book, you've already taken an important first step toward deepening your emotional and physical intimacy with your partner. Maintaining this connection over the long term isn't something that you do just once. It's a dynamic process that requires ongoing rebalancing, reassessment, and recommitment.

They say once you learn to ride a bike, you never forget. That unforgettable factor is balance. As any bike rider can tell you, balance isn't a static thing; it's a constant state of adjusting, correcting, subtly shifting to find the equilibrium that keeps you upright and moving forward. Relationships work in much the same way. To think that you can achieve balance once and be done with it is a fallacy that leads to disappointment and hurt. Balancing on a bike is an ongoing process, and the same is true for maintaining a vibrant relationship.

When you ride a bike, there are times when balance is easy, like cruising along a smooth, flat road. You're still balancing, but it doesn't require much effort or attention. In a relationship, this can be likened to those periods when everything seems to flow effortlessly—communication is smooth, connection is strong, and life feels in sync. It's easy to forget that balance is still happening during these times. You may even take it for granted, not realizing that the ease of the moment results from the work you've done to attune your body to slight changes or small but sudden bumps in the road.

But then there are those moments when the road gets rocky, or you're climbing a steep hill. On a bike, this might mean navigating muddy terrain or a road seamed with cracks and potholes. In these stretches, balancing feels like hard work, and you're hyperaware of every shift and adjustment. In a relationship, these are the times when challenges arise—conflicts, miscommunications, or external stressors like parenting or career pressures. Maintaining balance requires effort and attention during these times, and it can feel like you're barely staying upright. Sometimes, you may even need to pause and walk the bike for a bit, allowing yourselves to regroup and reassess.

This analogy helps normalize the ups and downs of relationships. When you're on a smooth road, losing sight of the work that balance requires is easy. So, when you hit that rocky uphill, it can feel like something's wrong—like you're falling apart. However, this is a natural part of every relationship. Just as riding a bike takes constant, subtle adjustments, relationships also require continuous effort, especially during tough times.

Sometimes, those rocky moments leave you breathless, gasping for air, or wondering if you need to stop altogether. But just like riding a bike, it's all part of the process. It's not a failure—it's a natural, essential part of finding and maintaining balance over the long term. The key is to make those adjustments during the easy and hard times to continue moving forward together.

It's easy to get off track, to feel disconnected from or misattuned to each other, like two ships passing at night. This is normal in any long-term relationship, especially when parenting is involved. Being romantic and life partners comes with challenges that make it difficult to stay in sync.

The key to maintaining that connection is tolerating the inevitable periods of disconnection and initiating reconnection. It's about finding a rhythm where you accept that these ebbs and flows are part of a long-term relationship. Rather than seeing these moments of distance as signs of trouble, we can view them as opportunities to realign and grow together. This ongoing process of disconnection and reconnection is what sustains a relationship over the long haul. Knowing that you will have to adjust and recalibrate throughout the years can help normalize the bumps in the road and make the journey smoother.

By picking up this book, you've already demonstrated a desire to improve your relationship, and that's an essential element. Awareness and intention are powerful tools. The fact that you're seeking guidance, insight, or even just reassurance shows that you're invested in making your partnership the best it can be. Acknowledging the need for growth and connection is a huge step, and it sets the stage for meaningful change.

If you and your partner share this interest in improving your relationship—whether through emotional reconnection, revitalizing your sex life, or simply becoming more attuned to each other—you're already on a winning path. That shared desire to make things better is an enormous advantage. Relationships that last are not the ones without challenges but rather the ones where both partners are willing to try to reconnect when needed.

The journey toward a joyful, satisfying, and vibrant relationship doesn't require perfection, just intention and consistent effort. With that, you and your partner are already well on your way to creating a deeply fulfilling emotional and physical bond that can withstand the ups and downs of life together. ♥

References

Basson, R. (2000). The female sexual response: A different model. *Journal of Sex & Marital Therapy, 26*(1), 51–65. https://doi.org/10.1080/009262300278641

Baumeister, R. F., Catanese, K. R., & Vohs, K. D. (2001). Is there a gender difference in strength of sex drive? Theoretical views, conceptual distinctions, and a review of relevant evidence. *Personality and Social Psychology Review, 5*(3), 242–273. https://doi.org/10.1207/S15327957PSPR0503_5

Baumeister, R. F., Vohs, K. D., Aaker, J. L., & Garbinsky, E. N. (2013). Some key differences between a happy life and a meaningful life. *The Journal of Positive Psychology, 8*(6), 505–516. https://doi.org/10.1080/17439760.2013.830764

Beeney, J. E., Wright, A. G. C., Stepp, S. D., Hallquist, M. N., Lazarus, S. A., Beeney, J. R. S., Scott, L. N., & Pilkonis, P. A. (2017). Disorganized attachment and personality functioning in adults: A latent class analysis. *Personality Disorders: Theory, Research, and Treatment, 8*(3), 206–216. https://doi.org/10.1037/per0000184

Bianchi, S. M., Robinson, J. P., & Milkie, M. A. (2006). *Changing rhythms of American family life.* Russell Sage Foundation.

Bode, A. (2023). Romantic love evolved by co-opting mother-infant bonding. *Frontiers in Psychology, 14*(1176067). https://doi.org/10.3389/fpsyg.2023.1176067

Bode, A., & Kushnick, G. (2021). Proximate and ultimate perspectives on romantic love. *Frontiers in Psychology, 12*(573123). https://doi.org/10.3389/fpsyg.2021.573123

Campbell, J. T., Bennett-Brown, M., Kaufman, E. M., Gesselman, A. N., Frederick, D. A., Garcia, J. R., & Mark, K. P. (2024). Women who experience more affectionate touch report better body satisfaction and relationship outcomes. *The Journal of Sex Research.* https://doi.org/10.1080/00224499.2024.2310705

Carver, D. N., & Peterson, Z. D. (2022). Couples with infertility and the desire to conceive: Examining the association between discrepancies in the desire to conceive and relationship and sexual satisfaction. *Sexual and Relationship Therapy,* https://doi.org/10.1080/14681994.2022.2058481

Cervilla, O., Álvarez-Muelas, A., & Sierra, J. C. (2024). Relationship between solitary masturbation and sexual satisfaction: A systematic review. *Healthcare, 12*(2), Article 235. https://doi.org/10.3390/healthcare12020235

Chivers, M. L., Seto, M. C., Lalumière, M. L., Laan, E., & Grimbos, T. (2010). Agreement of self-reported and genital measures of sexual arousal in men and women: A meta-analysis. *Archives of Sexual Behavior, 39*(1), 5–56. https://doi.org/10.1007/s10508-009-9556-9

Cowan, P. A., & Cowan, C. P. (2000). *When partners become parents: The big life change for couples.* Lawrence Erlbaum Associates.

Dana, D. (2018). *The polyvagal theory in therapy: Engaging the rhythm of regulation.* W. W. Norton.

Dana, D. (2021). *Anchored: How to befriend your nervous system using polyvagal theory.* Sounds True.

de Oliveira, L., Štulhofer, A., Tafro, A., Carvalho, J., & Nobre, P. (2023). Sexual boredom and sexual desire in long-term relationships: A latent profile analysis. *The Journal of Sexual Medicine, 20*(1), 14–21. https://doi.org/10.1093/jsxmed/qdac018

Delgado-Pérez, E., Rodríguez-Costa, I., Vergara-Pérez, F., Blanco-Morales, M., & Torres-Lacomba, M. (2022). Recovering sexuality after childbirth: What strategies do women adopt? A qualitative study. *International Journal of Environmental Research and Public Health, 19*(2), Article 950. https://doi.org/10.3390/ijerph19020950

Doherty, W. J., Harris, S. M., Hall, E. L., & Hubbard, A. K. (2021). How long do people wait before seeking couples therapy? A research note. *Journal of Marital and Family Therapy, 47*(4), 882–890. https://doi.org/10.1111/jmft.12479

Doss, B. D., Rhoades, G. K., Stanley, S. M., & Markman, H. J. (2009). The effect of the transition to parenthood on relationship quality: An eight-year prospective study. *Journal of Personality and Social Psychology, 96*(3), 601–619. https://doi.org/10.1037/a0013969

El Amiri, S., Brassard, A., Rosen, N. O., Rossi, M. A., Beaulieu, N., Bergeron, S., & Peloquin, K. (2021). Sexual function and satisfaction in couples with infertility: A closer look at the role of personal and relational characteristics. *The Journal of Sexual Medicine, 18*(2), 1984–1997. https://doi.org/10.1016/j.jsxm.2021.09.009

Ferreira, L. C., Narciso, I., Novo, R. F., & Pereira, C. R. (2014). Predicting couple satisfaction: The role of differentiation of self, sexual desire and intimacy in heterosexual individuals. *Sexual and Relationship Therapy, 29*(4), 390–404. https://doi.org/10.1080/14681994.2014.957498

Ferreira, L. C., Fraenkel, P., Narciso, I., & Novo, R. (2015). Is committed desire intentional? A qualitative exploration of sexual desire and differentiation of self in couples. *Family Process, 54*(2), 308–326. https://doi.org/10.1111/famp.12108

Frankenbach, J., Weber, M., Loschelder, D. D., Kilger, H., & Friese, M. (2022). Sex drive: Theoretical conceptualization and meta-analytic review of gender differences. *Psychological Bulletin, 148*(9–10), 621–661. https://doi.org/10.1037/bul0000366

Frederick, D. A., St. John, H. K., Garcia, J. R., & Lloyd, E. A. (2018). Differences in orgasm frequency among gay, lesbian, bisexual, and heterosexual men and women in a U.S. national sample. *Archives of Sexual Behavior, 47*(1), 273–288. https://doi.org/10.1007/s10508-017-0939-z

Frederick, D. A., Gillespie, B. J., Lever, J., & Garcia, J. R. (2021). Debunking lesbian bed death: Using coarsened exact matching to compare sexual practices and satisfaction of lesbian and heterosexual women. *Archives of Sexual Behavior, 50*(3). https://doi.org/10.1007/s10508-021-02096-4

Galizia, R., Theodorou, A., Simonelli, C., Lai, C., & Nimbi, F. M. (2023). Sexual satisfaction mediates the effects of the quality of dyadic sexual communication on the degree of perceived sexual desire discrepancy. *Healthcare, 11*(648). https://doi.org/10.3390/healthcare11050648

Girme, Y. U., Jones, R. E., Fleck, C., Simpson, J. A., & Overall, N. C. (2020). Infants' attachment insecurity predicts attachment-relevant emotion regulation strategies in adulthood. *Emotion, 21*(2), 276–288. https://doi.org/10.1037/emo0000721

Glass, J., Simon, R. W., & Andersson, M. A. (2016). Parenthood and happiness: Effects of work-family reconciliation policies in 22 OECD countries. *American Journal of Sociology, 122*(3), 886–929. https://doi.org/10.1086/688892

Gonzalez-Rivas, S. K., & Peterson, Z. D. (2020). Women's sexual initiation in same- and mixed-sex relationships: How often and how? *The Journal of Sex Research, 57*(3), 335–350. https://doi.org/10.1080/00224499.2018.1489489

Gottman, J. M. (1994). *What predicts divorce? The relationship between marital processes and marital outcomes.* Lawrence Erlbaum Associates.

Gottman, J. M., & Gottman, J. S. (2015). *The seven principles for making marriage work* (Revised ed.). Harmony Books.

Gottman, J. M., & Silver, N. (2015). *The seven principles for making marriage work.* Harmony Books.

Hansson, M., & Ahlborg, T. (2015). Factors contributing to separation/divorce in parents of small children in Sweden. *Nordic Psychology, 68*(1), 40–57. https://doi.org/10.1080/19012276.2015.1071201

Hays, S. (1996). *The cultural contradictions of motherhood.* Yale University Press.

Herbenick, D., Mullinax, M., & Mark, K. (2014). Sexual desire discrepancy as a feature, not a bug, of long-term relationships: Women's self-reported strategies for modulating sexual desire. *The Journal of Sexual Medicine, 11*(9), 2196–2206. https://doi.org/10.1111/jsm.12625

Hevesi, K., Horvath, Z., Miklos, E., Sal, D., & Rowland, D. L. (2022). Motives that mediate the associations between relationship satisfaction, orgasmic difficulty, and the frequency of faking orgasm. *Sexual Medicine, 10*(6), 100568. https://doi.org/10.1016/j.esxm.2022.100568

Holmberg, D., Blair, K. L., & Phillips, M. (2010). Women's sexual satisfaction as a predictor of well-being in same-sex versus mixed-sex relationships. *The Journal of Sex Research, 47*(1), 1–11. https://doi.org/10.1080/00224490902898710

Janssen, E., & Bancroft, J. (2006). The dual control model: The role of sexual inhibition and excitation in sexual arousal and behavior. In E. Janssen (Ed.), *The psychophysiology of sex* (pp. 197–222). Indiana University Press.

Jerath, R., Edry, J. W., Barnes, V. A., & Jerath, V. (2006). Physiology of long pranayamic breathing: Neural respiratory elements may provide a mechanism that explains how slow deep breathing shifts the autonomic nervous system. *Medical Hypotheses, 67*(3), 566–571. https://doi.org/10.1016/j.mehy.2006.02.042

Johnson, S. (2008). *Hold me tight: Seven conversations for a lifetime of love*. Little, Brown Spark.

Khoury, B., Lecomte, T., Fortin, G., Masse, M., Therien, P., Bouchard, V., Chapleau, M.-A., Paquin, K., & Hofmann, S. G. (2013). Mindfulness-based therapy: A comprehensive meta-analysis. *Clinical Psychology Review, 33*(6), 763–771. https://doi.org/10.1016/j.cpr.2013.05.005

Kleinplatz, P. J., & Ménard, A. D. (2020). *Magnificent sex: Lessons from extraordinary lovers.* Routledge.

Kleinplatz, P. J., Charest, M., Rosen, L. A., & Ménard, A. D. (2022). Optimal couple sexuality: A review of the (limited) literature. *Current Sexual Health Reports, 14*, 63–69. https://doi.org/10.1007/s11930-022-00327-w

Kraemer, S. (2000). The fragile male. *BMJ, 321*(7276), 1609–1612. https://doi.org/10.1136/bmj.321.7276.1609

Krejčová, L., Kuba, R., Flegr, J., & Klapilová, K. (2020). Kamasutra in practice: The use of sexual positions in the Czech population and their association with female coital orgasm potential. *Sexual Medicine, 8*(4), 767–776. https://doi.org/10.1016/j.esxm.2020.07.003

Leavitt, C. E., McDaniel, B. T., Maas, M. K., & Feinberg, M. E. (2017). Parenting stress and sexual satisfaction among first-time parents: A dyadic approach. *Sex Roles, 75*(6), 395–409. https://doi.org/10.1007/s11199-016-0623-0

Lévesque, S., Bisson, V., Charton, L., & Fernet, M. (2020). Parenting and relational well-being during the transition to parenthood: Challenges for first-time parents. Journal of Child and Family Studies, *29*, 1938–1956. https://doi.org/10.1007/s10826-020-01727-z

Lovie, K., & Marashi, A. (2022). Coital positions and clitoral blood flow: A biomechanical and sonographic analysis. *Sexologies, 31*(4), 423–429. https://doi.org/10.1016/j.sexol.2022.04.007

Masters, W. H., & Johnson, V. E. (1966). *Human sexual response*. Little, Brown and Company.

Meltzer, A. L., Makhanova, A., Hicks, L. L., French, J. E., McNulty, J. K., & Bradbury, T. N. (2017). Quantifying the sexual afterglow: The lingering benefits of sex and their implications for pair-bonded relationships. *Psychological Science, 28*(5), 587–598. https://doi.org/10.1177/0956797617691361

Menanno, J. (2023). *Secure love: Create a relationship that lasts a lifetime.* Harper Wave.

Metz, M. E., & McCarthy, B. W. (2011). *Enduring desire: Your guide to lifelong intimacy.* Routledge.

Mintz, L. (2017). *Becoming cliterate: Why orgasm equality matters—and how to get it.* HarperOne.

Muise, A., Kovacevic, K., Shoikhedbrod, A., & Uppot, A. (2023). The benefits (and costs) of sexual responsiveness in romantic relationships. *Current Opinion in Psychology, 52*, 101644. https://doi.org/10.1016/j.copsyc.2023.101644

Murray, S. H., Sutherland, O., & Milhausen, R. R. (2012). Young women's descriptions of sexual desire in long-term relationships. *Sexual and Relationship Therapy, 27*(1), 3–16. https://doi.org/10.1080/14681994.2011.649251

Nagoski, E. (2015). *Come as you are: The surprising new science that will transform your sex life*. Simon & Schuster.

Nagoski, E. (2024). *Come together: The science (and art!) of creating lasting sexual connections.* Ballantine.

Nimbi, F. M., Ciocca, G., Limoncin, E., Fontanesi, L., Uysal, Ü. B., Flinchum, M., Tambelli, R., Jannini, E. A., & Simonelli, C. (2020). Sexual desire and fantasies in the LGBT+ community: A focus on bisexuals, transgender, and other shades of the rainbow. *Current Sexual Health Reports, 12*(2), 162–169. https://doi.org/10.1007/s11930-020-00262-8

Pascoe, M. C., Thompson, D. R., Jenkins, Z. M., & Ski, C. F. (2017). Mindfulness mediates the physiological markers of stress: Systematic review and meta-analysis. *Journal of Psychiatric Research, 95*, 156–178. https://doi.org/10.1016/j.jpsychires.2017.08.004

Porges, S. W. (2022). Polyvagal theory: A science of safety. *Frontiers in Integrative Neuroscience, 16*, 871227. https://doi.org/10.3389/fnint.2022.871227

Real, T. (n. d.). *Relational parenting: Working like a team to raise connected children.* Relational Life Institute. https://relationallife.com/parenting

Real, T. (2022). *Us: Getting past you and me to build a more loving relationship.* Random House.

Rosen, N. O., Dawson, S. J., Leonhardt, N. D., Vannier, S. A., & Impett, E. A. (2021). Trajectories of sexual well-being among couples in the transition to parenthood. *Journal of Family Psychology, 35*(4), 523–533. https://doi.org/10.1037/fam0000689

Salisbury, C. M. A., & Fisher, W. A. (2014). "Did you come?" A qualitative exploration of gender differences in beliefs, experiences, and concerns regarding female orgasm occurrence during heterosexual sexual interactions. *The Journal of Sex Research, 51*(6), 616–631. https://doi.org/10.1080/00224499.2013.838934

Schore, A. N. (2017). All our sons: The developmental neurobiology and neuroendocrinology of boys at risk. *Infant Mental Health Journal, 38*(1), 15–52. https://doi.org/10.1002/imhj.21616

Séguin, L., Rodrigue, C., & Lavigne, J. (2018). Consuming ecstasy: Representations of male and female orgasm in mainstream pornography. *The Journal of Sex Research, 55*(3), 348–356. https://doi.org/10.1080/00224499.2017.1332152

Sims, K. E., & Meana, M. (2010) Why did passion wane? A qualitative study of married women's attributions for declines in sexual desire, *Journal of Sex & Marital Therapy, 36*(4), 360–380. https://doi.org/10.1080/0092623X.2010.498727

Sümer, N., Lubiewska, K., Aran, Ö., Głogowska, K., & Żegleń, M. (2024). Maternal reflective functioning and intergenerational transmission of attachment orientations in Poland, the Netherlands, and Turkey. *Journal of Child and Family Studies, 33*(4), 1–16. https://doi.org/10.1007/s10826-023-02753-3

US Department of Health and Human Services. (2024). *Parents under pressure: Struggling with stress and mental health.* Retrieved from https://www.hhs.gov/sites/default/files/parents-under-pressure.pdf

Vowels, L. M. (2023). An online sensate focus application to treat sexual desire discrepancy in intimate relationships: Contrasting case studies. *Sexual and Relationship Therapy, 38*(3), 411–430. https://doi.org/10.1080/14681994.2022.2026316

Vowels, L. M., Rosenkrantz, D. E., Brown, H. M., & Mark, K. P. (2020). Ebbs and flows of desire: A qualitative exploration of contextual factors affecting sexual desire in bisexual, lesbian, and straight women. *Journal of Sex & Marital Therapy, 46*(8), 807–823. https://doi.org/10.1080/0092623X.2020.1828207

Vowels, L. M., Sisson, N., Darwiche, J., & Impett, E. A. (2024). Placing a child's or partner's needs above my own: Impacts on a couple's sexual relationship. *Personal Relationships*, *31*(3), 776–795. https://doi.org/10.1111/pere.12560

Weiner, L. (2022). Sensate focus touch in sexual health and sex therapy: A critical literature review. *The Journal of Sexual Medicine*, *19*(5), S152. https://doi.org/10.1016/j.jsxm.2022.03.350

Weiner, L., & Avery-Clark, C. (2017). *Sensate focus in sex therapy: The illustrated manual.* Routledge.

Widman, L., Choukas-Bradley, S., Noar, S. M., Nesi, J., & Garrett, K. (2015). Parent-adolescent sexual communication and adolescent safer sex behavior: A meta-analysis. *JAMA Pediatrics*, *169*(12), 1172–1180. https://doi.org/10.1001/jamapediatrics.2015.2731

Winnicott, D. W. (1971). *Playing and reality*. Tavistock Publications.

Zhao, C., McNulty, J. K., Turner, J. A., Hicks, L. L., & Meltzer, A. L. (2022). Evidence of a bidirectional association between daily sexual and relationship satisfaction that is moderated by daily stress. *Archives of Sexual Behavior*, *51*, 3791–3806. https://doi.org/10.1007/s10508-022-02399-0

Acknowledgments

Lee—thank you for your unwavering support (especially when it's hard to give it), for being my rock and guiding light, and for being the kind of partner it's a joy to keep evolving with.

Gray and Kellan—you made me a mom. You are the best parts of me and the most amazing things I've ever done.

My parents—thank you for giving me the foundation of confidence, health, and a beautifully imperfect model of a relationship built on joy, commitment, and growth. I know what truly matters because of you.

Jannelle—thank you for always picking me up, having my back, and never letting me fall alone.

Sarah—thank you for all the life and business advice, and especially for being the sounding board behind the nervous system chapter. It's a joy to shape our life's work together.

Gretchen—thank you for your unwavering friendship, your calm presence, and your parenting wisdom. You've been a grounding force when I've needed it most.

Isabelle—thank you for inspiring me, walking beside me, and always understanding exactly what I mean. Your support has been a true gift.

Chaundera—thank you for your friendship, your PR wisdom, and for always telling me the truth, even when I don't want to hear it.

Jennie—thank you for your steady friendship and for being someone I can be real with. You make me feel less alone.

My sister-friends, Anne, Eliza, and Emma—thank you for all the advice, support, and for putting up with me even when I'm bossy.

To my clients and all the parents out there—this is especially for you. Your courage, honesty, and vulnerability have shaped this work more than you know. Thank you for trusting me with your stories.

About the Author

Rebecca Howard Eudy, PhD, LMHC, is an AASECT-certified sex therapist and coach who helps couples navigate sex, desire, and connection—even when life (and kids) make it feel impossible. Certified in emotionally focused couples therapy (EFCT), she specializes in the ever-changing dynamics of relationships, especially in the whirlwind of parenting.

Originally from the woods of New Hampshire, Rebecca now calls the Boston area home. As a mom to two spirited boys, she understands firsthand how relationships evolve under the weight of family life. Her personal survival toolkit includes exercise, cursing, meditation, cooking, gardening, reading trashy novels, and hiking with her husband, kids, and their aspiring therapy dog, Acorn. ♥